LEGENDARY LOCALS

OF

LATROBE

PENNSYLVANIA

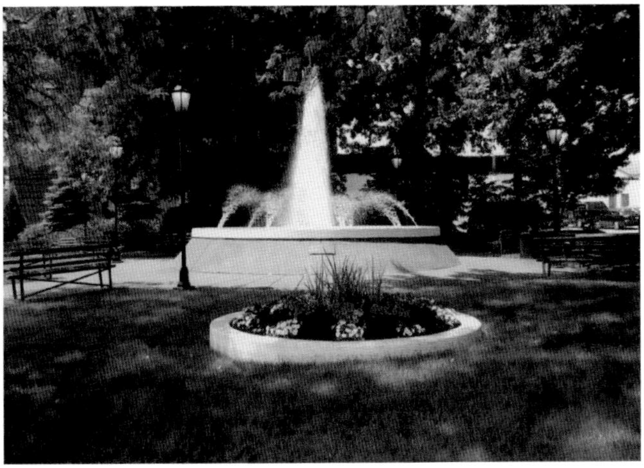

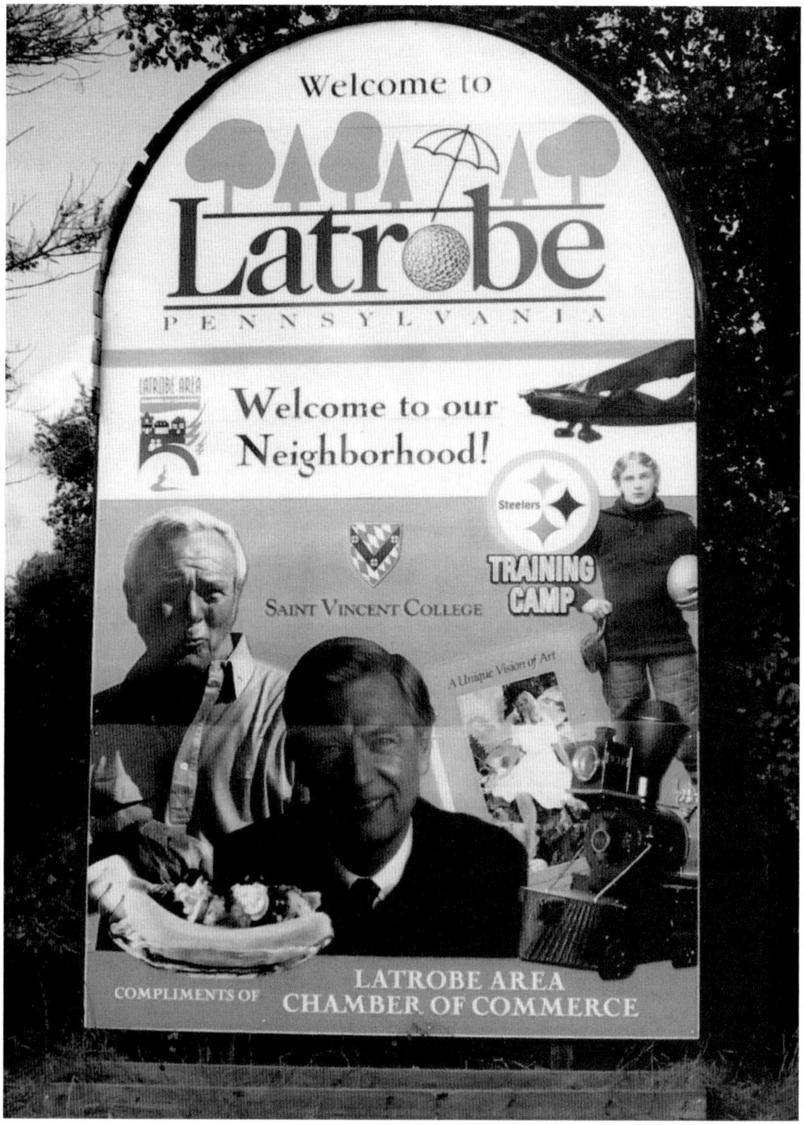

Welcome to the Neighborhood!

The Latrobe Area Chamber of Commerce, now the Greater Latrobe Laurel Valley Chamber of Commerce, added this attractive Welcome sign on Route 981 in 2007. It was designed by local artist George Fetkovich of Apollo Design. The featured images show famous firsts and legendary locals of Latrobe, including native sons Arnold Palmer and Fred Rogers; nearby St. Vincent College; the banana split; a bright red airmail plane; the Pittsburgh Steelers' training camp; old-time professional football legend John Brallier; a steam locomotive; and the cover of the Greater Latrobe School District (GLSD) Art Conservation Trust's book, *A Unique Vision of Art*, by Barbara H. Nakles. (Jim Wasylik/West Media Group.)

Page 1: James Hillis Rogers Memorial Park

The James Hillis Rogers Memorial Park and fountain offer welcome respite to Latrobe residents and visitors alike. (Author's collection; see page 107.)

LEGENDARY LOCALS

OF

LATROBE

PENNSYLVANIA

JOSEPH A. COMM

LEGENDARY LOCALS

ISBN 978-1-4671-0184-4

Legendary Locals is an imprint of Arcadia Publishing
Charleston, South Carolina

Printed in the United States of America

Library of Congress Control Number: 2014942235

For all general information, please contact Arcadia Publishing:
Telephone 843-853-2070
Fax 843-853-0044
E-mail sales@arcadiapublishing.com
For customer service and orders:
Toll-Free 1-888-313-2665

Visit us on the Internet at www.arcadiapublishing.com

Dedication
To my wife, Linda, who is always there with love when I need help

On the Front Cover: Clockwise from top left:
Fred McFeely Rogers, children's television pioneer (Copyright © The Fred Rogers Company, used with permission; see page 52), Rose Rubinoff, owner of the Rose Style Shoppe, and her brother, David Rubinoff, a violinist (Latrobe Area Historical Society; see page 32), John Brallier, one of the first professional football players (Latrobe Area Historical Society; see page 74), Arnold Palmer, professional golfer (Latrobe Area Historical Society; see page 72), the Steelers' training camp, held each year at St. Vincent College (author's collection; see page 79), George Hamilton Adams, railroad industrialist, and his wife willed proceeds from their estate to build Adams Memorial Library (Latrobe Area Historical Society; see page 44), the Sonics, Harry's Danceland's house band (Cathi Rhodes; see page 56), Jill Snyder, culinary artist (Jill Snyder; see page 65), and William Findley, first member of Congress from Westmoreland County (William Findley by Rembrandt Peale, from life, 1805, courtesy Independence National Historical Park; see page 14).

On the Back Cover: From left to right:
First all-pro football team (Latrobe Area Historical Society; see page 75) and Joseph E. "Ice Cream Joe" Greubel, restaurant owner (Author's collection; see page 27).

CONTENTS

ACKNOWLEDGMENTS

As an elementary schoolteacher, I have always had the good fortune to be assigned to a grade level in which local history is taught. This was true on the Eastern Shore of Maryland; in Alexandria, Virginia; and at my current position, teaching elementary students at Greater Latrobe School District (GLSD) in western Pennsylvania. Because of these experiences, I have developed a genuine appreciation for the events and people who shaped each community and a real love for local history. The study has provided my students a frame within which they can establish their roots and has helped to break down the barriers between school and the world outside, especially when "boots replace books" and the students visited local sites. Latrobe in particular has offered my students a unique and varied history and, perhaps best of all, some very famous and noteworthy local legends to emulate.

While working on this project, I have met the real historians, preservationists, volunteers, businessmen and women, and many others who exemplify the helpful spirit and kind nature of Latrobe-area citizens by offering a smile, a cup of coffee, or quick agreement whenever I asked for help. Chief among those who willingly came to my assistance are Mary Lou Townsend and Pamela Ferrero of the Latrobe Area Historical Society; Barbara H. Nakles and Jessica O. Golden of the Latrobe Art Conservation Trust; Robert and Harry Frye of Fantastic Fotographica; Ronald G. Cameron, chief executive officer of Cameron and Company, Inc.; Gabrielle K. Nastuck and Lauren Condon of the Latrobe Art Center; Steve Kittey of the *Latrobe Bulletin*; and Louise R. Tilzey-Bates, tourism coordinator for Westmoreland Heritage.

There are so many people of whom the Latrobe area can be proud. This volume attempts to highlight a number of them, but it is in no way all-inclusive. Although every local no doubt has his or her favorites, it is my sincere hope that the ones contained herein represent the spirit, ingenuity, kindness, creativity, and perseverance of all those who have contributed and continue to contribute to making Latrobe an ideal place to live, work, and raise a family.

Images provided by the Latrobe Area Historical Society are identified by the initials LAHS at the end of their captions. Photographs from Fantastic Fotographica are credited with FF, those from the author's collection with AC, and photographs by Linda Comm with LC. All others are individually credited.

INTRODUCTION

At the writing of this introduction, Latrobe is celebrating its 160th birthday. Founded in 1854 by Oliver W. Barnes, an engineer with the Pennsylvania Railroad Company, and named for his friend and college roommate, Benjamin Henry Latrobe, the city and the surrounding area have a rich history and a colorful variety of native sons and daughters. Most notably, it is the birthplace of David "Doc" Strickler, inventor of the banana split; the first all-professional football team; the first nonstop airmail pickup; children's television pioneer Fred Rogers; and golf legend Arnold Palmer. Latrobe is the original home of the Latrobe Brewery (the brewer of Rolling Rock beer), St. Vincent College, and the training camp of the Pittsburgh Steelers.

Nestled in the beautiful rolling foothills of the Laurel Mountains in western Pennsylvania, the Latrobe area was originally a hunting ground for Native Americans, including the Delaware, Shawnee, Seneca, and Mingo. The first European to give a detailed description of the region was Christopher Gist, an accomplished colonial British explorer and frontiersman. According to Gist's journal, he came over the scenic Chestnut Ridge into "Loyalhannan" (present-day Ligonier) and followed the waters into the area known today as Latrobe. He wrote, "It is good land for farming, covered with large white and red oaks and fine runs for mills." Three years later, Gist would accompany a young George Washington on a road-building expedition across the area.

The French and Indian War brought more Europeans over the mountains from the east. In 1758, British general John Forbes ordered construction of a new road across Pennsylvania, guarded by a chain of fortifications, the final link being the "Post at Loyalhannan," or Fort Ligonier. Forbes and his army of 8,000 British soldiers cleared a road through this area on their way from Philadelphia to Pittsburgh. The path they created is now called Forbes Road.

The village of nearby Youngstown, Pennsylvania, was established 50 years before Latrobe started and was a post town, or stopping place, along the historic Forbes Road. Because it was at the foot of the mountains, Youngstown was a convenient place for pack horses, wagons, and stagecoaches to stop before ascending or after descending Chestnut Ridge. Some travelers decided to stay in the area because they found good land for farming here. But western Pennsylvania was hostile country then. For at least 25 years, European settlers suffered attacks from Native Americans.

To protect themselves, early farmers built blockhouses, or log homes, made of heavy timbers for military defense. The upper floor walls were "loopholed," or pierced, for gunfire. One such structure was recently discovered near St. Vincent College by Floyd Eiseman of the Latrobe Area Historical Society. The blockhouse, believed to have belonged to county lieutenant Archibald Lochry, was fully restored by students from Derry Area High School.

In 1790, Fr. Theodore Brouwers, a member of the Orders of Friars Minor, purchased 300 acres of land in the Latrobe area called Sportsman's Hall Tract and founded Sportsman's Hall Parish. The parish was later placed under the patronage of Saint Vincent de Paul and called St. Vincent Parish. By 1846, Fr. Boniface Wimmer was installed as pastor and established the first Benedictine college in the United States. The St. Vincent Archabbey and College was founded from modest beginnings but grew rapidly, and on April 18, 1870, the state legislature of Pennsylvania incorporated the school, empowering it to grant and confer degrees in the arts and sciences.

Not long after St. Vincent was founded, the Pennsylvania Railroad mainline from Harrisburg to Pittsburgh was being surveyed. Oliver W. Barnes, one of the railroad's engineers, was planning to build an extensive rail yard in the Loyalhanna Creek Valley just west of the Chestnut Ridge at the site of present-day Latrobe. Instead, he built the rail yards four miles northeast at what he called Derry

Station. At the original location, Barnes made plans for a town that he named Latrobe in honor of his friend Benjamin Latrobe, the Baltimore & Ohio Railroad's chief engineer.

In about 1870, immigrant laborers began digging for coal in mines under many parts of the community. Many miners and their families moved near the coal mines to small villages called "patches." Coal from local mines was used to heat homes and businesses and to make steam engines run. Coal was also baked to make coke in beehive ovens. Steel mills in Latrobe and Pittsburgh burned the coke with iron ore to make steel. The geographic and natural features of the area made it ideal for the production of steel.

Between 1880 and 1900, Latrobe grew at a dramatic rate. Owing most of the population growth to the expansion of industry, the borough continued adding more and more areas of Derry and Unity Townships. Immigrants arrived from around the world, especially from Europe: Irish, German, Italian, Polish, and Slovak. Major employers were the coal mine companies and the first steel mill.

About 1908, the public schools became increasingly overcrowded, and it was necessary to build additional schools. The First Ward School was constructed in 1909, followed by a new high school, dedicated on September 24, 1914. The Latrobe Area Hospital was built in 1909 to serve the growing community, and a public library was established in 1927.

During both world wars, the people living in the Latrobe district were first in the line of duty when called to serve. Many of the young men enlisted and left home, while a large number of others were registered under special inductions by the Selective Service Board located in Latrobe. On the home front, the Red Cross played an important part, providing comfort and service to the men overseas, and Latrobe businesses and its citizens supported the troops in a variety of ways that would make any community proud. Following victory in both wars, joyful crowds lined the streets to welcome home returning soldiers with cheers as confetti and church bells proclaimed the good news.

With downtown businesses thriving, the 1950s are fondly recalled as the "Golden Years" in Latrobe. The decade saw the community recognized by the National Football League as the birthplace of professional football, the grand spectacle of a weeklong centennial celebration in 1954, and local legends Fred Rogers and Arnold Palmer beginning careers that would soon bring national attention to their hometown, Rogers for his pioneering work in children's television and Palmer for his record-breaking achievements in professional golf.

By 1960, Latrobe had reached its peak in population growth and industry. Over the next several decades, like so many other cities in the country, downtown shopping districts gave way to suburban shopping centers, and family-owned shops were overtaken by large national chains. Many Latrobe residents, however, remained determined to preserve the economic and cultural vitality of downtown and surrounding neighborhoods. Thanks to their efforts and community-driven programs like the Latrobe Community Gardens Project and the Latrobe Community Revitalization Program, the city is once again moving forward, encouraging new business, promoting tourism, and making the streets clean and green in appearance.

Latrobe's notoriety today comes from being a region of modern industry, recreation, and expanding technology. It is a special place known for its close neighborhood feel and the quality of its people, intriguing characters and everyday citizens who have made Latrobe's history legendary.

CHAPTER ONE

Pioneers and Early Settlers

Pennsylvania was unique among the original 13 colonies. It was granted solely to an individual and not to a company or colony, as the others had been. King Charles II granted land to William Penn for services that his father, Adm. Sir William Penn, had rendered the English government in various European wars. Penn established an American sanctuary, "Penn's Woods," that protected freedom of conscience, and he chose a policy of peace in securing his new land from the Native Americans. Although the lands were already his by a royal grant, Penn chose to repurchase them from the native peoples, traveling unarmed and negotiating peacefully. But these principals could not keep up with rapid westward expansion, and by the time western Pennsylvania was being settled, they were forgotten or disregarded. This led to a period of much bloodshed in the region and a dispute with Virginia over western borders. Virginia claimed the land between the Monongahela and the Ohio Rivers, and the Native Americans saw it for the sum of its uses as a resource to be shared, not owned. Few people settled west of the Alleghenies before April 3, 1769, when the Pennsylvania Land Offices were opened in this territory. The Penns never willingly permitted anyone to settle on land that had not been purchased, but the Native Americans gradually receded before the progressive and aggressive early settlers. This, combined with a British victory in the French and Indian War, fairly secured the area for the state of Pennsylvania.

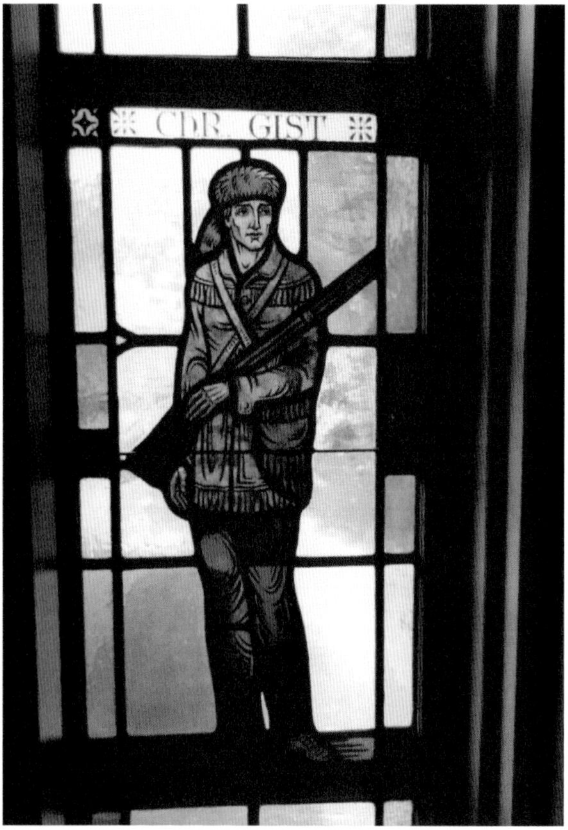

Christopher Gist

Christopher Gist (1706–1759) was an accomplished colonial British explorer, surveyor for the Ohio Company of Virginia, and frontiersman. He is credited with providing the first detailed description of the Latrobe area in 1750 and was a guide for the young George Washington. Gist's image (left) is one of eight historical figures immortalized in stained glass at the front of Unity Chapel in Latrobe. The other subjects lit in leaded glass are Gen. John Forbes, Col. Henry Bouquet, John Smith, Col. John Proctor, William Findley, William Penn, and George Washington. (LC.)

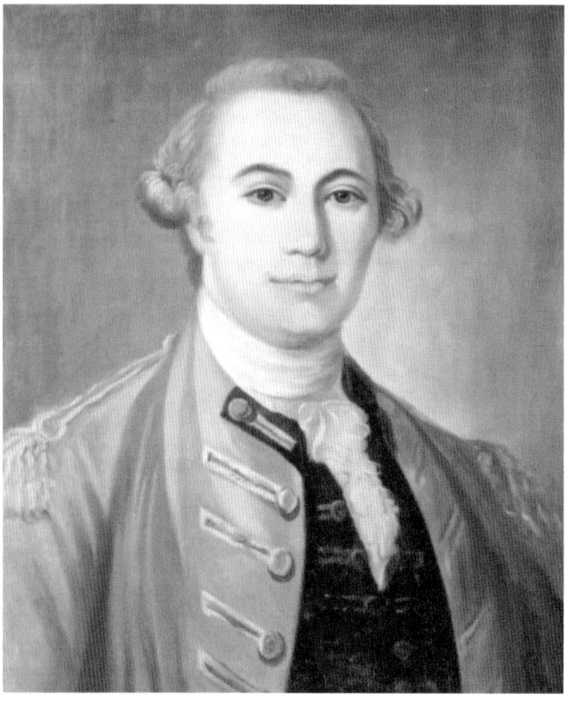

John Forbes

John Forbes (1707–1759) was a British general in the French and Indian War. Eight years from Gist's stay in the area, Forbes and his army of 8,000 men cut a wagon road over the Allegheny Mountains and constructed a series of fortifications to serve as supply depots. Today, US Route 22 largely follows portions of Forbes Road from Monroeville to Latrobe, and US Route 30 follows it from Latrobe to Bedford. Forbes eventually captured the French outpost at Fort Duquesne, renamed it Fort Pitt, and named the new settlement Pittsburgh in honor of British secretary of state William Pitt the Elder. (Carnegie Library of Pittsburgh.)

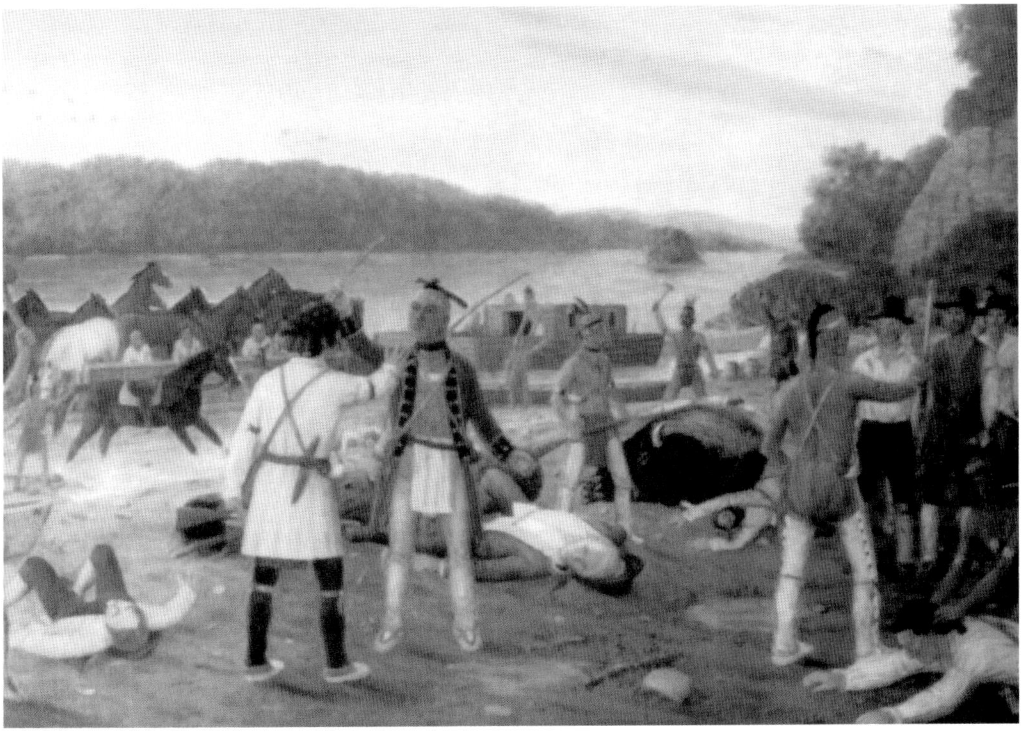

Archibald Lochry
Archibald Lochry (1733–1781) immigrated to the colonies from Northern Ireland and settled in Pennsylvania. He joined the militia and later became a justice in the newly formed Westmoreland County. In 1781, Lochry was made a colonel and given command over 100 men. His Pennsylvania Rangers were dispatched to "discomfort Indian and British forces" in the Ohio Valley. They traveled in relative safety along the Ohio River, but when hunger forced them ashore, his battalion was ambushed by the British and their Native American allies. The party fought bravely until their ammunition ran out. Thirty-seven of his men were killed, and some others, including Lochry, were executed in the aftermath of what has become known as "Lochry's Defeat." (*Lochry's Defeat* by artist Hal Sherman.)

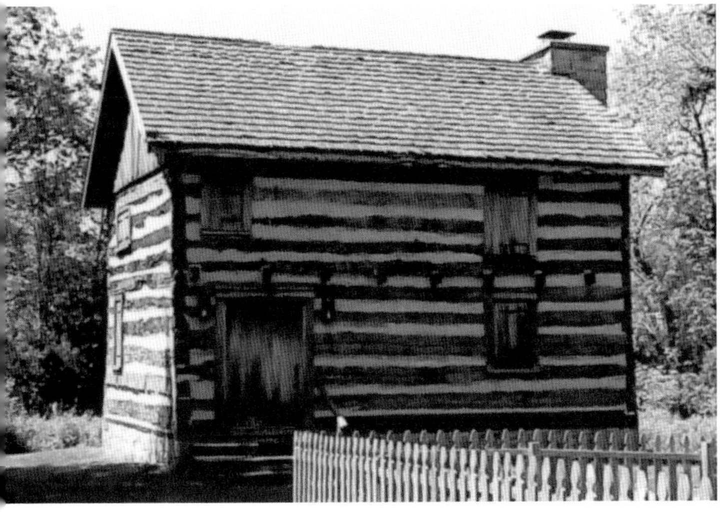

Lochry's Blockhouse
Col. Archibald Lochry acquired large tracts of land, which he used to support his fellow settlers in the Latrobe area. These early pioneers were vulnerable to attack by Shawnee, Delaware, and Sandusky Native American tribes, necessitating Lochry to erect a blockhouse as a safe haven between the forts at Hanna's Town and Ligonier. Today, the 25 acres around Lochry's Blockhouse have been designated as the Winnie Palmer Nature Reserve. (LC.)

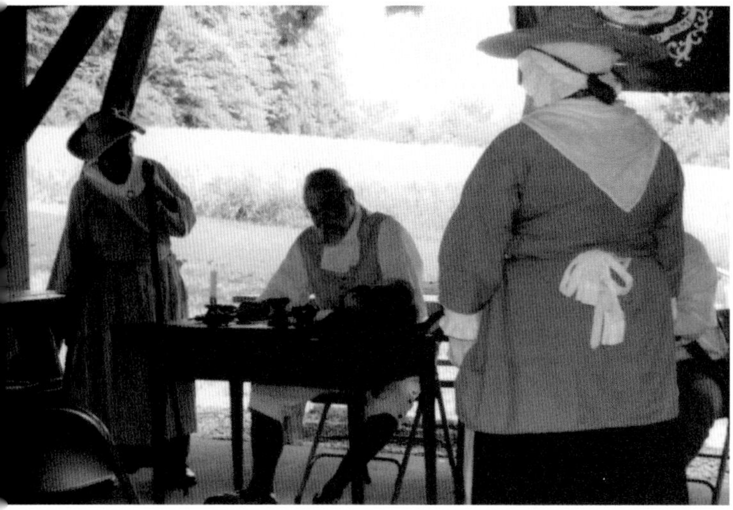

Robert Hanna

Robert Hanna (1738–1786) established his tavern at Hanna's Town as the first English court west of the Alleghenies and presided as judge on April 6, 1773. He and others drew up the "Hanna's Town Resolves," agreeing to take up arms if necessary to resist further "tyrannical" acts of Parliament. Shown during a modern reenactment of an 18th-century trial at Hanna's Town are (from left to right) Helen Auman, Richard Auman as Archibald Lochry's brother Judge William Lochry, and Tiffany Kolbolsky. (AC.)

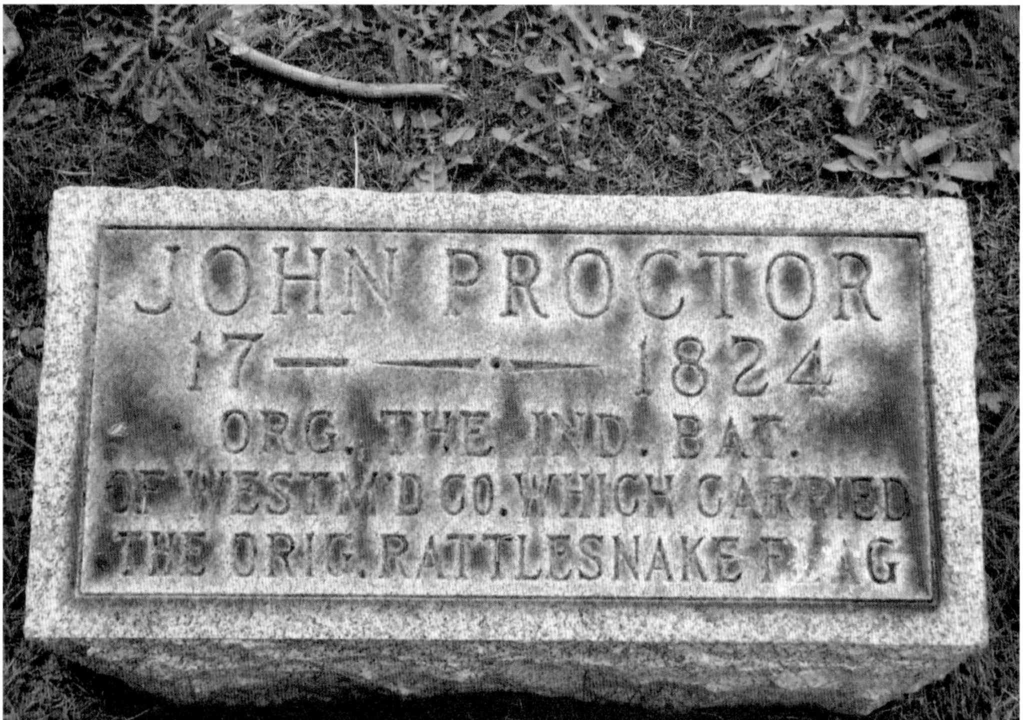

John Proctor

John Proctor (unknown–1824) first appears in the Westmoreland County records as having been elected sheriff in 1773. Shortly after the "Hanna's Town Resolves" were drawn up, Proctor served as colonel of the 1st Battalion and led his men to Philadelphia to help fight the war with the British. However, Native Americans raided quite often in western Pennsylvania, and Proctor was called back to protect the frontier. Proctor's farm was located between the St. Xavier property and historic Unity Cemetery. Although no one knows with any certainty, Proctor is believed to be buried near his old neighbor William Findley at Unity. (AC.)

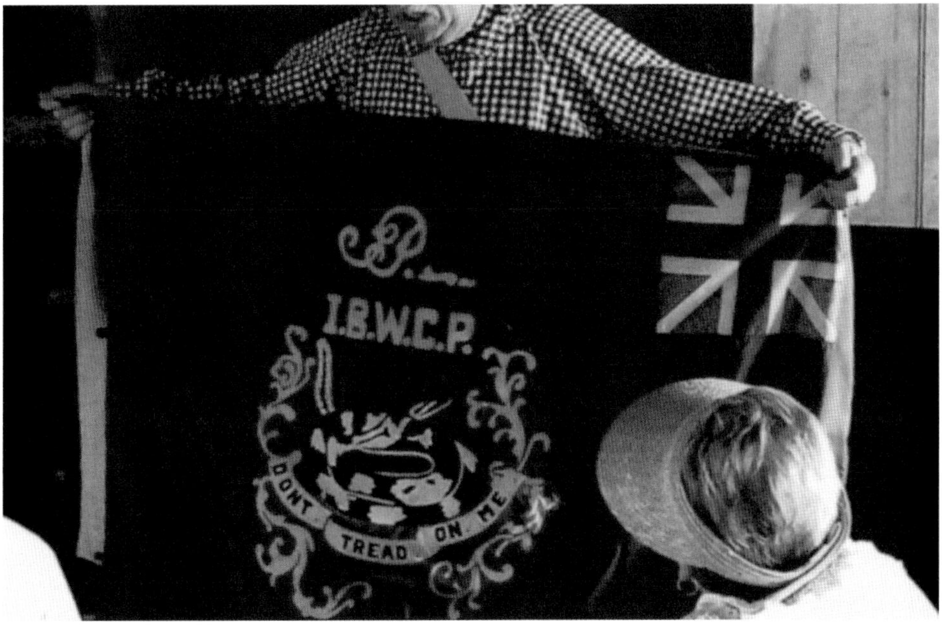

1st Battalion Westmoreland County Militia

The 1st Battalion Westmoreland County Militia marched under its own battle flag. The "Don't Tread on Me" rattlesnake flag predates the Stars and Stripes by two years. The letters stitched on the square red flag, "JP IBWCP," stand for "John Proctor's Independent Battalion of Westmoreland County Provincials." Richard Sheats, a volunteer tour guide, is shown (above) displaying a replica flag to visitors at the Historic Hanna's Town Tavern. The original flag (below) is currently on display at the Fort Pitt Museum at Pittsburgh's Point State Park, on loan from the William Penn Memorial Museum in Harrisburg, Pennsylvania. (Both, AC.)

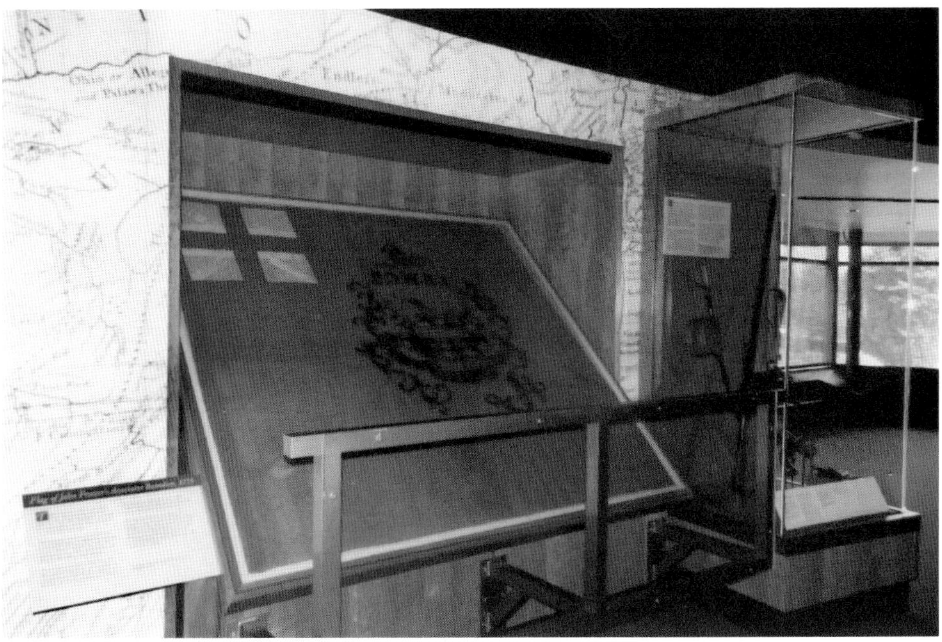

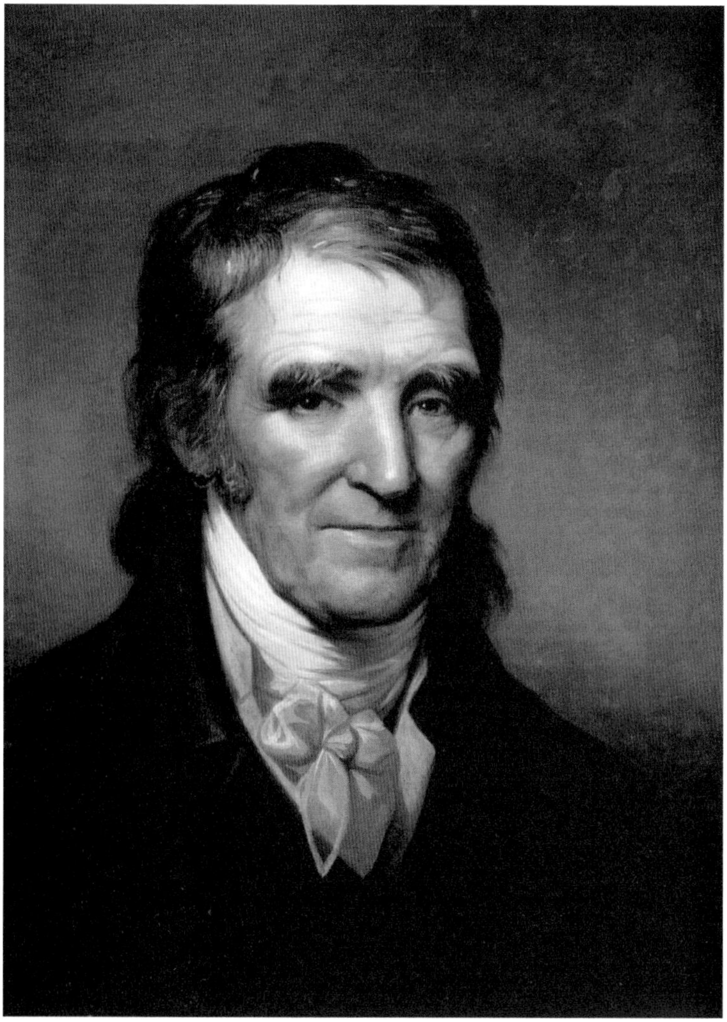

William Findley

William Findley (1741–1821) was the first member of Congress elected from Westmoreland County. Coming from Ireland in 1763, his first intention was to go to Carolina, but he changed his mind and came to Pennsylvania over the issue of slavery. "He chose to hold his own plow and reap his own grain here rather than raise a family where slavery prevailed," wrote George Dallas Albert in his book *History of the County of Westmoreland*. Findley was elected to represent Pennsylvania's 8th and 11th Congressional Districts and served in the US House of Representatives. He urged for peaceful protest of the whiskey tax during the Whiskey Rebellion and later wrote a book arguing that Alexander Hamilton had deliberately provoked the insurrection. He also was a member of the convention to ratify the Constitution of the United States. Findley is often noted in history books for his size and manner of dress. Albert recorded, "Mr. Findley was a large man; his complexion was florid; he wore no beard, and was very tidy and tasteful in his dress. When at home he dressed in homespun, but on going out in fair weather wore a complete suit of white, with white hat having a broad rim, silk stockings, and cue." A Pennsylvania roadside historic marker describing the location of Findley's log home was spotted on October 28, 1994, west of Route 981 just after it crosses Loyalhanna Creek in downtown Latrobe. Findley's gristmill was the first industry in the Latrobe area. Pictured is a portrait of William Findley by Rembrandt Peale, painted from life in 1805. (Independence National Historical Park.)

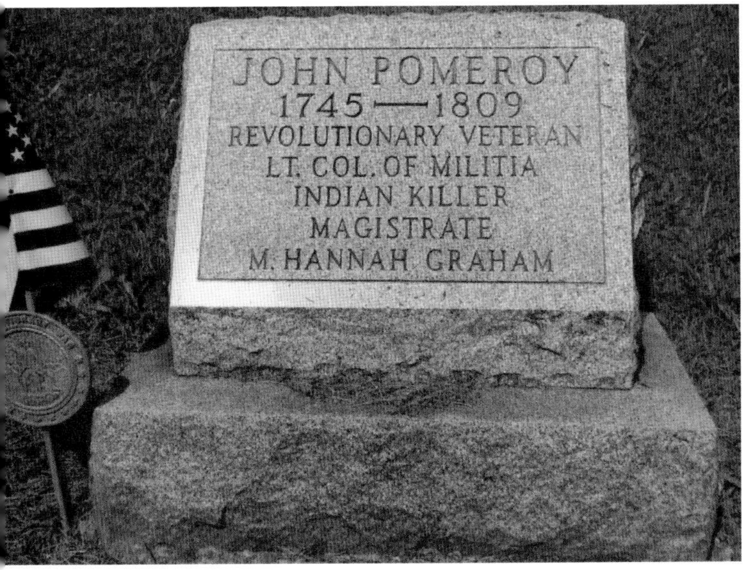

John Pomeroy

John Pomeroy (1745–1809) received a commission from the government as lieutenant colonel for the 1st Battalion, Westmoreland County Militia and served on the frontier. He held the grim moniker of "Indian Killer" when he took command of Fort Ligonier on October 31, 1777. By 1785, Pomeroy was one of the commissioners to locate a county seat for Westmoreland County. His final resting place is Old Salem Church and Cemetery in Derry, Pennsylvania. (AC.)

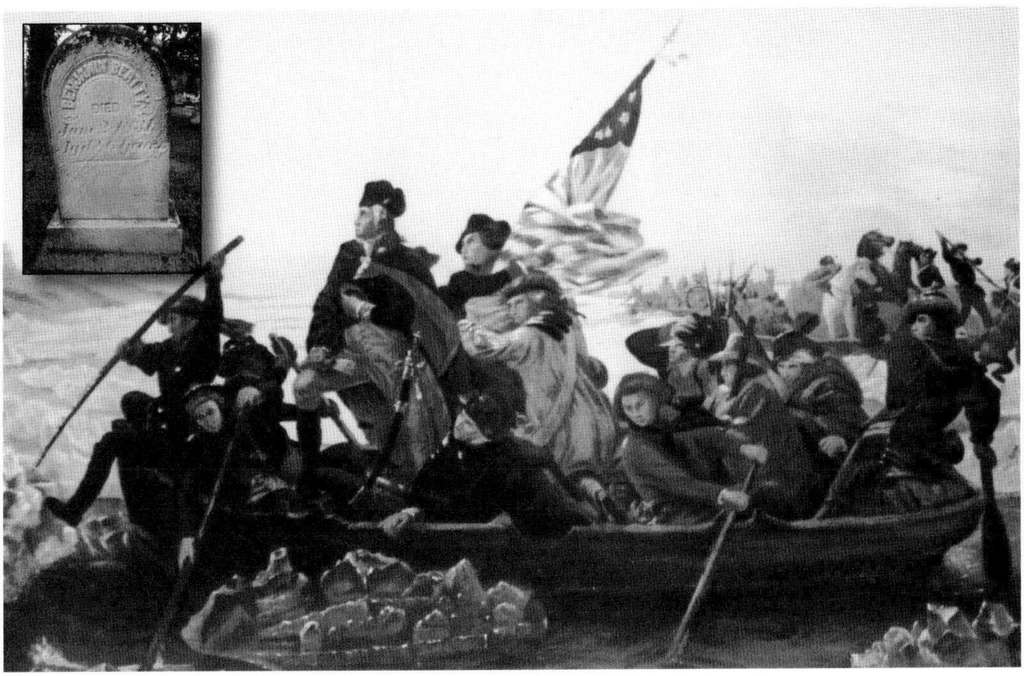

Benjamin Beatty

Benjamin Beatty (1745–1834) fled religious persecution in Scotland through Ireland and arrived on the shores of America in time to sign up to fight for democracy at the start of the Revolutionary War. He served as an ensign in the 1st Battalion of the York County Militia in Pennsylvania and is said to have crossed the Delaware River with George Washington on December 24–25, 1776. Beatty came to western Pennsylvania shortly after the war ended and established a homestead near Unity Cemetery, where he was laid to rest (inset). Beatty Station and Beatty Crossroads were named for him. (Inset, LC; above, AC.)

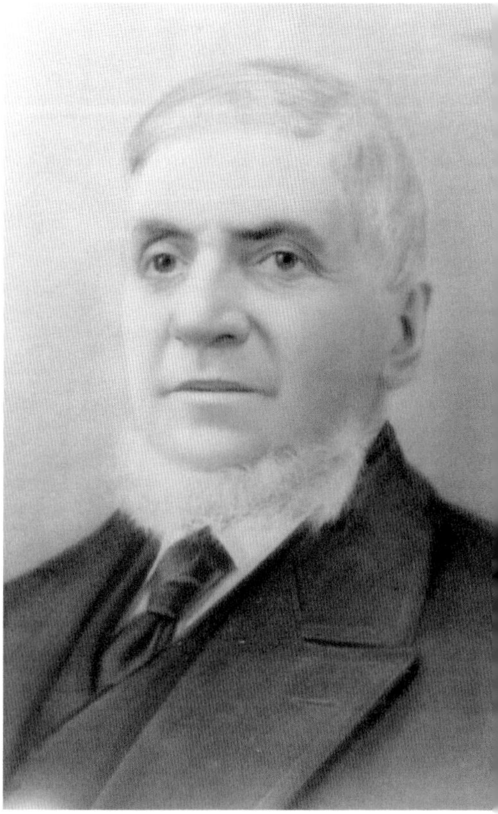

Thomas Kirk

Thomas Kirk (1809–1907) sold his 140-acre farm to Oliver W. Barnes, an engineer with the Pennsylvania Railroad Company, in 1851 for $7,400. His property would become downtown Latrobe. Kirk then moved to Pittsburgh, only to return to Latrobe years later. According to *History of Westmoreland County*, volume 1, "Kirk paid nearly as much for his residence lot as he had received from Barnes for his entire farm." The land purchased was on Chestnut Street, where he built a brick homestead. The house was occupied by his grandson John Kelley in the 1950s and included some of the original furniture and a framed portrait of Thomas Kirk (right), now located in the Latrobe Historical Society. When he died in 1907, at the age of 98, Kirk was the oldest citizen in Latrobe. Below is an 1851 sketch of the town. The road in the picture roughly parallels present-day Ligonier Street. The rendering is dated 1851, but the first train did not arrive until 1852. (Both, LAHS.)

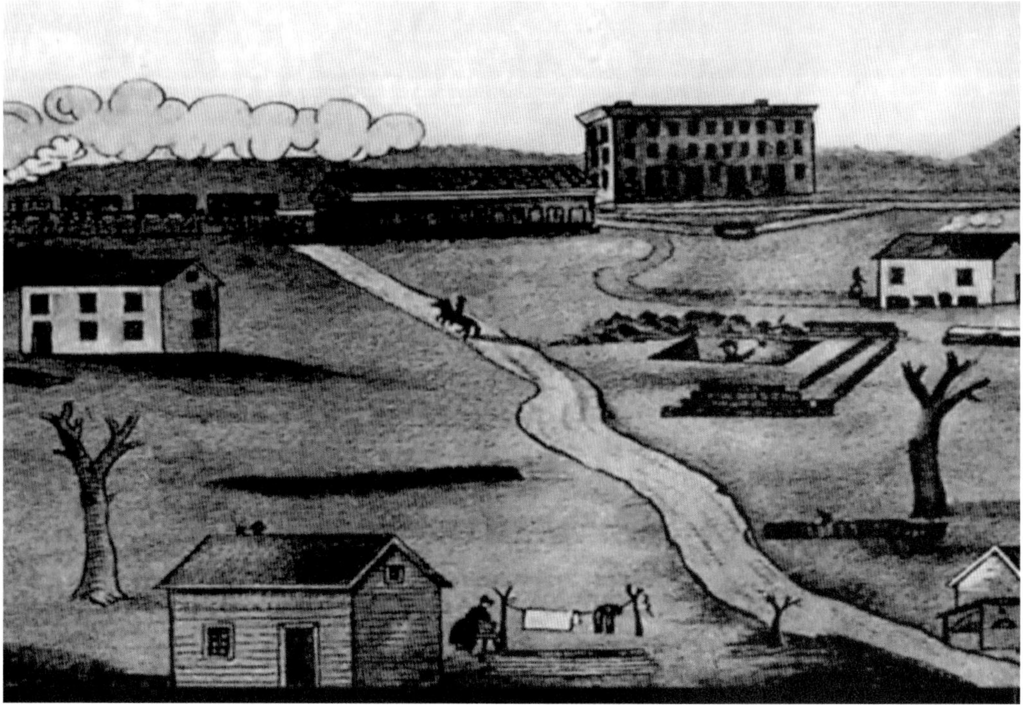

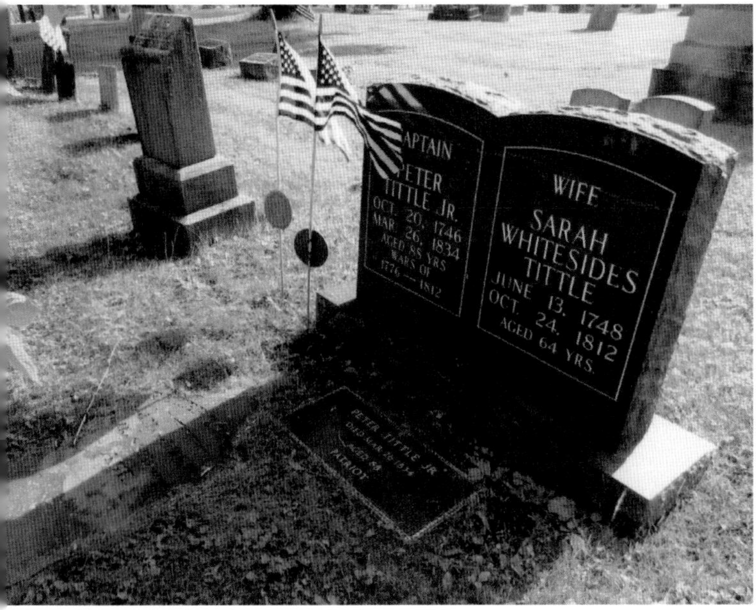

Peter Tittle Jr.
Capt. Peter Tittle Jr. (1746–1834) was a veteran of the American Revolution who joined the growing settlement in Westmoreland County. He served in the army as part of Capt. John McClelland's Rangers, Westmoreland County Militia. He and his wife, Sarah Whitesides Tittle (1748–1812), are buried in the old section of Unity Cemetery. The old headstone lies flat on the ground, but a new stone was recently erected that lists him as having served in the wars of 1776 and 1812. (LC.)

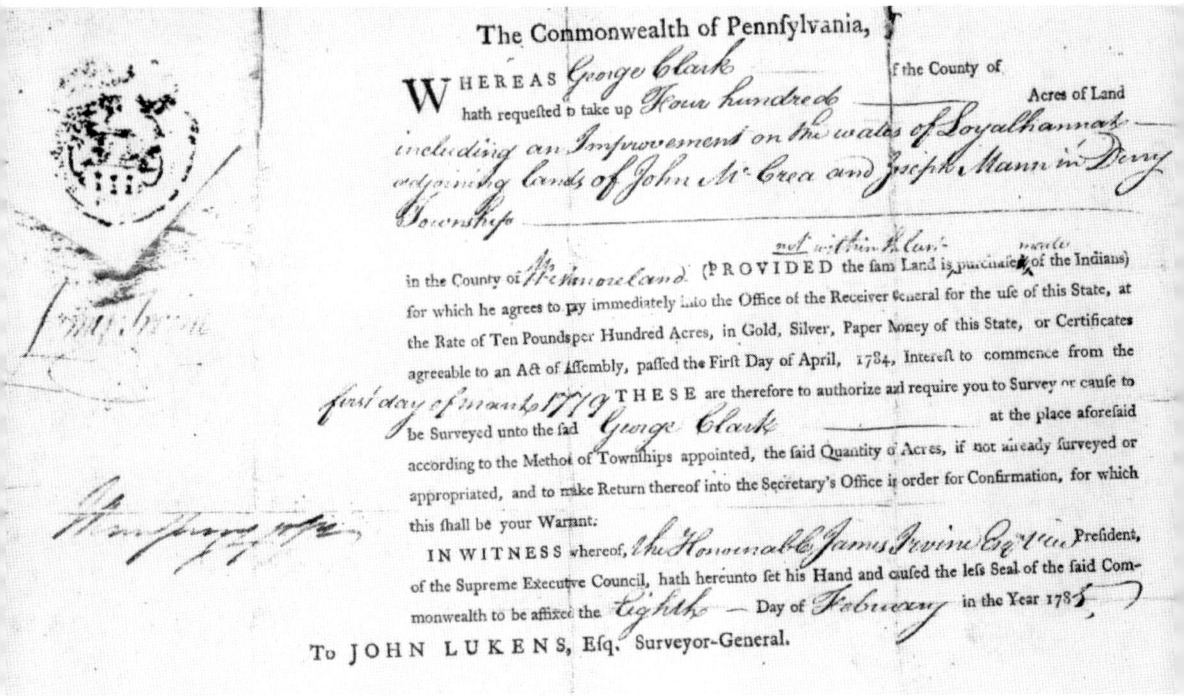

The Commonwealth of Pennſylvania,

WHEREAS George Clark of the County of hath requeſted to take up Four hundred Acres of Land including an Improvement on the waters of Loyalhannah adjoining lands of John McCrea and Joseph Mann in Derry Township

in the County of Westmoreland (PROVIDED the ſaid Land is not within the Lan- purchaſe made of the Indians) for which he agrees to pay immediately into the Office of the Receiver General for the uſe of this State, at the Rate of Ten Pounds per Hundred Acres, in Gold, Silver, Paper Money of this State, or Certificates agreeable to an Act of Aſſembly, paſſed the First Day of April, 1784, Intereſt to commence from the first day of March 1779 THESE are therefore to authorize and require you to Survey or cauſe to be Surveyed unto the ſaid George Clark at the place aforeſaid according to the Method of Townſhips appointed, the ſaid Quantity of Acres, if not already ſurveyed or appropriated, and to make Return thereof into the Secretary's Office in order for Confirmation, for which this ſhall be your Warrant.

IN WITNESS whereof, the Honourable James Irvine Esq. Vice President, of the Supreme Executive Council, hath hereunto ſet his Hand and cauſed the leſs Seal of the ſaid Commonwealth to be affixed the Eighth Day of February in the Year 1785.

To JOHN LUKENS, Eſq. Surveyor-General.

George Clark
After the Pennsylvania Land Offices were opened on April 3, 1769, George Clark was issued one of the first land titles granted for the Latrobe area under the name "Shillelagh" near Derry. Pictured is the Pennsylvania Land Warrant, dated February 8, 1785, showing that this tract comprised some 400 acres for which George Clark paid the commonwealth £10 per 100 acres, roughly the equivalent of $6,000 today. In 1840, Clark's heirs sold the land to George Lehmer, a farmer and hotel keeper. Lehmer then deeded 140 acres, which are now the central part of Latrobe, to Thomas Kirk. (AC.)

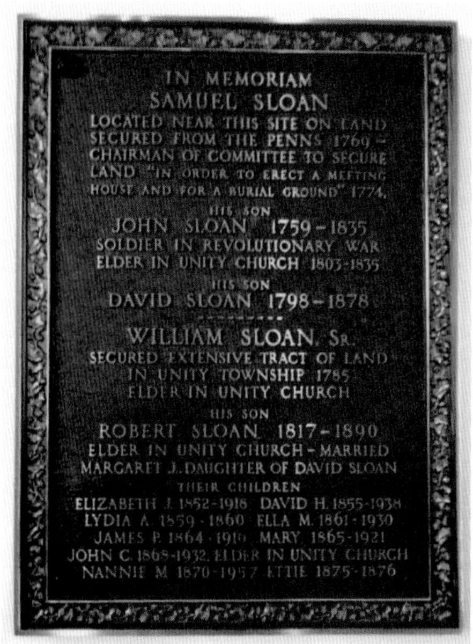

Samuel Sloan Sr.

Samuel Sloan Sr. (1724–1791) built the first house in what is now the city of Latrobe, having applied for a land patent on April 3, 1769, for 320 acres, which he called Happy Discovery. The property was located on the east side of the Loyalhanna Creek opposite the mouth of Fourteen Mile Run. Sloan also helped to establish the Unity Presbyterian Church and graveyard in 1774. On a wall of the church is a bronze plaque dedicated to Samuel Sloan, his son John Sloan, and John Sloan's son David, all of whom were elders. (LC.)

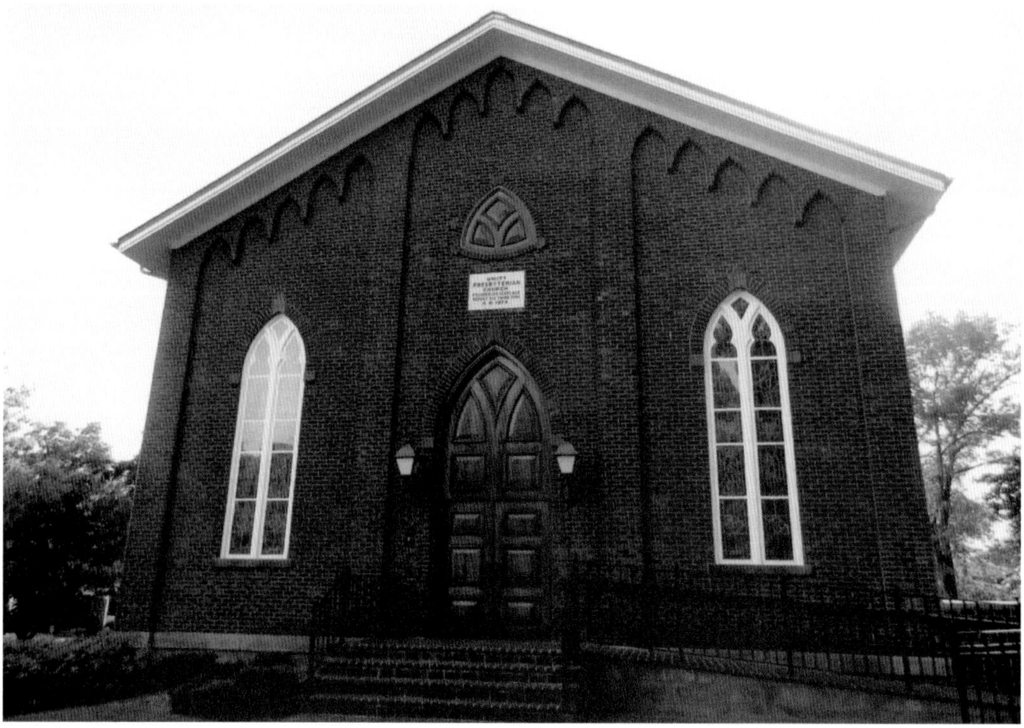

Unity Chapel and Cemetery

On March 1, 1774, sixty acres of land were deeded by Thomas and John Penn, grandsons of William Penn, to the Unity trustees "for the use of the Presbyterian Congregation, in order to erect a Meeting House and Burial Ground." On this tract, a log church was built, perhaps as early as 1776. About 14,000 people have been buried in the church's cemetery since it was established 240 years ago, including many local legends and soldiers who fought in every American war. (LC.)

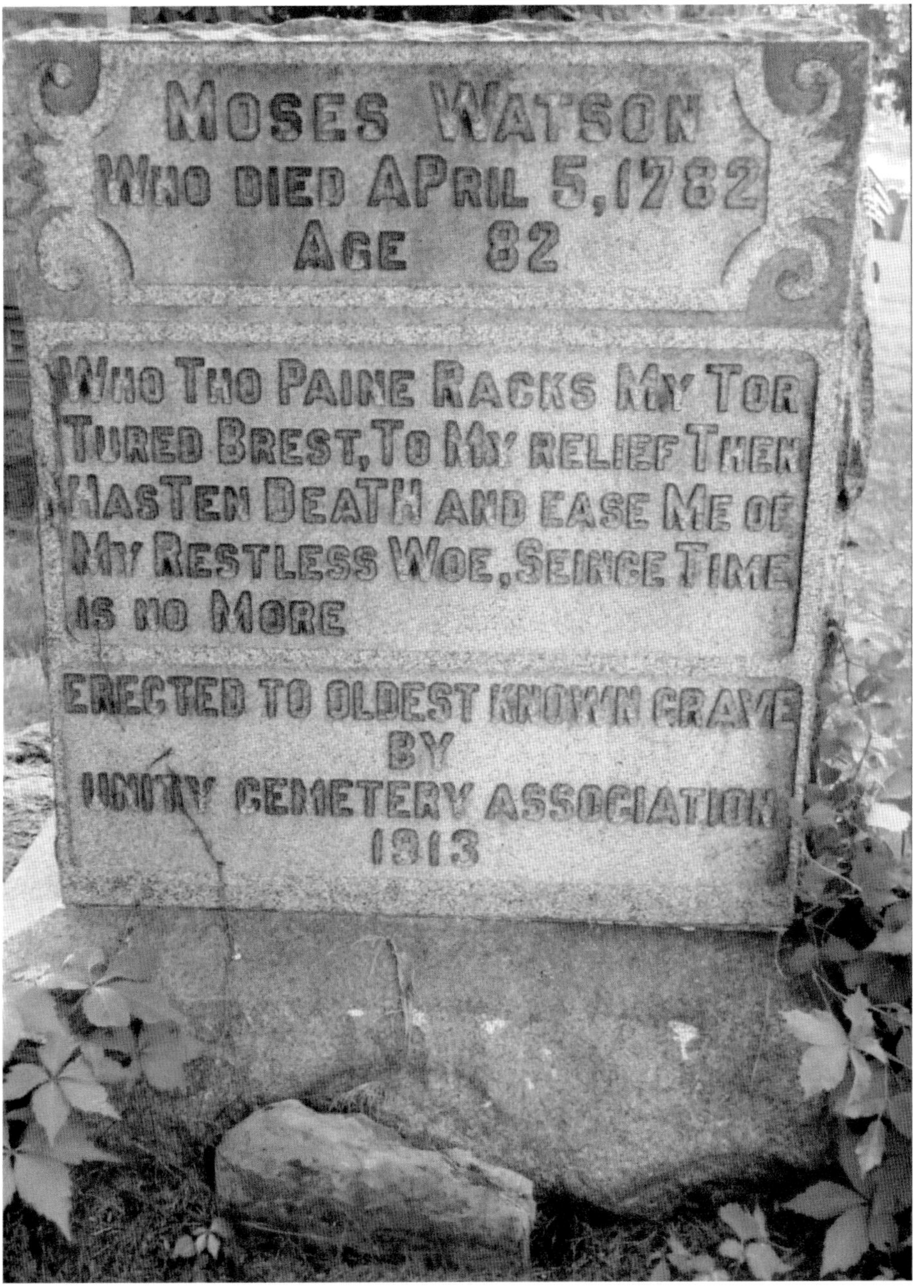

Moses Watson

Moses Watson (1700–1782) was a Revolutionary War soldier. He served as a private in Capt. William Donaldson's Company in the Cumberland County Militia and later as quartermaster under Col. John Proctor of the Westmoreland County Militia. According to the *Commemorative Biographical Record of Central Pennsylvania* (1898), Watson received seven bullet wounds during the war. He is noted in the history of Unity Chapel as having the first recorded burial there. His marker (above) was erected in 1913 by the Unity Cemetery Association and replaced the nearly unreadable original flagstone. It gives Watson the distinction of having the "oldest known grave." (LC.)

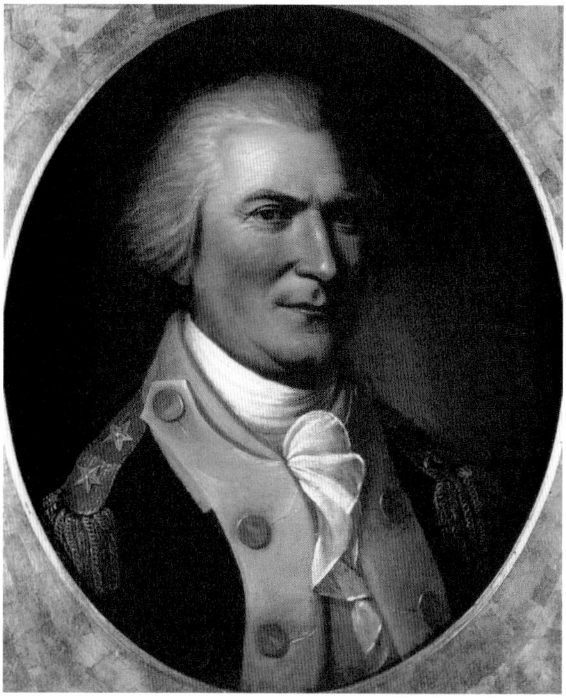

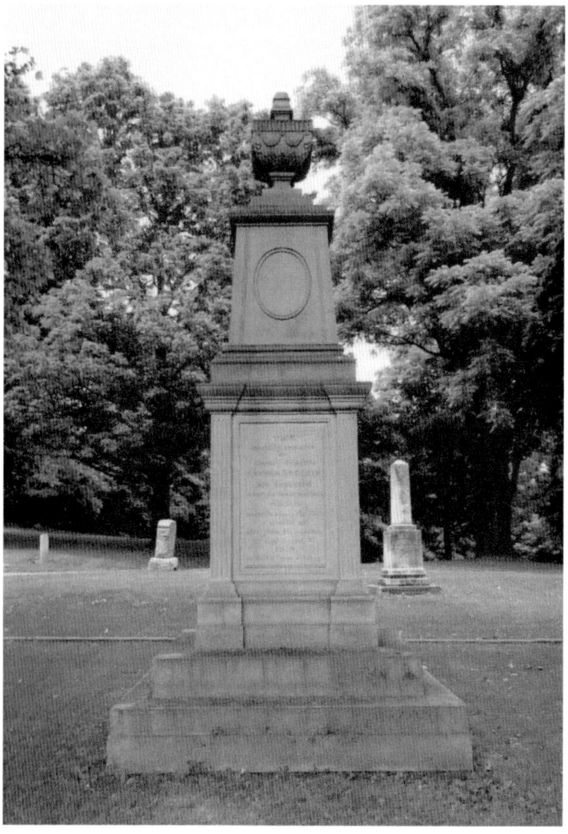

Arthur St. Clair

Gen. Arthur St. Clair (1737–1818) was an American soldier and politician. Born in Scotland, he served in the British army during the French and Indian War before settling in Pennsylvania, where he held local office. During the American Revolution, he became a supporter of the patriot cause. He rose to the rank of major general in the Continental Army but lost his command after a controversial retreat. In his later days, St. Clair lived and ran a tavern at the top of Chestnut Ridge on Forbes Road. Nearby Youngstown served as his market place and post office. He died in poverty, as his vast wealth had been exhausted by generous gifts and loans, by business reverses, and, mainly, by the refusal of Congress to reimburse him for money he loaned during the Revolution and while governor of the Northwest Territory. Pictured above is a portrait of Arthur St. Clair by Charles Willson Peale, painted from life from 1782 to 1784. Pictured below, St. Clair's remains lie buried under a Masonic monument in St. Clair Park in downtown Greensburg, Pennsylvania. (Above, Independence National Historical Park; below, LC.)

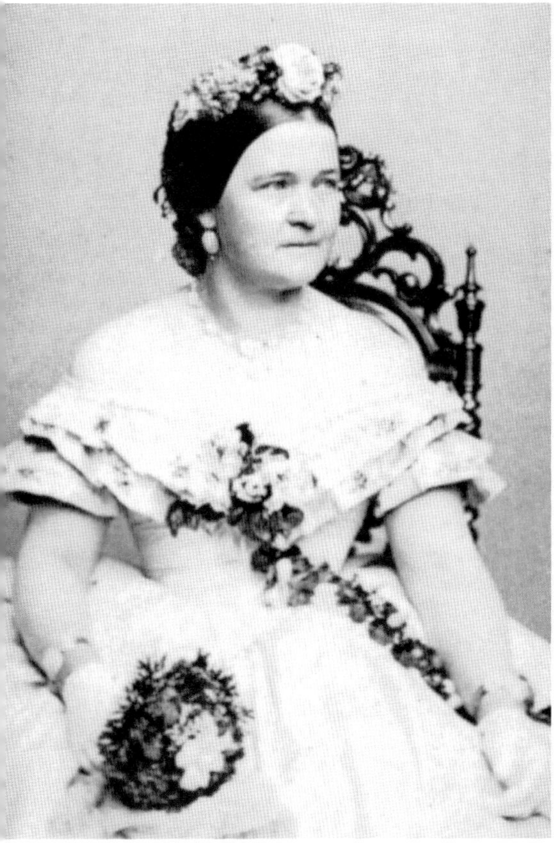

William Todd

William Todd (1739–1810) was an American soldier and politician from Pennsylvania. He fought in the French and Indian War, was involved in the capture of Fort Duquesne, and later fought bravely for independence during the Revolution. A contemporary of Arthur St. Clair, Todd settled west of Youngstown on Forbes Road. He represented Westmoreland County on the Supreme Executive Council, the convention to ratify the federal constitution, and was an associate judge of the county. Pictured is Todd's grandniece Mary Todd, who would later become Abraham Lincoln's wife and first lady of the United States of America. (AC.)

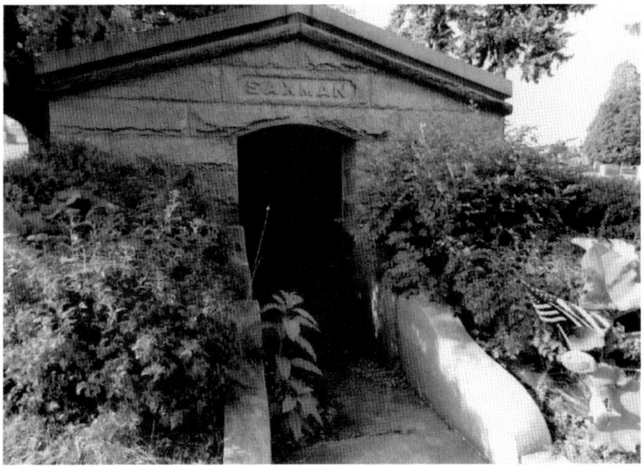

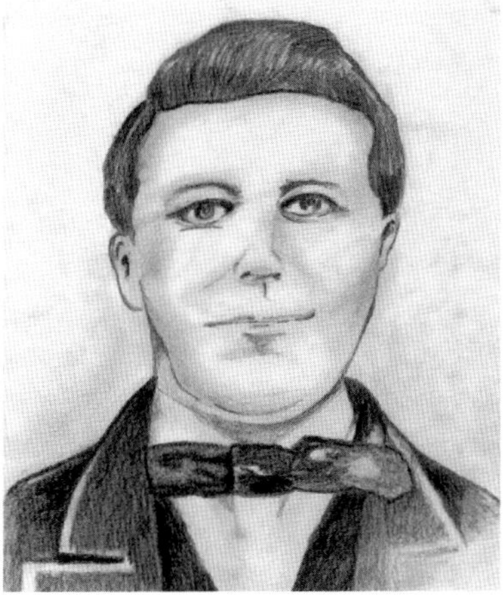

Christian Saxman

Christian "Christopher" Saxman (1733–1836) was living east of Latrobe near what is now Machesneytown in 1765. He is among the early settlers of Latrobe and operated a gristmill on the banks of the Loyalhanna Creek where Saxman's Run enters from the east. His mill ground grain for farmers throughout Ligonier Valley and from as far away as Fort Pitt. Saxman's descendants would have a profound effect on the Latrobe area in the coal and steel industries. The semi-subterranean Saxman family mausoleum (left) is located in the old section of Unity Cemetery. (Both, AC.)

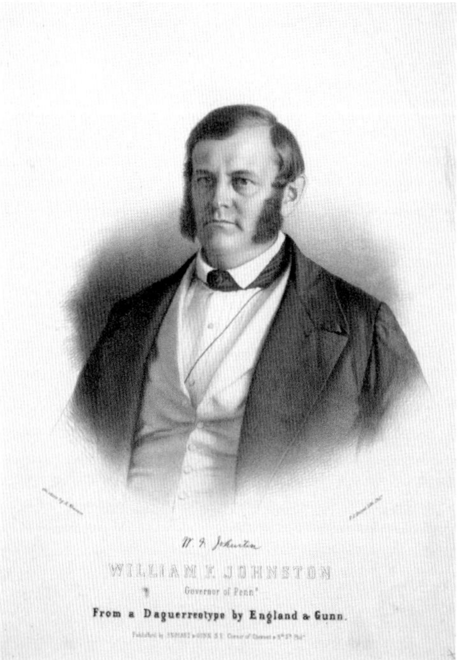

William Freame Johnston

William Freame Johnston (1808–1872) served as governor of Pennsylvania from 1848 to 1852. Born in Greensburg, Johnston grew up at Kingston House, on Loyalhanna Creek, about three miles from Latrobe. His father, Alexander Johnston, arrived in Westmoreland County in 1797 and was an iron manufacturer. He built the stone home and, along with the governor's mother, Elizabeth Freame, raised a family of eight sons and two daughters in what is now referred to as the Historic Johnston House. Governor Johnston is perhaps best known for succeeding in having the state legislature pass a new appropriation to finish the South Fork Dam on Lake Conemaugh—the same dam that later collapsed, causing the Great Johnstown Flood. (Division of Home and Community Life, National Museum of American History, Smithsonian Institution, Harry T. Peters, "America on Stone" Lithography Collection.)

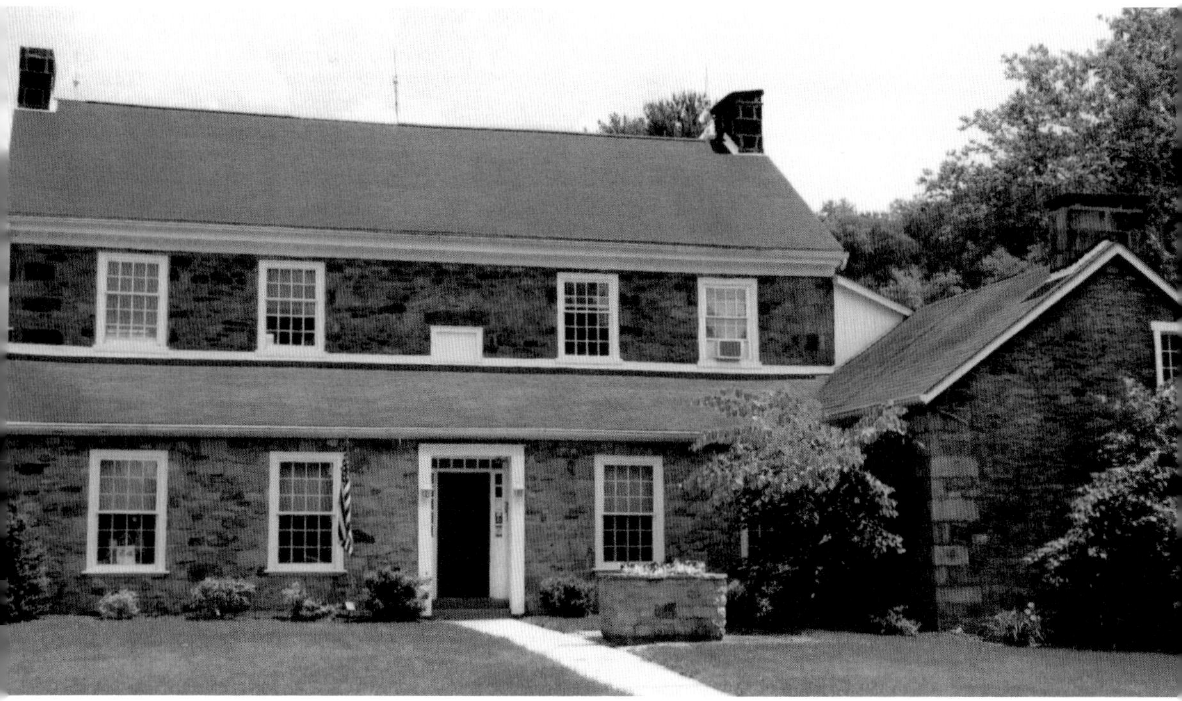

Historic Johnston House

Built in 1815, as a tablet on its front wall indicates, the Historic Johnston House, boyhood home of Pennsylvania governor William Freame Johnston, was transformed in 2012 into the Lincoln Highway Experience on US Route 30 near the Kingston Bridge in Latrobe. The museum is dedicated to America's first transcontinental highway and is one of the oldest structures along its path. (LC.)

CHAPTER TWO

Business and Industry

At the time of the early settlers and pioneers, the Latrobe area was defined by its geography—the green rolling hills of Chestnut Ridge to the east, the patchwork quilt of forests and farmlands, and the winding narrow ribbon of Loyalhanna Creek, bending so severely in the west it practically tied itself in a knot. The small town of Latrobe, however, would soon be defined by the railroad. On April 13, 1846, J. Edgar Thompson, chief engineer for the newly incorporated Pennsylvania Railroad, was required to select a line route between Altoona and Greensburg. Initially, three different routes were considered: a northern route near Blairsville, a southern route through Ligonier, and a middle route through Derry. Thompson chose the middle route for the main line because it reduced the amount of time required to reach Pittsburgh. Civil engineer Oliver W. Barnes was then commissioned to obtain ground in the area now known as Latrobe for the railroad yard. He successfully negotiated on behalf of the Pennsylvania Railroad for Thomas Kirk's farm, but the Pennsylvania Railroad reversed course and chose instead to build the rail yard approximately five miles east in Derry. Barnes saw a business opportunity and decided to purchase the Kirk land for himself. According to Latrobe author and attorney Richard L. Jim in his book, *The Making of Latrobe*, "He [Barnes] negotiated directly with Thomas Kirk and purchased the land for $7,400. He paid only $1,000 down and executed a purchase money mortgage for $6,400, to be paid to Thomas Kirk and his wife, over a period of six years." In 1852, Barnes laid out plans for his new town that would be incorporated in 1854 as the Borough of Latrobe. Soon the familiar grid of city streets began to appear, and in the distance, the bright orange glow of burning coke ovens filled the night skies from the surrounding coal patch communities. Bituminous coal produced in the 200 square miles surrounding Latrobe fed the booming railroad industry while local steel mills devoured the coke made in beehive ovens. Today, the area is still known for its steel, especially for its production of carbide. With industry in the late 18th and early 19th centuries came more thriving businesses producing a wide variety of materials and services and, along with them, the entrepreneurs and inventors who would become some of the region's most notable and legendary locals.

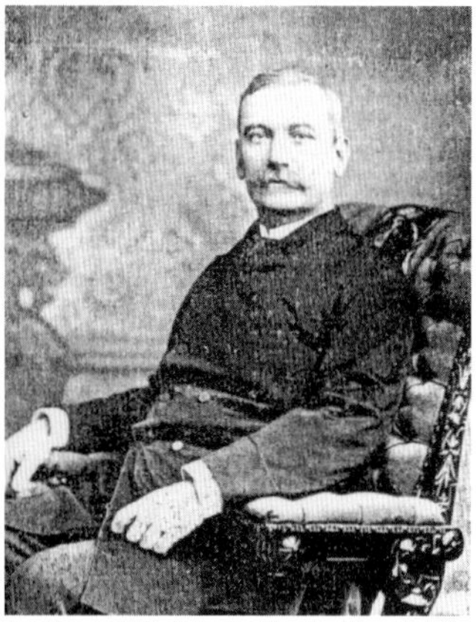

Oliver W. Barnes

Oliver W. Barnes (1823–1908) was Latrobe's founder and a railroad engineer. Knowing the railroad coming from the east would pass through Thomas Kirk's farm and wooded property, Barnes bought the land, laid out a plan for the town, and immediately began to sell lots. According to author and historian John Newton Boucher in his *History of Westmoreland County, Volume I* (1906), it was said to be "the most beautifully located town in Westmoreland County" for its topography. Barnes also knew the needs of the railroad and built the town's first hotel, constructed a water and wood station, and established the Pennsylvania Car Works, often cited as the borough's first industry. (LAHS.)

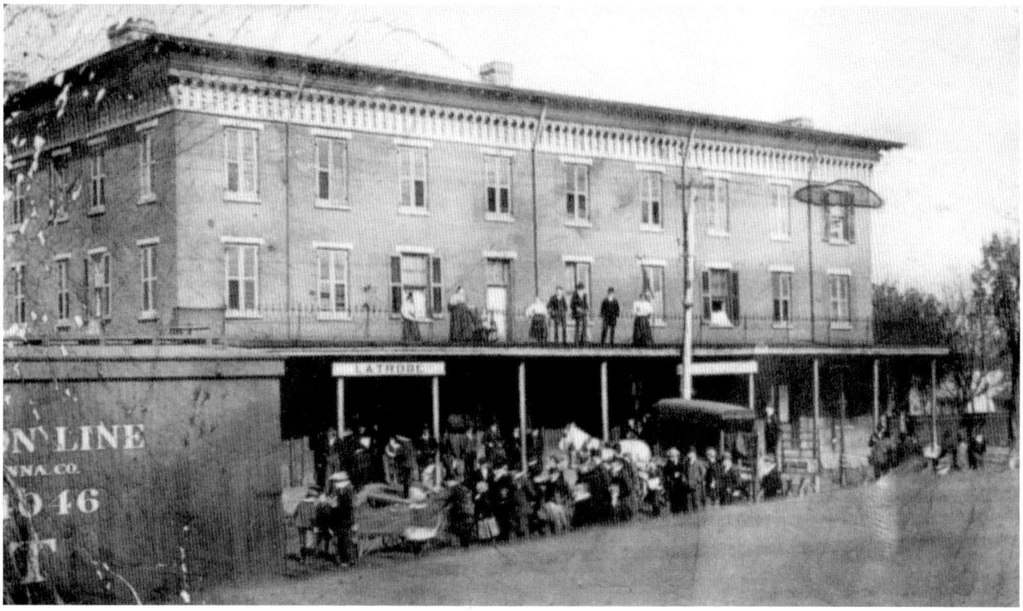

Clifford House

The Clifford House was the first hotel to accommodate Latrobe's visitors and stood where the old passenger station is located today. It was erected by Oliver W. Barnes and operated by Joseph Clifford. The three-story building served both as a hotel and as the railroad station. "Passengers delighted in the famous Clifford House pancakes and sausage," according to the book *Historic Latrobe: A Glance or Two at Earlier Times*. The building was razed in 1902, when the railroad tracks were elevated. (LAHS.)

Benjamin Henry Latrobe

Benjamin Henry Latrobe (1806–1878) was a friend and college roommate of Oliver W. Barnes and became Latrobe's namesake. According to his granddaughter, Latrobe never visited the town named after him. He was the chief engineer for the Baltimore & Ohio Railroad and the son of Benjamin Henry Boneval Latrobe, architect of the US Capitol. Latrobe's greatest standing accomplishment as construction chief for the B&O is the Thomas Viaduct, the railroad's first bridge built on a curved alignment. (AC.)

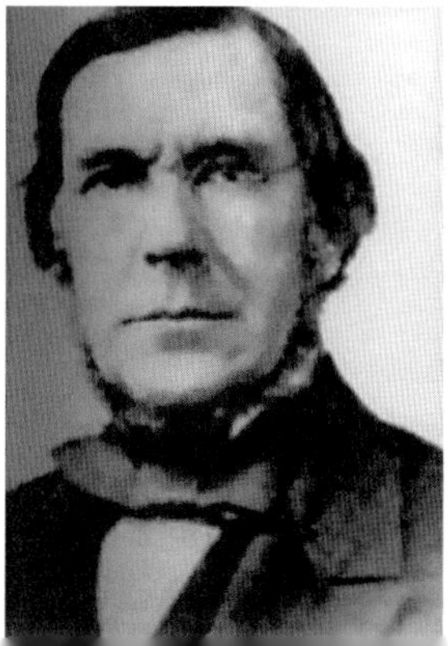

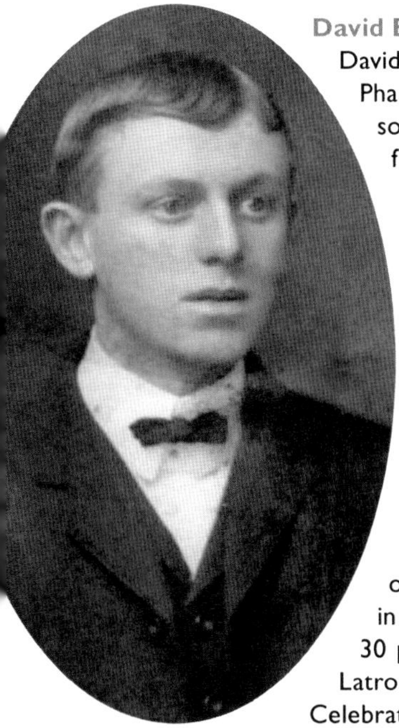

David Evans Strickler

David Evans "Doc" Strickler (1881–1971) was a 23-year-old apprentice at Tassell Pharmacy in Latrobe. In 1904, while experimenting one day at the store's soda fountain, Strickler cut a banana lengthwise, smothered it with assorted flavors of ice cream, and topped it with sweet syrups, marshmallows, chopped nuts, whipped cream, and a maraschino cherry. He dubbed his creation the "Banana Split" and began selling the frozen treats for 10¢ apiece. The confection became an instant hit with students from nearby St. Vincent College. "When a guy took his best girl out," Strickler's son William explained in the August 1, 2004, edition of the *Tribune-Review*, "he bought her a banana split. Other girls just got ice-cream cones." Within a few years, druggists and ice cream parlor owners across the country learned of the new sundae, and its popularity and notoriety quickly spread. Strickler went on to buy the Latrobe pharmacy where he invented the banana split. Although he is most noted for his triple sundae, "Doc," as he was known locally, was a man of many accomplishments. He was an optometrist, community leader, and pharmacist who created his own furniture polish, headache remedy, and homemade root beer. He died in 1971 at age 90. Pictured below is a banana split jelly bean mural utilizing 30 pounds of jelly beans and created by 28 children who took part in the Latrobe Art Center's Kid's Art Camp during the Great American Banana Split Celebration in 2013. (Left, LAHS; below, AC.)

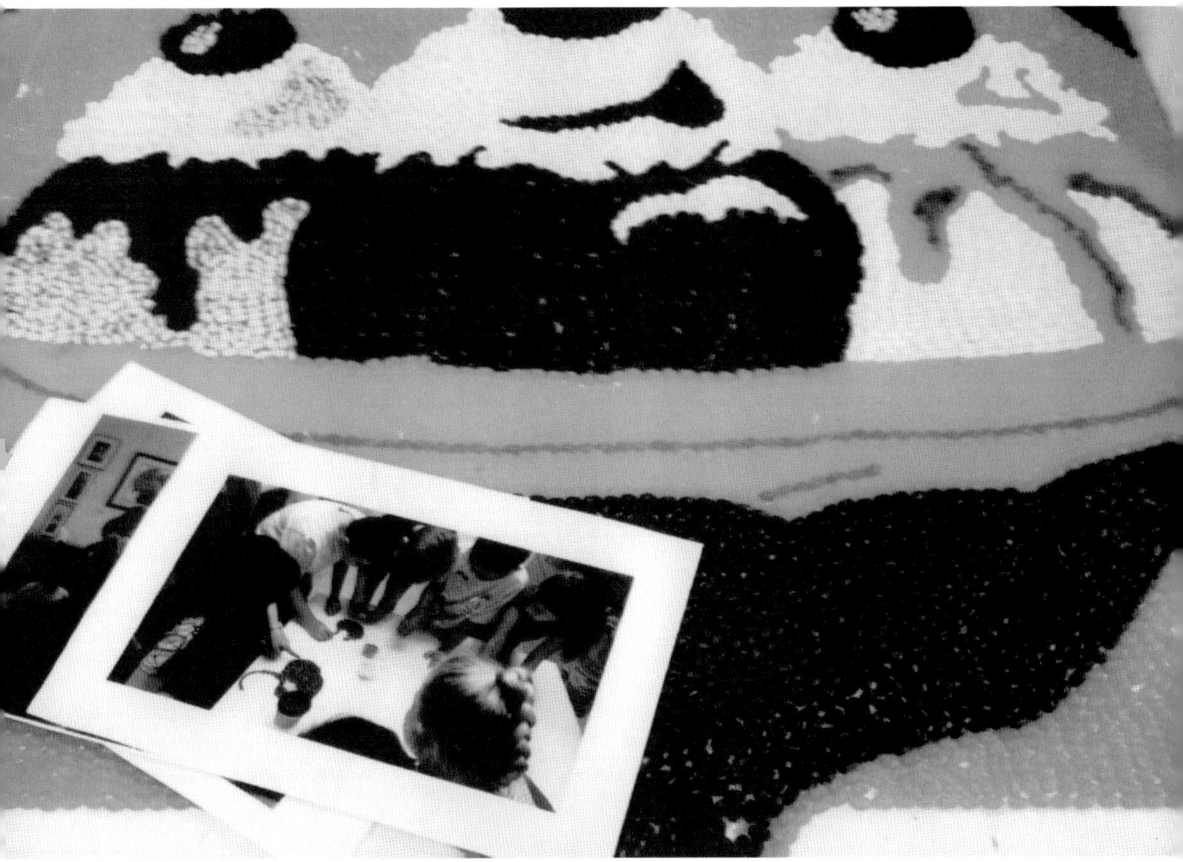

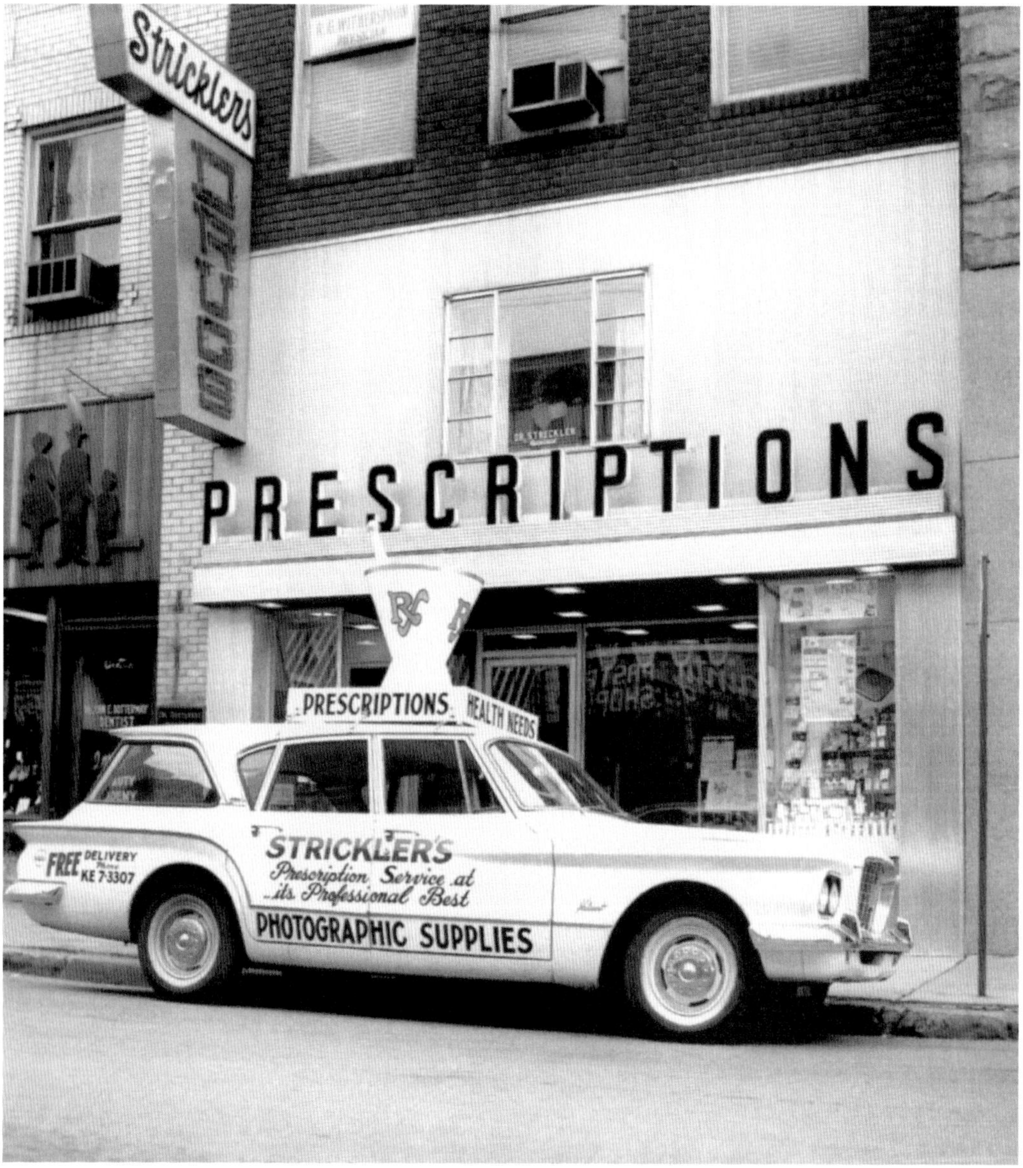

Strickler's Drug Store

Strickler's Drug Store at 805 Ligonier Street is shown with its 1960 Plymouth Valiant delivery car in front. The building that housed Tassell Pharmacy, and later Strickler's, was still standing in downtown Latrobe as recently as 2009, when Valley Dairy's Joe Greubel said, in the June 2009 edition of *American Profile* magazine, he hoped the building would be transformed into a banana split museum. Since that time, it has been razed, and in its place, a narrow grassy plot holds the recently unveiled banana split historical marker. At the time the photograph was taken, Charles T. Poorman was the owner. Tom Lazarchik bought the drugstore in 1966 and kept the Strickler name until the business closed its doors for the final time in 2000. (FF.)

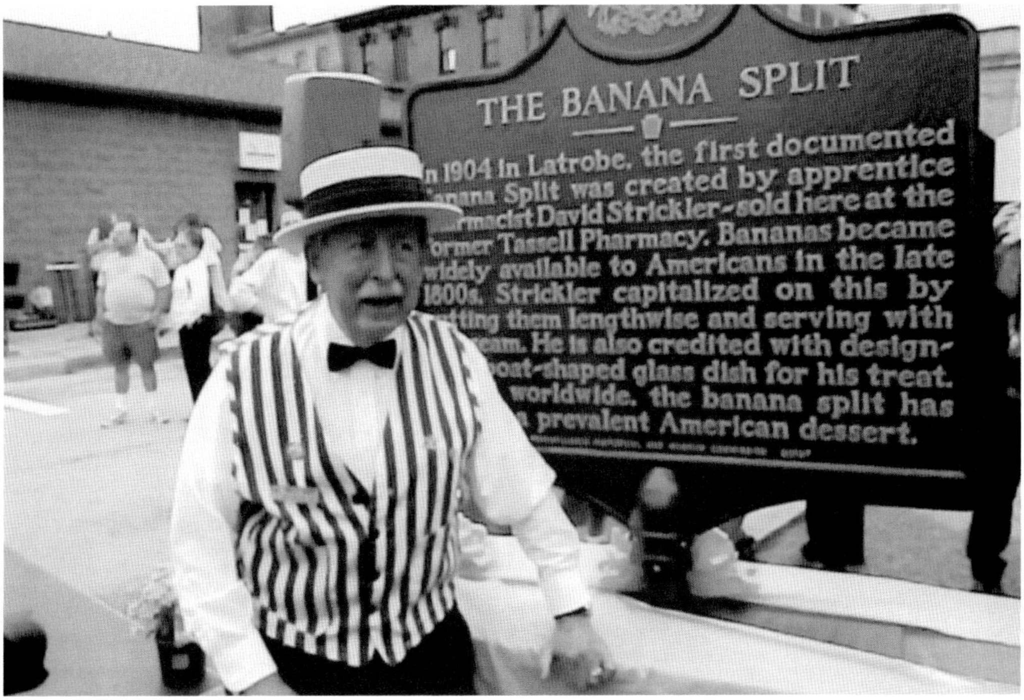

Joseph E. Greubel

Joseph E. "Ice Cream Joe" Greubel transformed his family's ice cream–centered dairy stores into the thriving Valley Dairy Restaurant chain. He says his joy in creating a pleasing product has remained unchanged since he learned to make ice cream at his father's side as a boy. Greubel's great-grandfather Joseph A. Greubel is credited with being Westmoreland County's first ice cream maker at his bakery in Derry in 1884. Greubel is shown wearing his traditional ice cream vendor outfit at the banana split historical marker dedication. His father, Joseph F. Greubel, was the first to don the iconic red and white–striped vest to greet the public and man an ice cream cart at special events. (AC.)

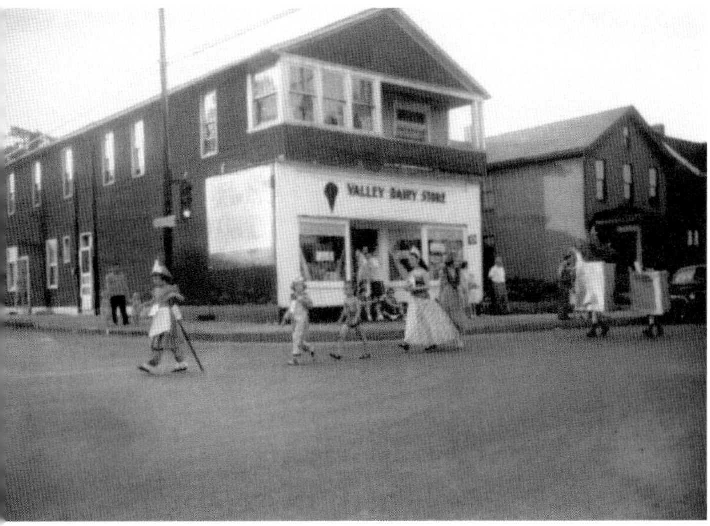

Valley Dairy Store

This photograph, taken in 1955, shows one of "Ice Cream Joe's" Valley Dairy Stores, located on the corner of Lloyd Avenue and Unity Street. In the foreground, children in costume march during the annual Halloween Parade. It must have been a warm October day, as a young Tarzan walks along in a loincloth and onlookers in short sleeves line up for a cold treat at Joe's. (FF.)

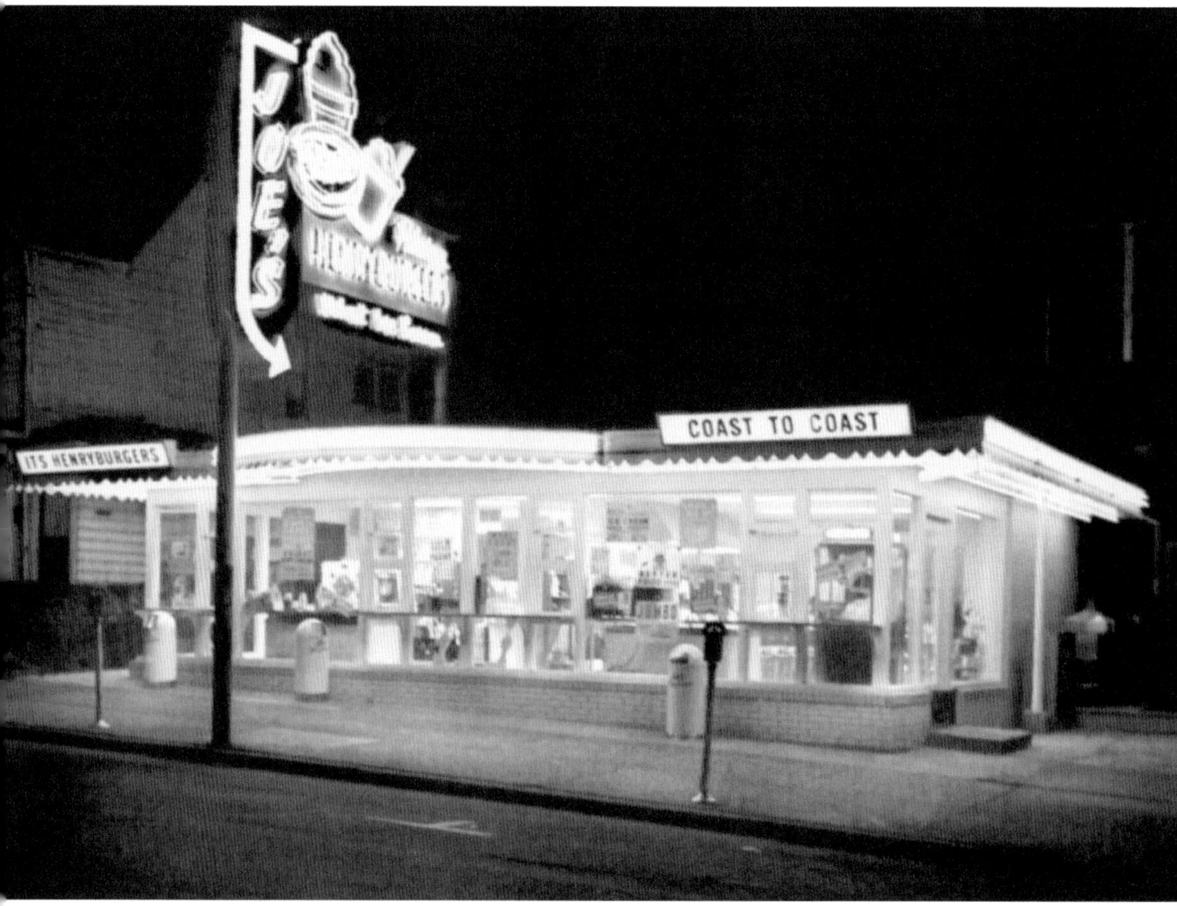

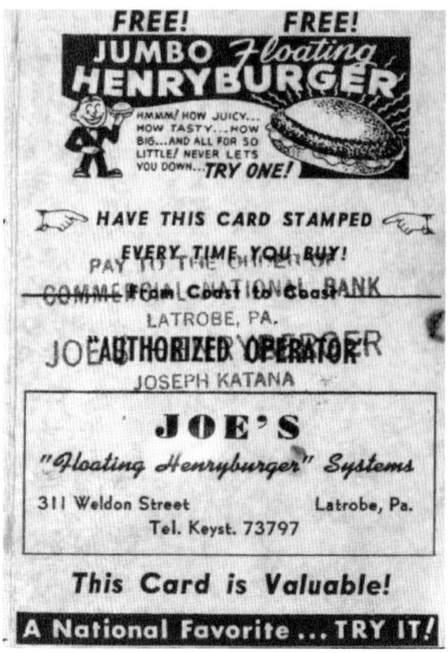

Joseph Katana

Joseph "Joe" Katana's burger joint, Joe's Henryburger at 311 Weldon Street, Latrobe, was the hangout for local teenagers in the 1950s. Area residents fondly recall getting four "Floating Henryburgers" for a dollar. The Floating Henryburger System and the "Coast to Coast" motto originated with the Jesse & Jesse Company of Wichita, Kansas. An article in *Time* magazine dated December 27, 1954, explained the cooking process: "K.M. Jesse, president of the Floating Henryburger System (38 hamburger stands in 12 states), has developed an automatic hamburger cooker. The hamburgers are shaped by hand, then loaded on a conveyor belt that automatically carries them through the cooker, dips them in sauce, and turns them out at the rate of 480 an hour." Katana offered his patrons a stamp card featuring buy six burgers and get the seventh one free. The stamp card (left) is on display at the Latrobe Area Historical Society. (Above, FF; left, LAHS.)

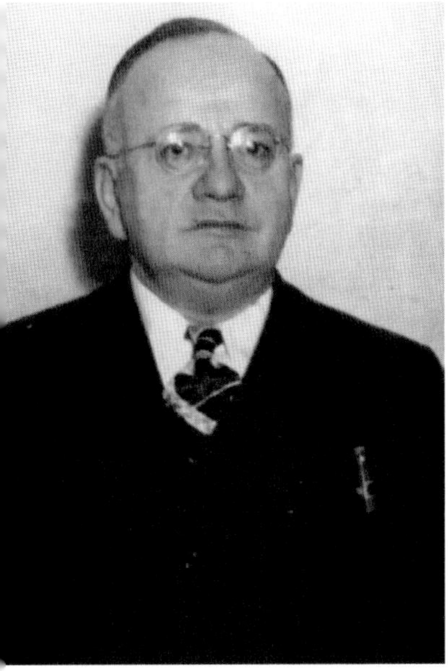

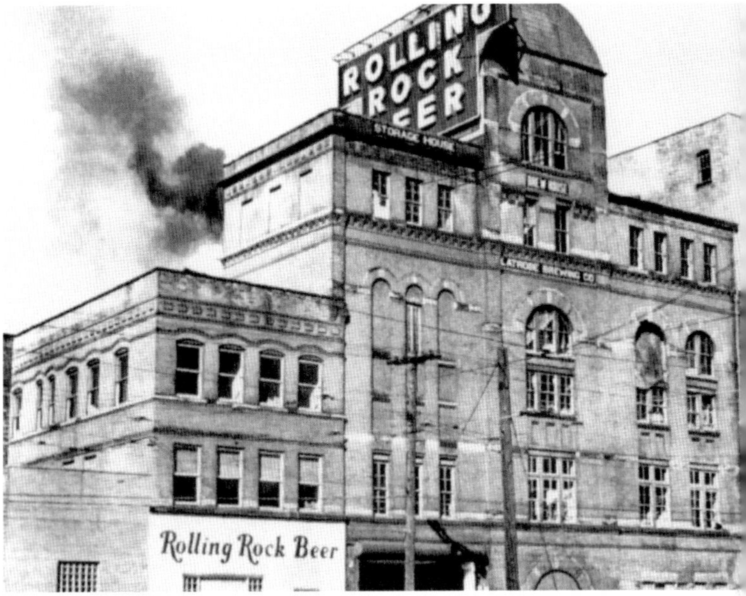

Tito Brothers

Monks of the Benedictine Society of St. Vincent's Abbey were the first brewmasters in the Latrobe area, having opened their brewery in 1856. The Latrobe Brewing Company opened its doors more than three decades later as a cadet brewery of Pittsburgh Brewing in 1893. After Prohibition, Pittsburgh decided to drop some of its smaller breweries, and Latrobe was sold to the Tito brothers—Frank, Joseph, Robert, Ralph, and Anthony—who reopened it in 1933. For six years, the Tito brothers brewed Latrobe Old German and Latrobe Pilsner varieties. Then, in 1939, Rolling Rock was introduced. On those very first silk-screened green bottles, the pledge read: "Rolling Rock. From the glass lined tanks of old Latrobe we tender this premium beer for your enjoyment, as a tribute to your good taste. It comes from the mountain springs to you." At the end of the motto is the number 33. While others have speculated that the 33 signifies the year Prohibition was repealed (1933) or that Latrobe test-brewed 33 batches of beer before coming up with the final formula, James L. Tito, former chief executive officer of Latrobe Brewing, explained that the number most likely signifies the 33 words in the pledge of quality. It was noted as a word count only and putting the number on the label was nothing more or less than an accident. The errant 33 was not removed when the design was sent off to the bottle maker and was subsequently painted on the back label at the end of the 33-word pledge. The "accident" turned out to be good for marketing. It seems nothing helps sell a product like a little mystery. Pictured above are Joseph Tito, vice president of the Latrobe Brewing Company, and the brewery and brew house on Ligonier Street with the familiar neon Rolling Rock Beer sign on top. (Left, LAHS; right, FF.)

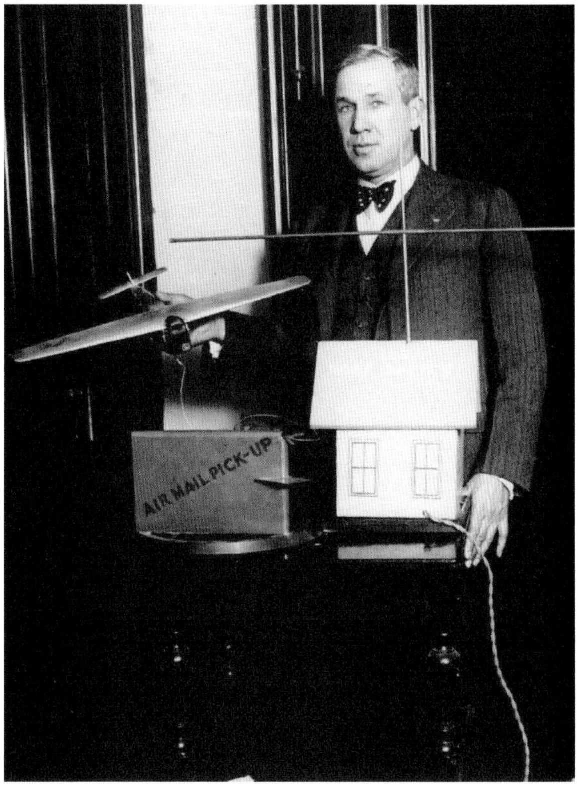

Lytle Schooler Adams

Dr. Lytle Schooler "Doc" Adams (1881–1970) of Irwin, Pennsylvania, was an oral surgeon and part-time inventor who believed airmail service could be expanded to rural areas. Pictured in 1927 exhibiting his models, Adams began experimenting with a pickup device that enabled airplanes to collect and deliver mail loads while in full flight. Twelve years later, the first officially scheduled nonstop airmail pickup flight took place at Latrobe Airport as onlookers snapped photographs and filmed the historic event. (Copyright © Willis Adams, 2014, all rights reserved. Reprinted with permission.)

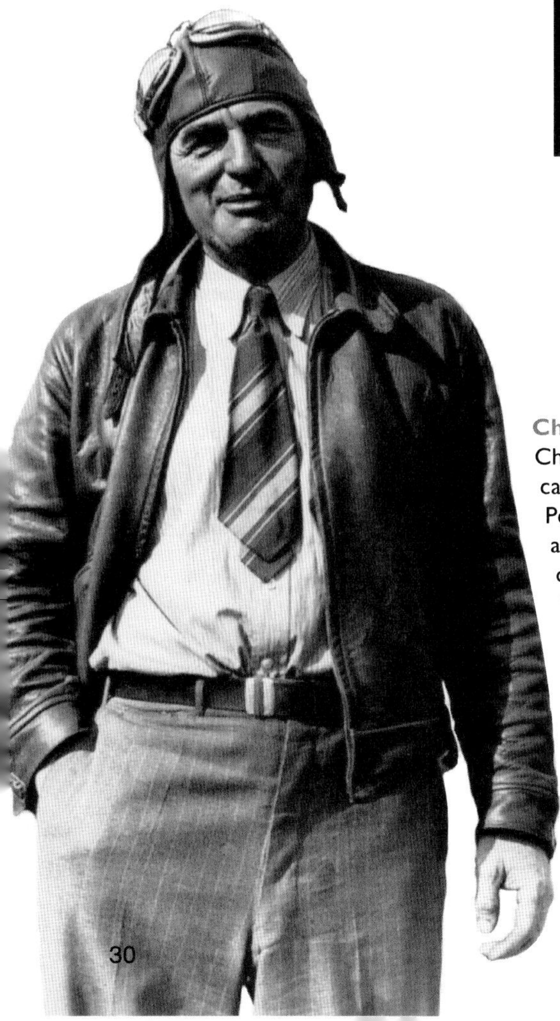

Charles B. Carroll

Charles B. "Charlie" Carroll (1890–1973) was a car salesman and mechanic from nearby Scottdale, Pennsylvania. He caught the aviation bug and bought an old army surplus Curtiss JN-4 "Jenny." After flying over the Latrobe area and landing in a field at St. Vincent College, he noticed the property across the Lincoln Highway, known as the Kerr Farm. He convinced the owner to lease his cow pasture as an airfield and established a permanent flying field there in 1919. This was the humble beginning of Longview Flying Field in 1924, J.D. Hill Airport in 1928, Latrobe Airport in 1935, Westmoreland County Airport in 1978, and today's Arnold Palmer Regional Airport. (Lloyd Santmeyer and St. Vincent College's Center for Northern Appalachian Studies [SVCCNAS] *Place in the Sky*.)

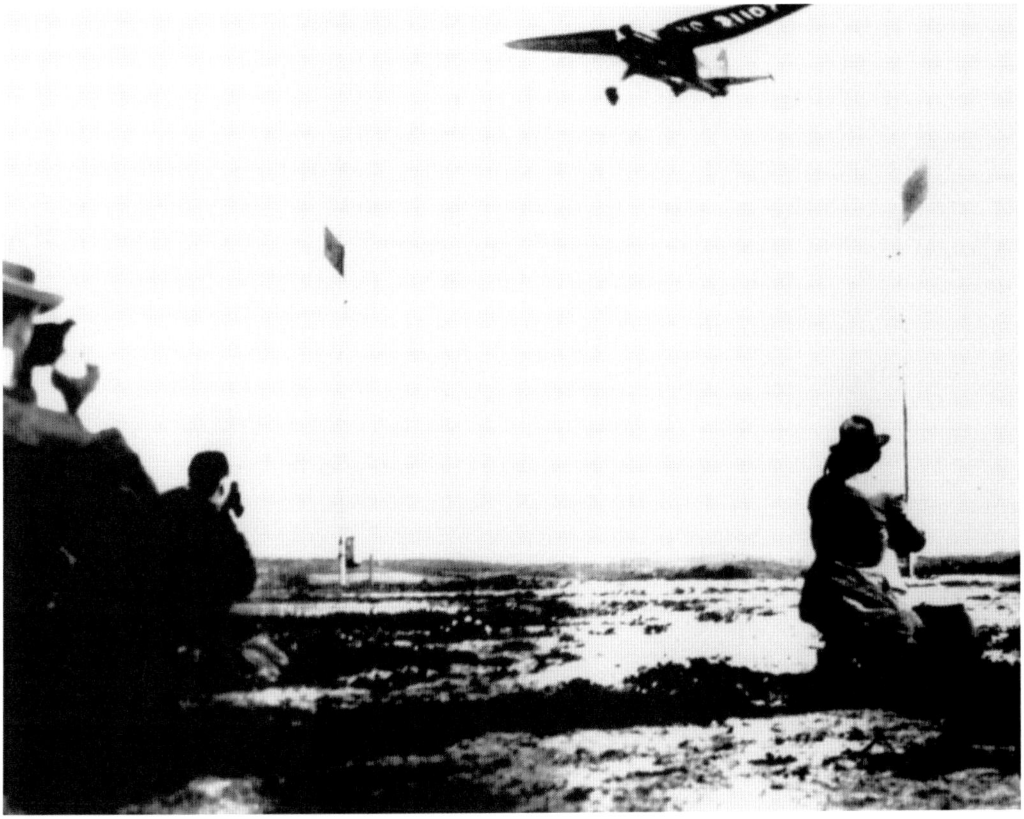

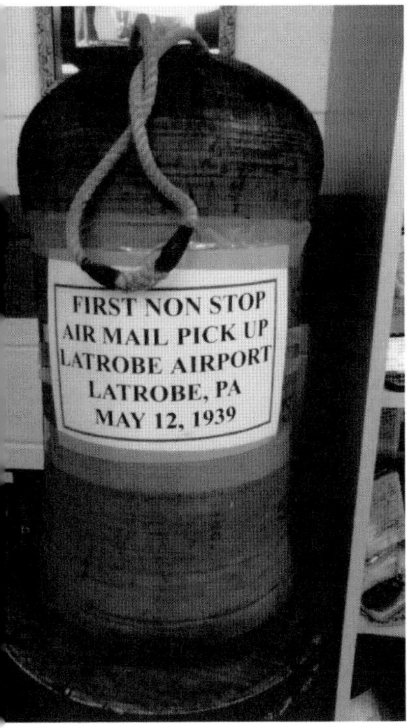

First Nonstop Airmail Pickup

The first nonstop airmail pickup (above) was witnessed as a bright red Stinson Reliant plane swooped down out of the sky in Latrobe, snatching a saltshaker-shaped container of mail suspended on a rope between two poles on May 12, 1939. At that time, airmail service was restricted almost exclusively to metropolitan centers, out of reach of the majority of the country's population. The Stinson Reliant planes were chosen for their rugged reliability and tight-turning flying capability around hills and through valleys. For 10 years, a fleet of these planes provided airmail pickup to locations in the northeast United States that could not be served by regular airmail service. Dr. Lytle Schooler Adams modeled the pickup technique on the Railway Mail Service's Mail-on-the-Fly service. A display at the Smithsonian National Postal Museum in Washington, DC, reads, "The Stinson, painted bright red for easy identification, had a long take up boom with a hook and a winch that operated through an opening in the fuselage. Traveling between towns at 110 miles per hour, the Stinsons collected and delivered mail and express packages at each community without landing." An original airmail pickup container (left) is on display at the Latrobe Area Historical Society. The container is open on the bottom with an upside-down mailbag inside. (Above, LAHS and SVCCNAS *Place in the Sky*; left, LC.)

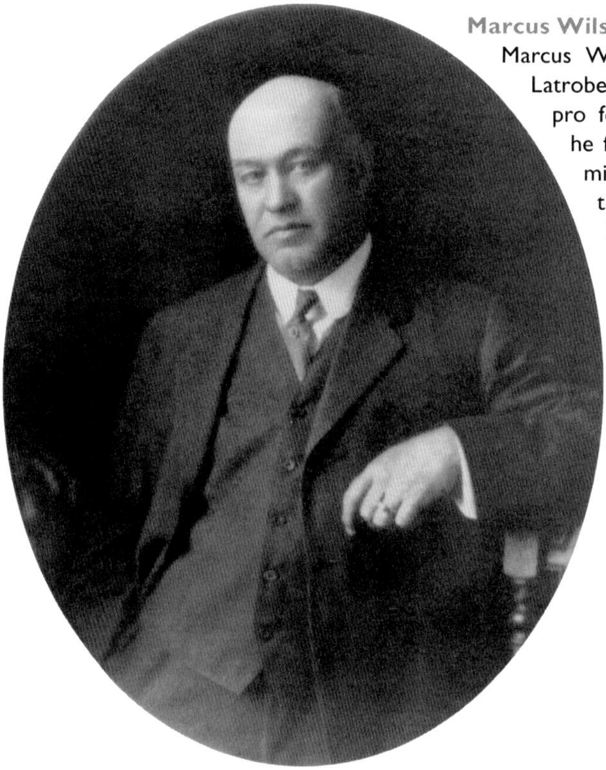

Marcus Wilson Saxman

Marcus Wilson Saxman (1867–1934) was born in Latrobe and played left halfback for the first all-pro football team. In the early 20th century, he followed his father, Mathias, into the coal mining business, and in 1913, he cofounded the Latrobe Electric Steel Company, where he served as the first president until his death in 1934. Latrobe Electric Steel revolutionized American steel making with North America's first electric arc furnace and developed the first mirror-finished cutlery in the United States. In 2013, Latrobe Steel—now Latrobe Specialty Metals, a Carpenter Company—celebrated its 100th birthday under a banner that read, "Steel Forging Strong." (LAHS.)

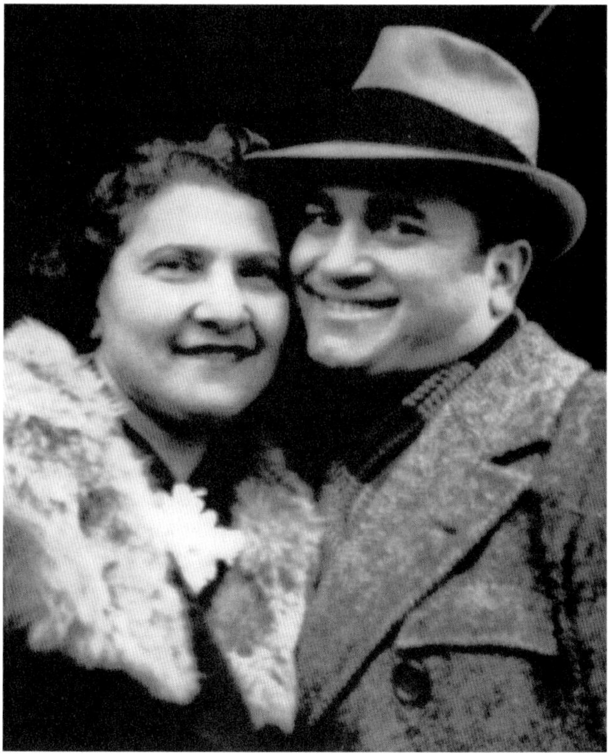

Rose Rubinoff Buchman

Rose Rubinoff Buchman (1892–1951) opened her Rose Style Shoppe in June 1932 in the Miller Hotel on the corner of Ligonier and Depot Streets. Born in Grodno, Russia, Buchman came to the area thanks to her brother's extraordinary skill on the violin. In the photograph, Buchman (left) is pictured with her brother, David Rubinoff, who was heard during the 1930s and 1940s on various radio programs playing his $100,000 Stradivarius violin. In 1945, Rose Style Shoppe moved to its present site at 906 Ligonier Street. Today, the business celebrates its over-80-year-old history by displaying generations of family photographs above the checkout counter. (Rhonda Goetz/LAHS.)

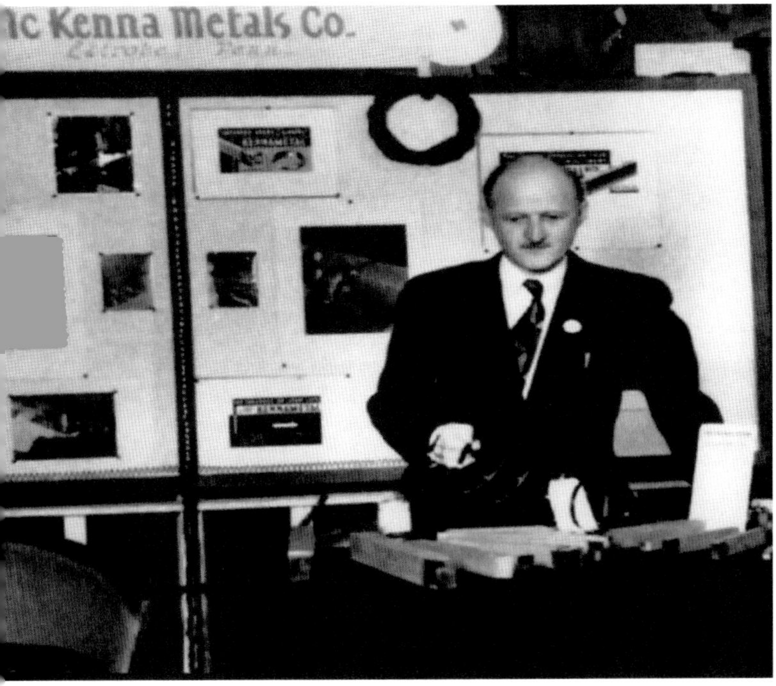

Philip Mowry McKenna
Philip Mowry McKenna (1897–1969) founded McKenna Metals Company in 1938 and created a hard metal carbide for cutting steel. "Kennametal tools cut faster and lasted longer," early advertisements read. In 1943, the organization was incorporated under its present name. Kennametal Corporation has become a world leader in the metalworking industry and remains headquartered in Latrobe. (LAHS.)

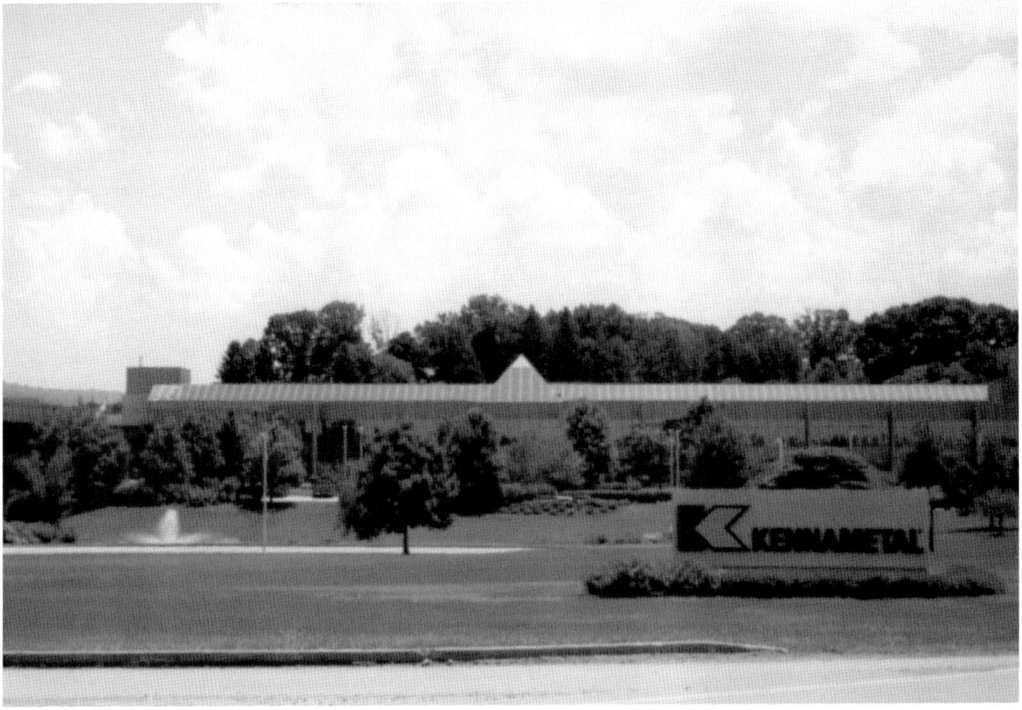

Kennametal Corporation
Kennametal Corporation employs nearly 13,000 worldwide with annual sales at around $3 billion. Headquartered in Latrobe, it has operations in over 60 countries and is the global market leader in tooling for the mining and highway construction industries. (AC.)

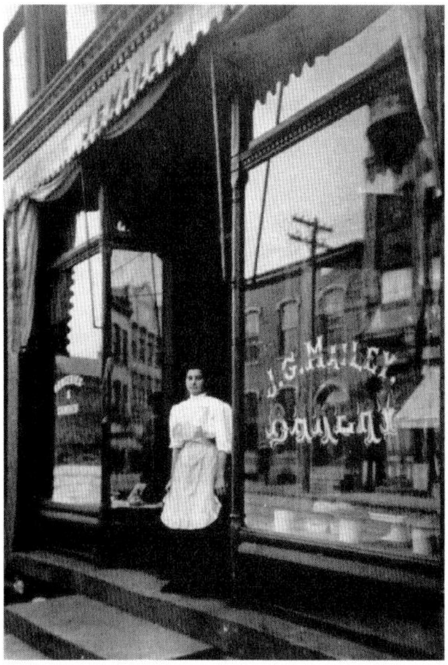

John Gottlieb Mailey

Mailey's Bakery on Main Street has a long history in Latrobe. John Gottlieb Mailey's uncle, J.A. Maier, began serving breads and sweets from his bakery on Ligonier Street, near the railroad tracks, in 1880. By the time Mailey was 16 years old, he was given the responsibility of running the business, which at that time was in the Riddell building on Main Street. The current owners, Richard Duncan and "Butch" Burkey highlight the business's history with antiques and still use the original 1898 brick oven to bake treats. (LAHS.)

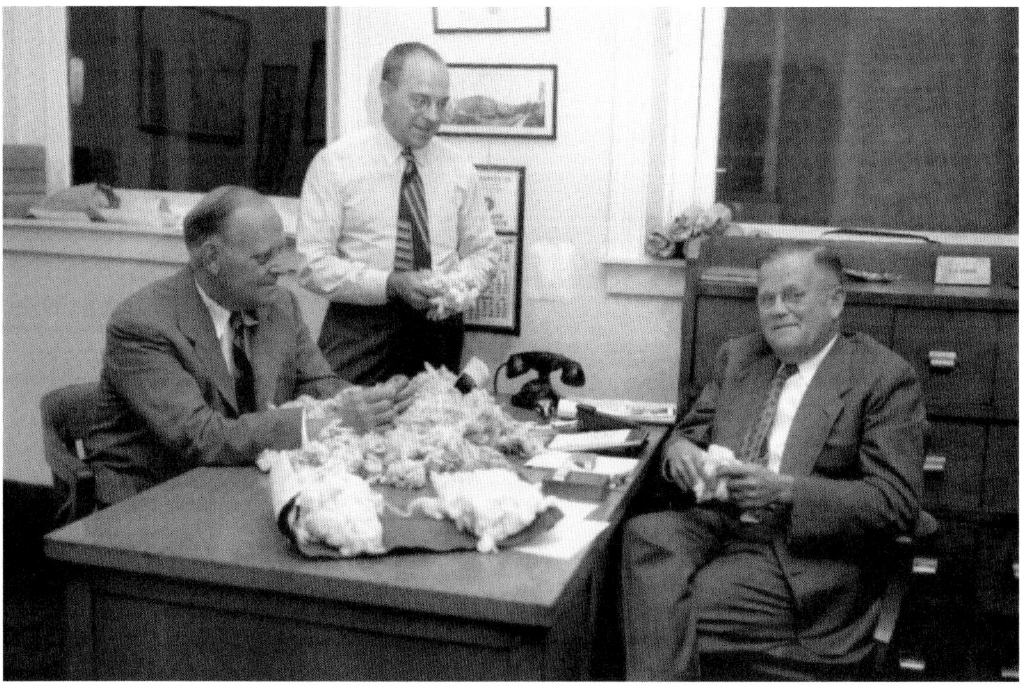

James B. Corson

James B. Corson (1896–1957), seated at right, was president of Pearce Woolen Mills in Latrobe. For many years, the principal product of the company was Pearce all-wool blankets. The first mill was established in 1805 at Harmony, Pennsylvania. In 1885, operations moved to Greenville, Pennsylvania, and continued there until a fire in 1904 destroyed the plant. The company then moved to Latrobe, where "adequate facilities were available for immediate operations," according to an advertisement from 1954, which began, "Pearce: America's Oldest Blanket Mill." Corson, a World War I army veteran, was described as a pillar of the area's society, and his company is remembered for contributing much to the community and those in need. (FF.)

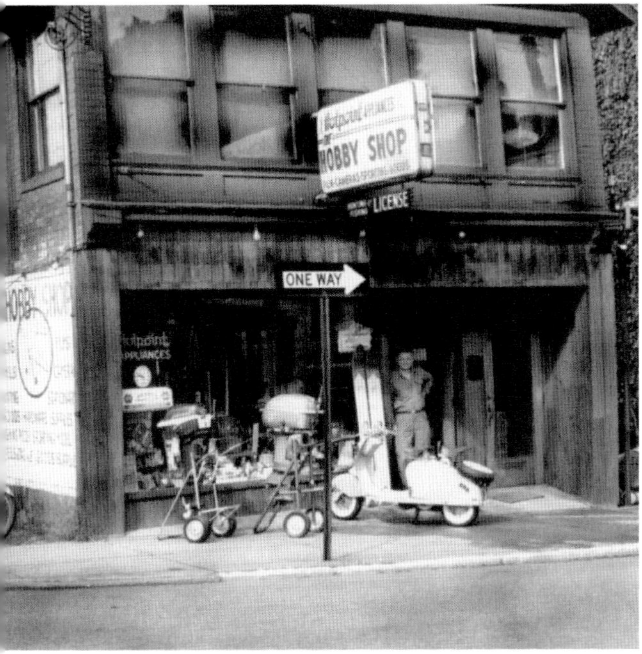

James J. Stumpf

James J. "Jim" Stumpf (1912–1987) owned the Hobby Shop, located on Ligonier and Fairmont Streets in Latrobe for 33 years. He is pictured standing in the doorway in the late 1950s. The outboard motors on the sidewalk and fishing gear in the display window reflect Stumpf's own hobbies. He was a member of the State Fish Commission for 12 years and president for four. From 1954 to 1956, Stumpf operated a marina on the Youghiogheny Flood Control Reservoir and held a captain's license to carry passengers for hire. He was also a deputy game warden for 30 years. In 1979, Stumpf was inducted into both the Westmoreland County Sportsmen's Hall of Fame and the Pennsylvania Federation of Sportsman's Clubs Hall of Fame. (FF.)

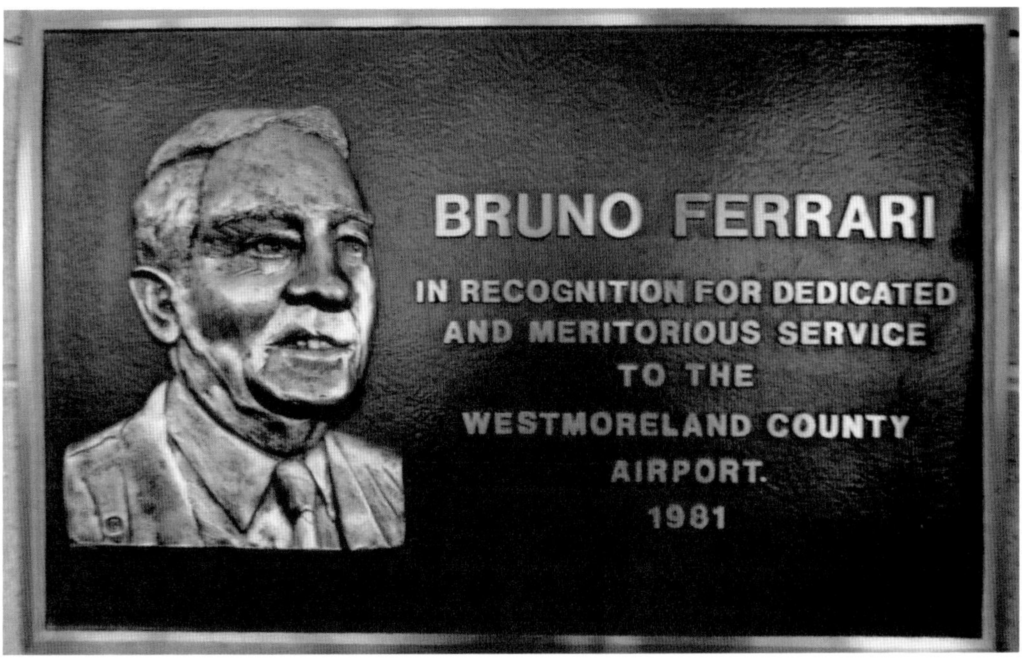

Bruno Ferrari

Bruno Ferrari (1902–2008) was the owner and operator of the Latrobe Construction Company. He was born in Fayette County, Pennsylvania, on April 1, 1902, to Italian immigrant parents. In the early 1930s, Bruno moved to Latrobe and started B. Ferrari General Contracting, which later became known as Latrobe Construction Company. Ferrari was instrumental in building parts of the Westmoreland County Airport and constructing highways in the Latrobe area. Pictured is the Bruno Ferrari Plaque mounted at the entrance to Arnold Palmer Regional Airport. (AC.)

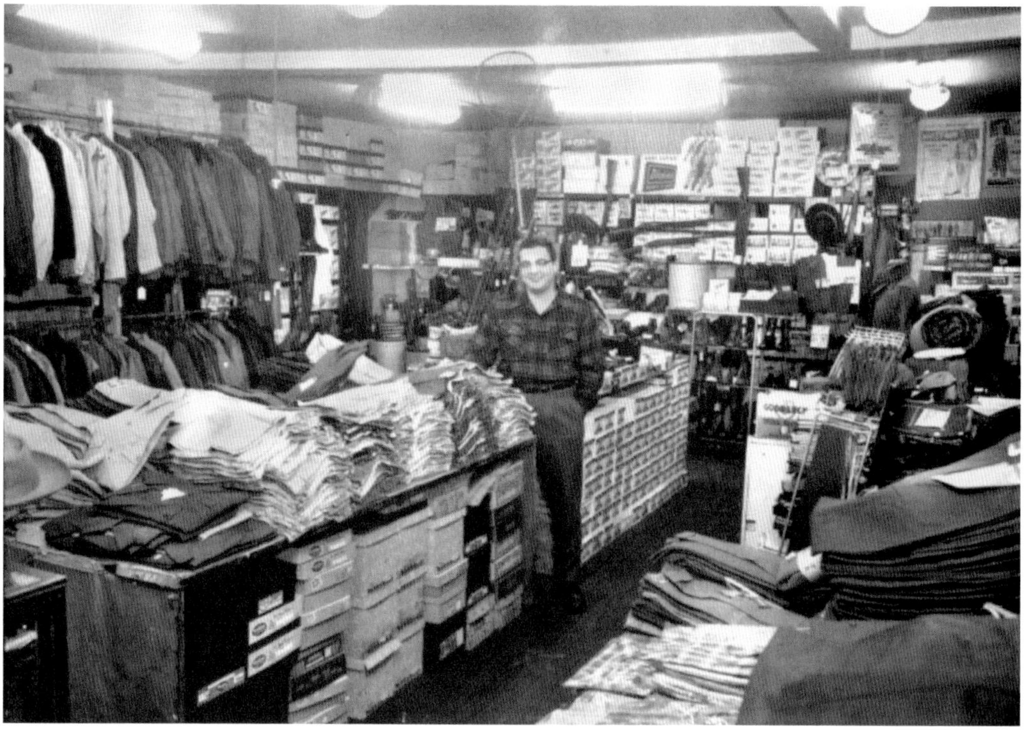

Charles Boerio

Charles Boerio (1928–1990) is pictured in 1955 in his family's Army Navy Store at 1201 Ligonier Street. The Army Navy Store in Latrobe is one of the oldest continually family-operated businesses in the city, having opened in December 1920 under the ownership of Victor J. Boerio. Originally, it sold military surplus, but it has expanded over the years to include sporting goods, uniforms, work clothes, and firearms. (FF.)

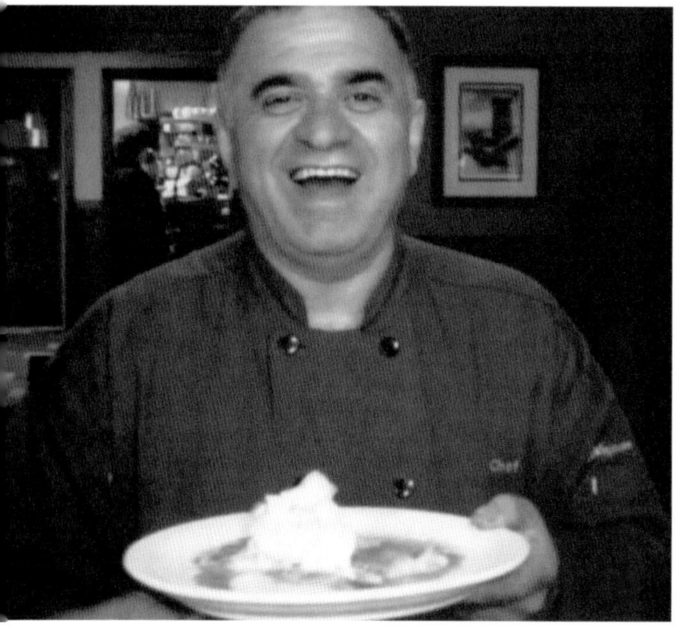

David Kadagishvili

David "Chef Dato" Kadagishvili (1960–2011) came to the area in 2002 to work at Mountain View Inn as the executive sous chef. He went on to have his own restaurant and catering business at the Tin Lizzy in Youngstown, Pennsylvania, and then purchased his own building in Latrobe, near Derry, in May 2010, calling it Chef Dato's Table. Kadagishvili came to the United States in 1994 from the former Soviet republic of Georgia and became an American citizen on January 16, 2009. He proudly displayed a large American flag outside his restaurant and often donated his time and talents to charitable events. Tragically, Chef Dato died in a car accident in 2011, though his restaurant continues on with his family and team of chefs, keeping his famous dishes and creativity alive today. (AC.)

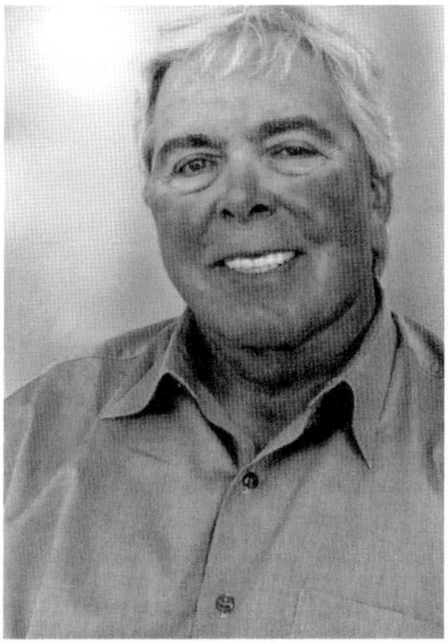

Herbert W. Boyer

Dr. Herbert W. "Herb" Boyer was born on July 10, 1936, in Derry, Pennsylvania. He received his bachelor's degree in biology and chemistry from St. Vincent College and his doctorate at the University of Pittsburgh. Boyer is a biology scientist and cofounder of Genentech. He served as vice-president of Genentech from 1976 through his retirement in 1991 and is most noted for producing synthetic insulin. He was featured on the cover of *Time* magazine in 1981 and was named one of the Greatest Innovators of the Past 75 Years in *Business Week* (2004). In 2007, St. Vincent College announced that it had renamed the School of Natural Science, Mathematics, and Computing the Herbert W. Boyer School. (Jane Gitschier/PLoS Genetics.)

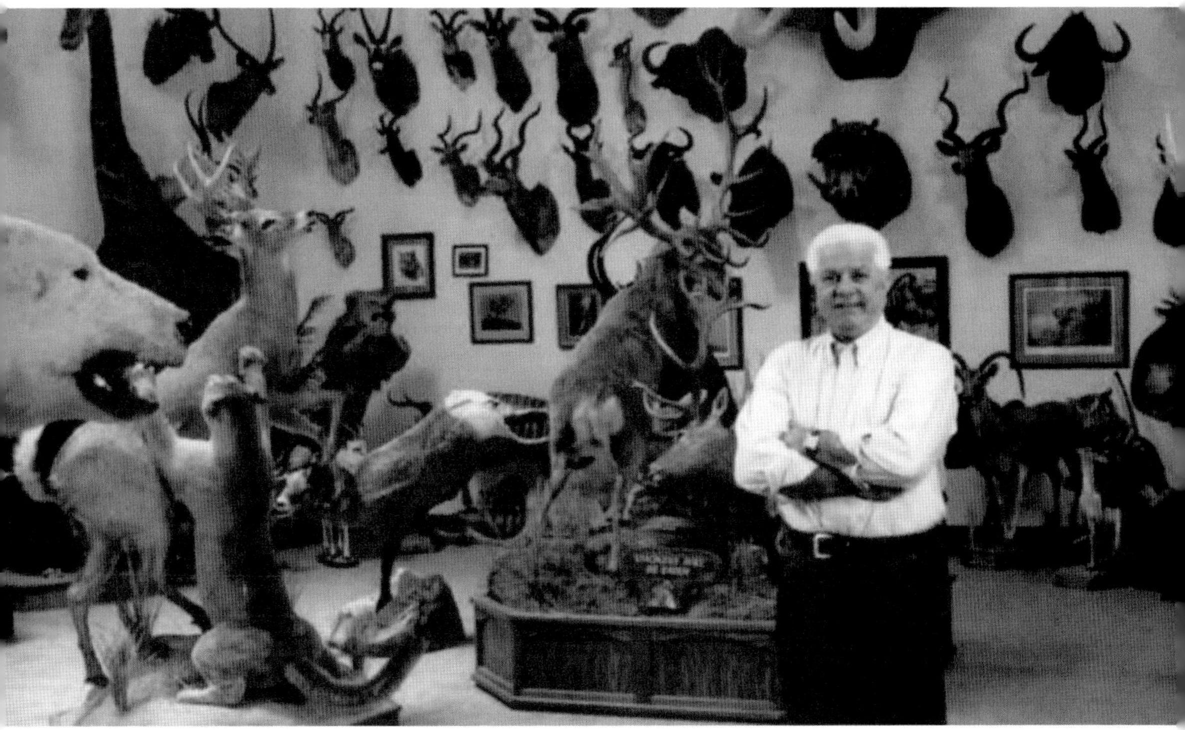

Carl Ross

Carl Ross was born in Latrobe on March 1, 1936, and graduated from Latrobe High School in 1953. His story and that of Lynx Golf, the company he pioneered, have been described by *Golf* magazine (1978) as "the greatest rags to riches saga in golf history." His first job, at age seven, was collecting scrap metal in town. In 1960, he became Arnold Palmer's first employee, selling Palmer golf clubs until leaving in 1969 to start his own company. In three years, Lynx was the bestselling premium golf club in the United States. Since that time, Ross has been in the industrial real estate business. His safari-themed complexes feature life-size bronze giraffes and elephants. Ross, who began hunting squirrels and rabbits as a boy, is pictured with a sample of the 183 prized game trophies he bagged while on many safaris to remote locales across the globe. (Carl Ross.)

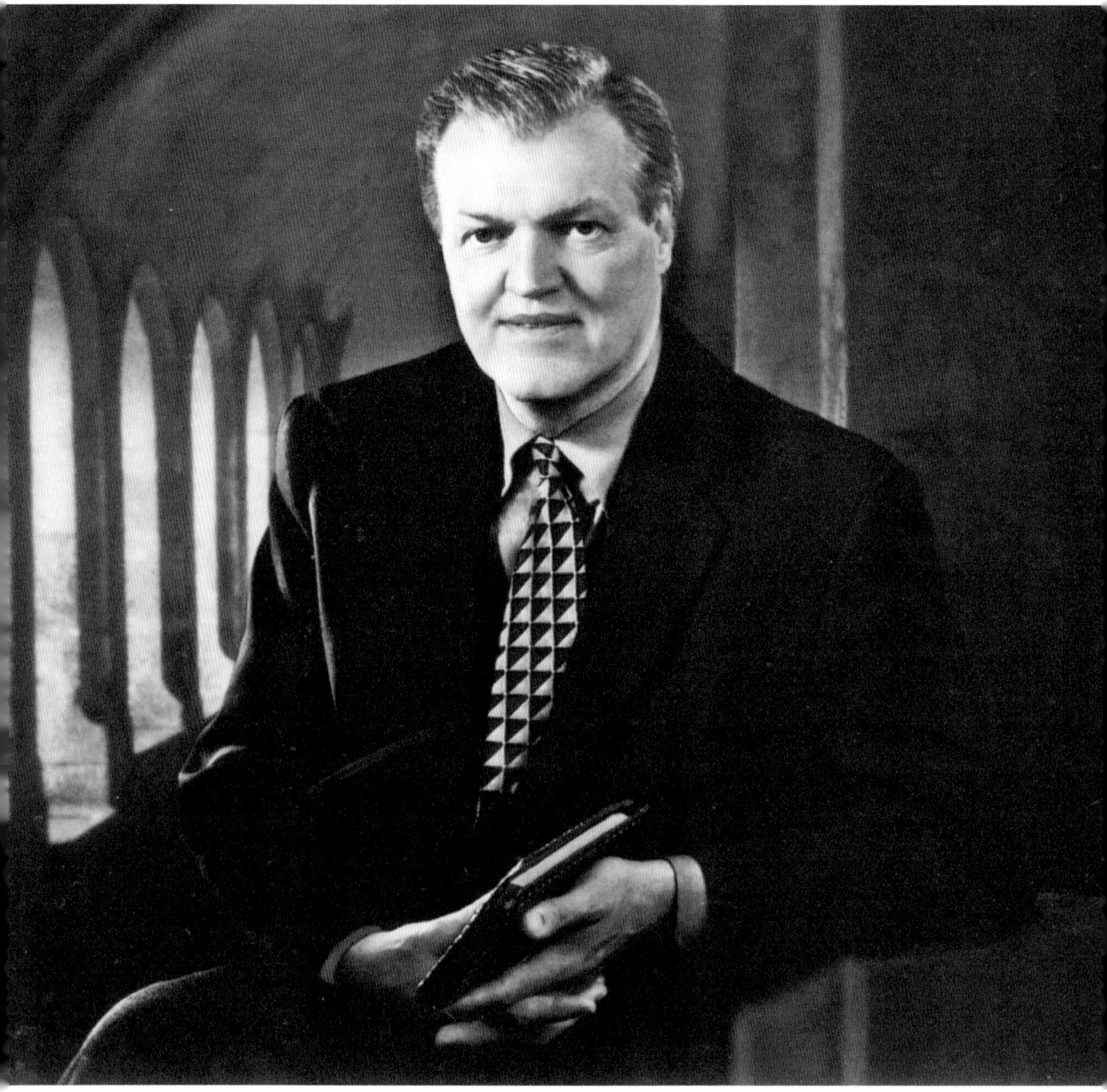

Terry J. Deglau

Terry J. Deglau was born in Latrobe on August 17, 1940, as a third-generation photographer in his family's portrait business. Though he tinkered in his father's studio as a youngster, he did not decide on a career until college. He earned his bachelor's of science in photographic science from Rochester Institute of Technology in 1964 and a master of photography degree with the Professional Photographers of America Association. He served for many years as Eastman Kodak's liaison to the professional photographic community. The recipient of many honors—including the Professional Photographers of America Director's Award, Wedding and Portrait Photographers International's Lifetime Achievement Award, and two Professional Photographers of Pennsylvania National Awards—Deglau was selected to photograph the heads of state portrait at the United Nations Millennium Conference in 2000. In attendance were 149 heads of state, including British prime minister Tony Blair, French president Jacques Chirac, and US president Bill Clinton. (Terry J. Deglau.)

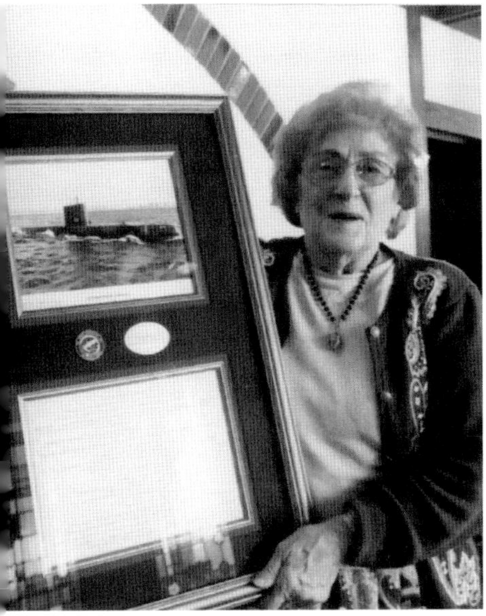

Natalie Carbone Mangini

Natalie Carbone Mangini was born on August 24, 1928, to Nat and Mary Carbone. Her family originally settled in the area to work in the coal mines. Today, she is a waitress at the family's restaurant, Carbone's in Crabtree, but customers are often surprised to learn that she is also recognized as the first woman to be hired as a nuclear scientist at Westinghouse's Bettis Atomic Power Division. She attended Seton Hill College and did her graduate work at Carnegie Tech. In 1957, she married Vincent Mangini, and when she became pregnant in 1960 with the first of two daughters, she quit her job, worried about what the exposure to radiation might do to the unborn child. She delivered a healthy girl and gave up her career to spend time with her new family and work at the restaurant. In 1958, she appeared on the popular game show *What's My Line?* to discuss her life and work. (Chris Kasprak/ Copyright © *Pittsburgh Post-Gazette*, 2014, all rights reserved. Reprinted with permission.)

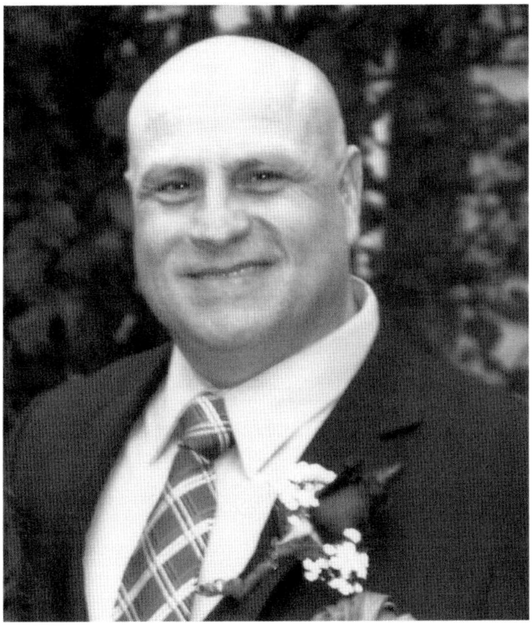

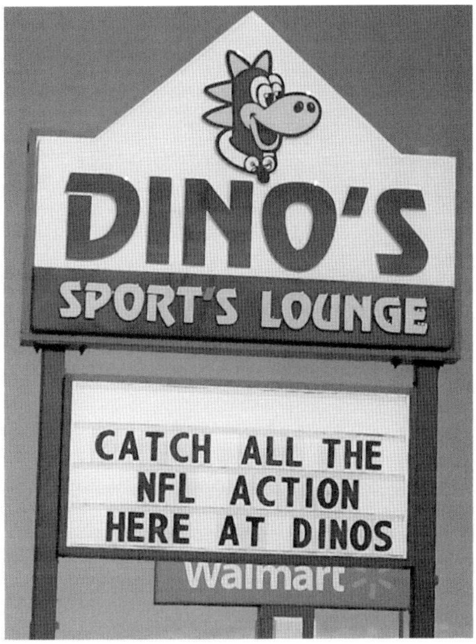

Dino DeCario

Dino DeCario was born in Latrobe and grew up in New Derry, Pennsylvania. He is an avid hunter and owner of Dino's Sport's Lounge on Route 30 in Latrobe (and Greensburg). Dino's was voted to have the "best wings in Pennsylvania" in 1995 and listed among the top 10 sports bars in *USA Today.* It is a favorite among locals and visitors year-round and a beloved part of the annual pilgrimage of Steelers' fans to training camp at St. Vincent College in late summer. In fact, most of the sports memorabilia on the walls at Dino's is dedicated to the Steelers, and the delicious menu of "Giant Sandwiches" and gourmet burgers includes the Steeler Burger, which promises to "knock you out without fines." Dino's most popular fare, however, is the "Wings of Joy," served every Monday and Tuesday night. (Left, Dino DeCario; right, AC.)

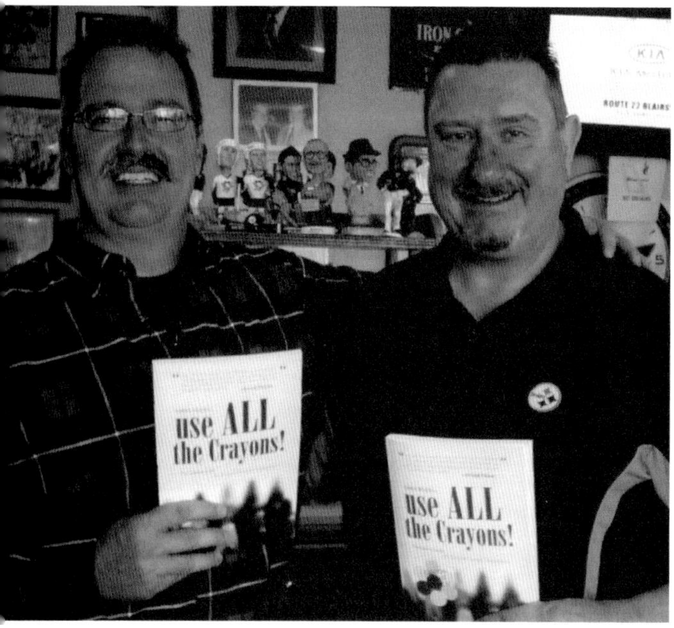

Dave Carfang

Founded in 1954 by brothers Ed and Dick Carfang, the Pond Tavern & Grille is now owned by Dick's son Dave Carfang. When locals go "fishing at the Pond," there are no rods or reels required, only barstools and bent elbows on the tavern side. But regular customers frequent the Pond for its good food, varied menu, and daily specials featuring prices that reflect the working person's wallet. Not much has changed at the Pond over the past 60 years. The restaurant accepts cash only—no credit or debit cards. And it does not deliver. Even local authors—like Chris Rodell, pictured (left) with owner Dave Carfang—choose the Pond for their book signing events, and Latrobe legend Arnold Palmer once told Carfang his daughters were raised on Pond pizza. (Chris Rodell.)

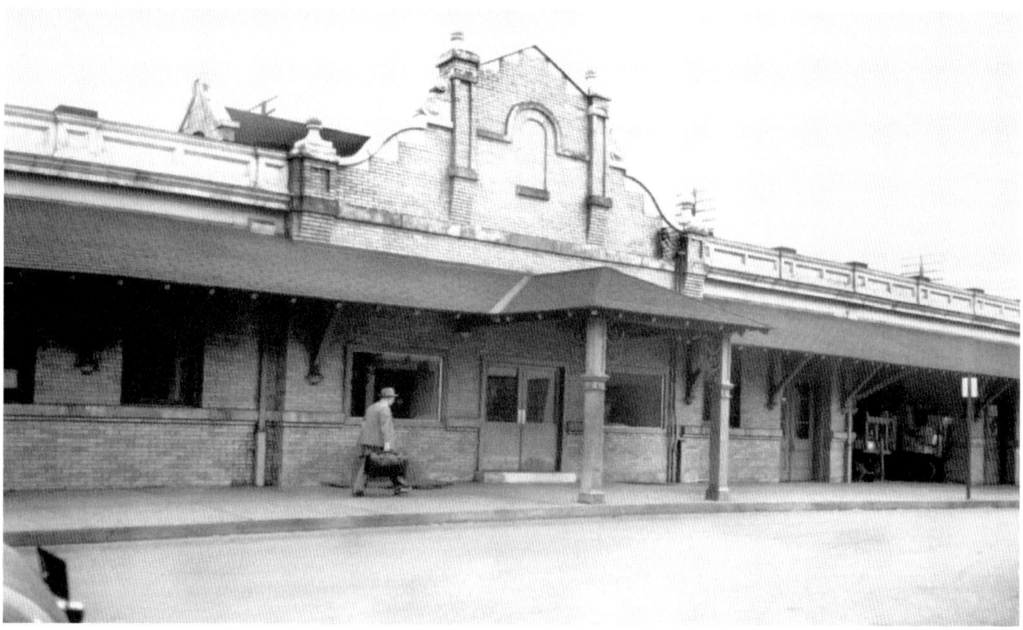

Joey DiSalvo

Joey DiSalvo and his mother and father purchased the Latrobe train station, now DiSalvo's Station Restaurant, in 1989 and resurrected the 16,000-square-foot historical landmark, making it part museum and part restaurant. The restaurant features dining and entertainment; à la carte Italian cuisine, complemented with wine, beer, and spirits from around the world; a banquet facility; and Joey D's Cigar Bar, the area's only cigar bar and retail store. The Prima Classe dining car is a restaurant within the restaurant, offering a five-course menu that features only fresh products and ingredients bought at market that day. Latrobe currently has two sites in the National Register of Historic Places: the Pennsylvania Railroad Station (1903) and the Quatrini Rafferty Law Firm building (1926). (FF.)

CHAPTER THREE

Public Service and Community Leaders

Latrobe has been blessed with many notable public servants and community leaders since it was established in 1854. Many volunteered their time, neighbor helping neighbor, while others moved the area forward through their representation at the local, state, and national levels. Politicians, such as Latrobe's first female mayor, Barbara Griffin, have helped the area evolve by encouraging new businesses and applying for grants to make Latrobe a better place to live.

Everyday people from all walks of life have also stepped forward to enrich the Latrobe area with their time, their treasures, and their ideas. George Hamilton Adams was an employee with the Pennsylvania Railroad who had no heirs. He recorded in his will that he would like to donate money to provide a new building for the library, which was done in 1954. As an honor to Adams, the library was renamed the Adams Memorial Library. John Wandrisco is a retired steel executive and the originator of Latrobe's Mini Gardens and community vegetable gardens. According to an article in the September 22, 2005, edition of the *Pittsburgh Post-Gazette*, "Wandrisco looked around Latrobe and saw a gray, grim landscape. So he decided to give it some flowers, some color." The Mini Gardens began with 16 plots near Legion Keener Park and have grown to 29 plots at various locations throughout the city. Wandrisco says the garden project is a testimony to the cooperative spirit of Latrobe and Unity. Volunteers and parks and recreation employees provide labor, storage space, equipment, and skills.

Latrobe is rich in volunteerism, with the Latrobe Volunteer Fire Department; Mutual Aid Ambulance; Rotary, Lions, and Elks Clubs; the American Legion; and the Veterans of Foreign Wars providing service to the community. The men and women in this chapter have put service before self, and while they are great examples of Latrobe's public servants and community leaders, they are just a few of many. Latrobe has truly been fortunate, and continues to be, to have great people who have accepted the responsibility passed on from the founders. Their dedication and hard work will ensure that the next generation enjoys the same strong community amenities and opportunities that they have had.

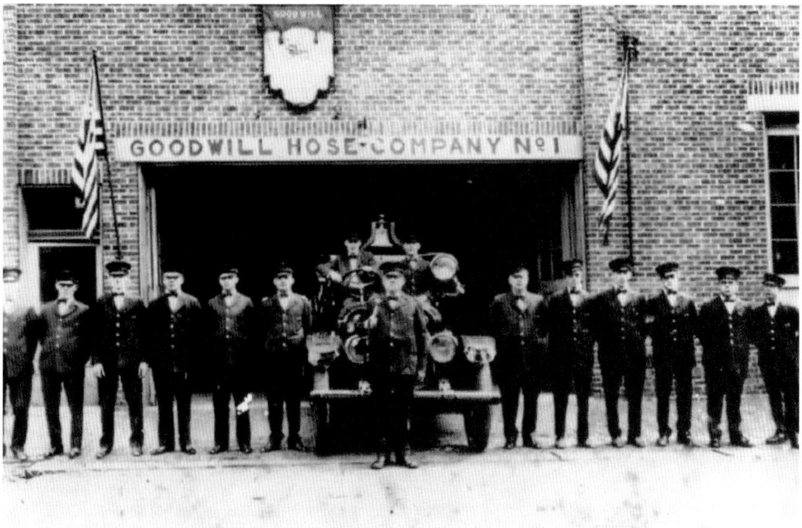

A.J. Keepers

A.J. Keepers was Latrobe's first fire chief. He was endorsed by council shortly after the first organized fire protection in the city of Latrobe was established on December 19, 1879, when "15 individuals gathered to form Goodwill Hose Co. No. 1," according to the book *Historic Latrobe, A Glance or Two at Earlier Times* (1985). The first piece of equipment purchased by the borough was a small hand-pulled cart. It cost $800 and sported a chemical tank, a hand ladder, pike poles, and 10 leather buckets. As the community expanded, the need for fire protection grew. Hook & Ladder Co. No. 2 and Freewill Hose Co. No. 3 were organized in 1886. In 1906, Free Services Fire Unit No. 6 was organized, followed by Good Friend Hose Co. No. 5. On April 20, 1908, the various companies combined forces to make what is known today as Latrobe Volunteer Fire Department. Pictured above are Chief J.L. Aukerman (center) and the men of Goodwill Hose Co. No. 1 in 1928, and below is Hose Co. No. 6. In 2012, the Latrobe Fire Department adopted a Dalmatian mascot and named him Keeper after the first fire chief. (Above, Steven Patterson; below, FF.)

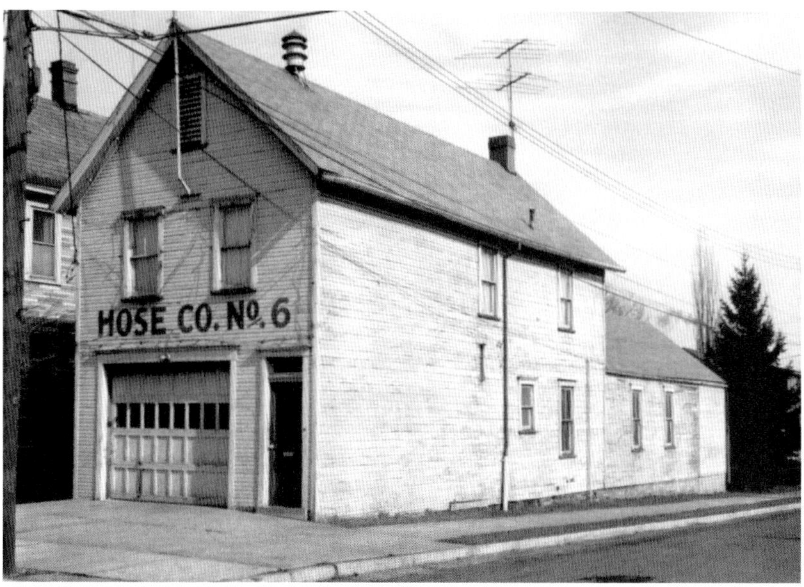

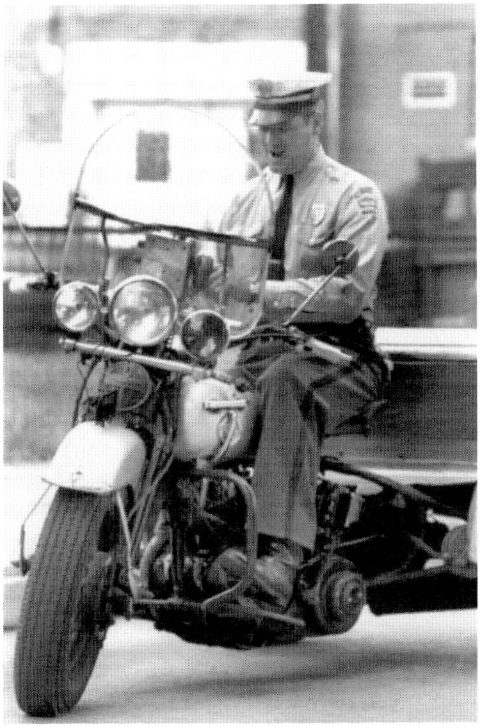

William Barkley

Officer William Barkley is shown (left) while on cycle patrol in Latrobe Borough in the late 1950s. At the time, the police force consisted of Chief Chester A. College (1912–2011), two lieutenants, and nine patrolmen. Barkley and College are listed among a roll call of others at the present police station on Jefferson Street. It honors those who faithfully served the community of Latrobe with a bronze plaque reading, "O' Ye citizen, look upon these police officers as our hope for a safer community." Pictured below is Latrobe's police force around 1910. From left to right are (first row) Robert Gillis, Charles Butz, Frank Ondriezek, and Joseph Stahl; (second row) George Galloway, H. Cramer, Jerry Hall, and Milton Dodds. (Left, FF; below, Steven Patterson.)

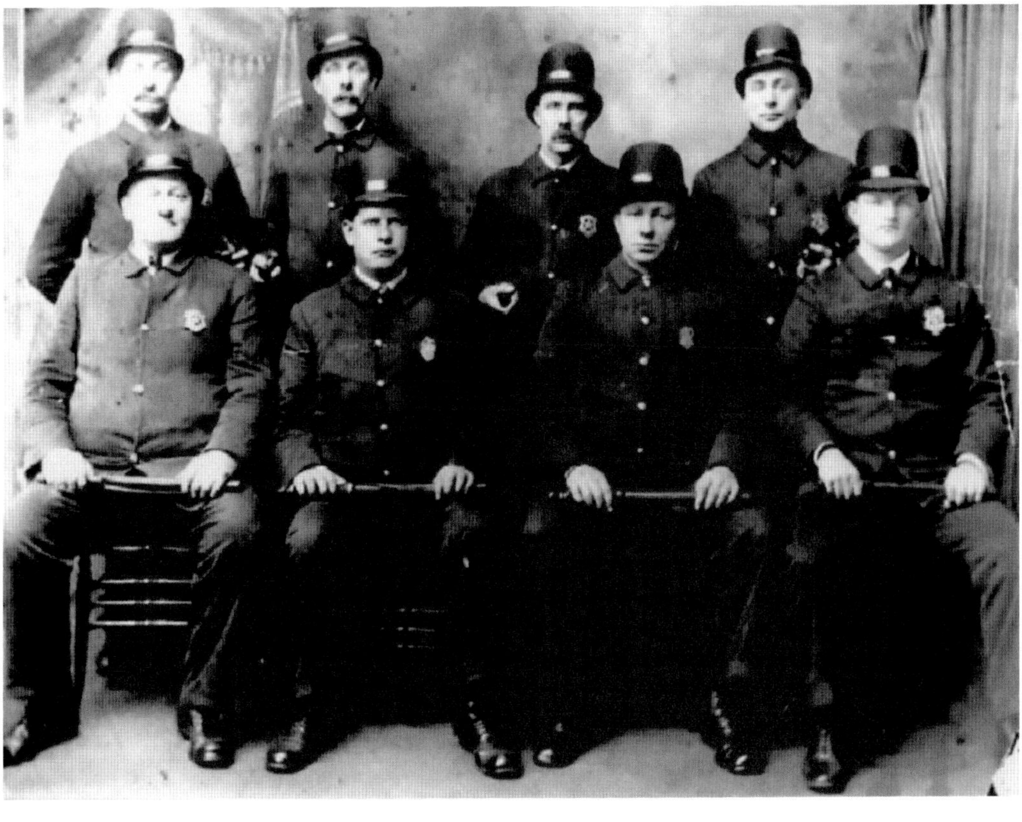

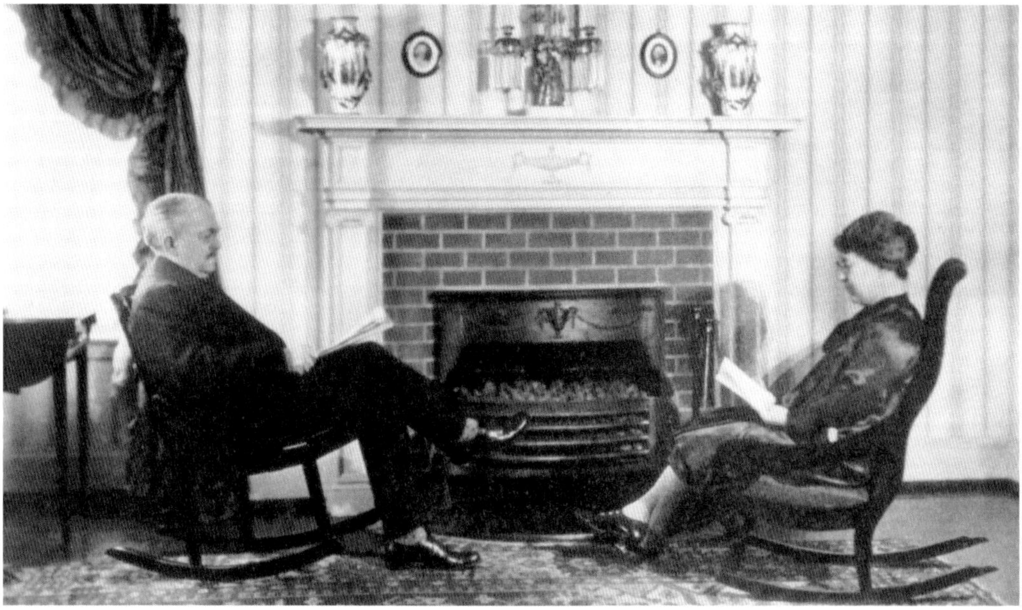

George Hamilton Adams

George Hamilton Adams (1860–1954) was an employee of the Pennsylvania Railroad in Latrobe. He served the railroad for 57 years, starting as a boy in his father's office at Beatty Station. Adams was appointed station agent at Beatty upon the death of his father in 1880 and continued there until he was promoted to agent in Latrobe on September 15, 1891. Beatty Station was named in honor of Adams's maternal great-grandfather Benjamin Beatty, who was one of the soldiers in Washington's army. Adams left no heirs, and proceeds from his estate were used to build Adams Memorial Library in 1954. The library, pictured below under construction, continues to proudly serve the Latrobe community and surrounding areas. (Above, LAHS; below, FF.)

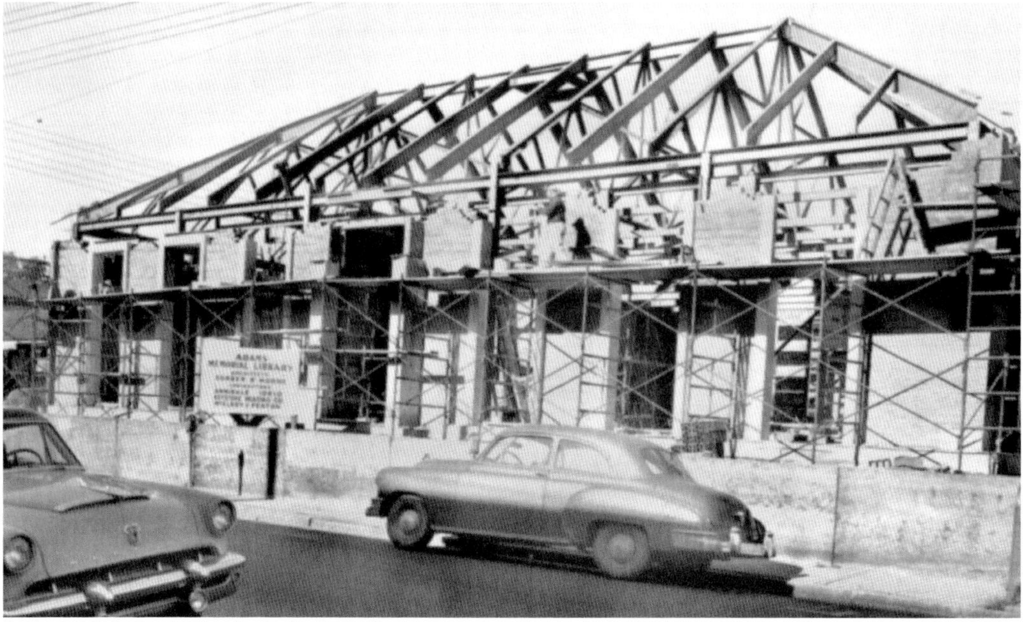

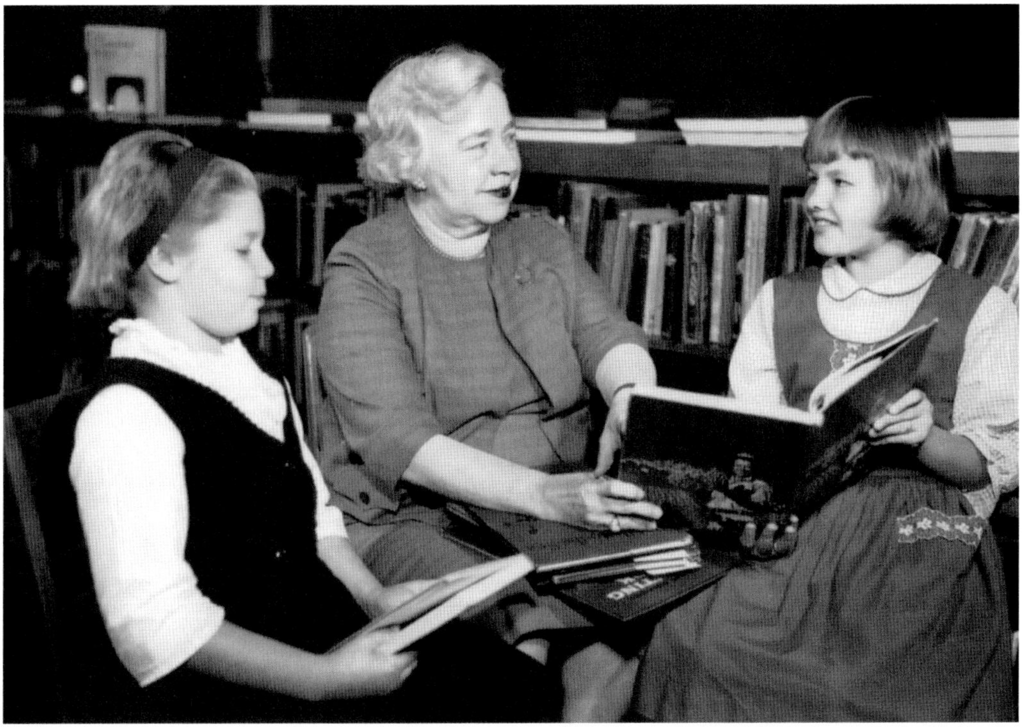

Sara Carr McComb
Dr. Sara Carr McComb (1905–1978) was a Latrobe librarian and civic leader. She has been described as a "legendary" librarian for the early Latrobe Public Library, founded on September 1, 1927, in the Masonic building on the first block of Spring Street. Her estate has made scholarships available to St. Vincent College students who register in the continuing education program. McComb was awarded an honorary doctor of letters degree from St. Vincent in 1958. (LAHS.)

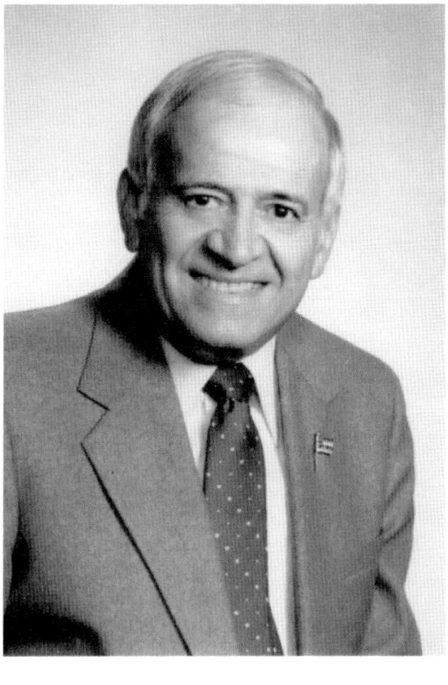

Anthony M. Angelo
Anthony M. "Tony" Angelo (1924–2011) spent his life serving the area in various organizations, including the March of Dimes and Fraternal Order of the Eagles. In the Eagles, he became known as the "singing secretary" because of his tenor voice. A lifelong resident of the community he loved, his name is synonymous with Latrobe, in particular its Fourth of July celebration, often referred to as "Tony's Picnic." (*Latrobe Bulletin.*)

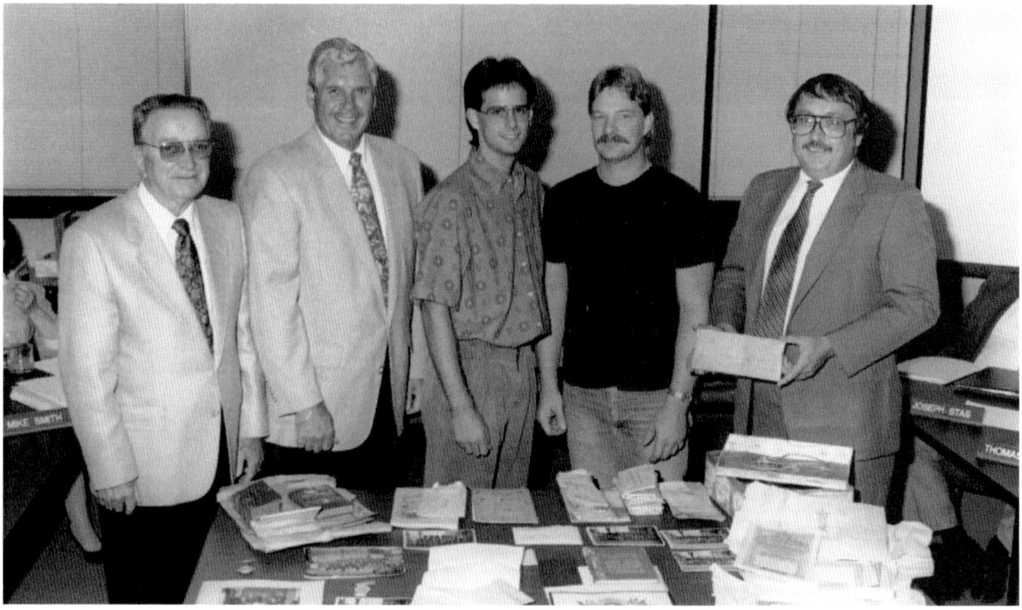

Jack B. Townsend

Jack B. Townsend (1945–2013) was self-employed in insurance sales but devoted much of his time to community service. He was president of the Rotary Club and was instrumental in developing the Rotary Community Park/School near Youngstown, Pennsylvania. He was a member of the Unity Chapel Committee and served on the boards of the Art Conservation Trust, the Latrobe Area Historical Society, and the Greater Latrobe School District Board of Directors. In the photograph, Townsend holds an 1882 tin box time capsule discovered in the 1980s when the district was making renovations to the Second Ward School. Standing are, from left to right, Joseph Newcomer, president of the Greater Latrobe Historical Society; Richard Marshall, school board member; Michael Naeger and John Scott Weirs, who discovered the box; and Jack Townsend, school board president. (LAHS.)

James R. Okonak

James R. Okonak was born in Latrobe and graduated from Latrobe Schools in 1967. He attended West Virginia Wesleyan College, graduating in 1971 with a bachelor's of science degree in business administration. Since 1973, he has worked for the McFeely-Rogers Foundation and is currently the organization's secretary/executive director. He is also secretary to Rogers Enterprises, Inc.; vice president of the Latrobe Foundation; on the advisory board of the Fred Rogers Center for Early Learning and Children's Media; and organizational cochairman of the Latrobe Community Revitalization Program. In 1981, Okonak arranged to have Fred Rogers visit Latrobe High School when the school was celebrating its 100th anniversary. (James R. Okonak.)

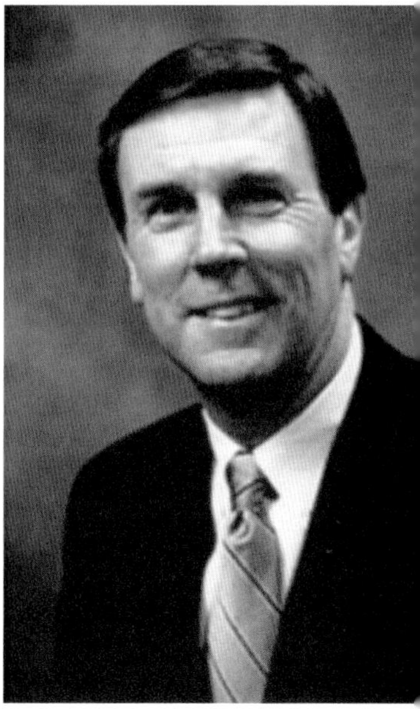

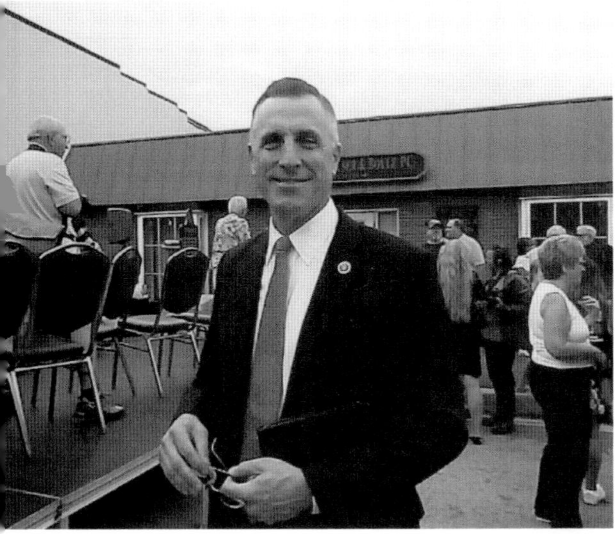

Timothy F. Murphy
Timothy F. Murphy is a US congressman serving Latrobe and the 18th District of Pennsylvania. He was a featured speaker at the dedication ceremony of the banana split historical marker. In addition to delivering the official congressional recognition to Mayor Barbara Griffin, he read an original poem entitled "The Ode to the Banana Split." It brought to mind Clement C. Moore's "'Twas the Night Before Christmas" and ended with the line, "So raise high your spoons in celebration, for this treat known all over the globe. From May to September, grab your scoop and remember, that it all started, here, in Latrobe." (AC.)

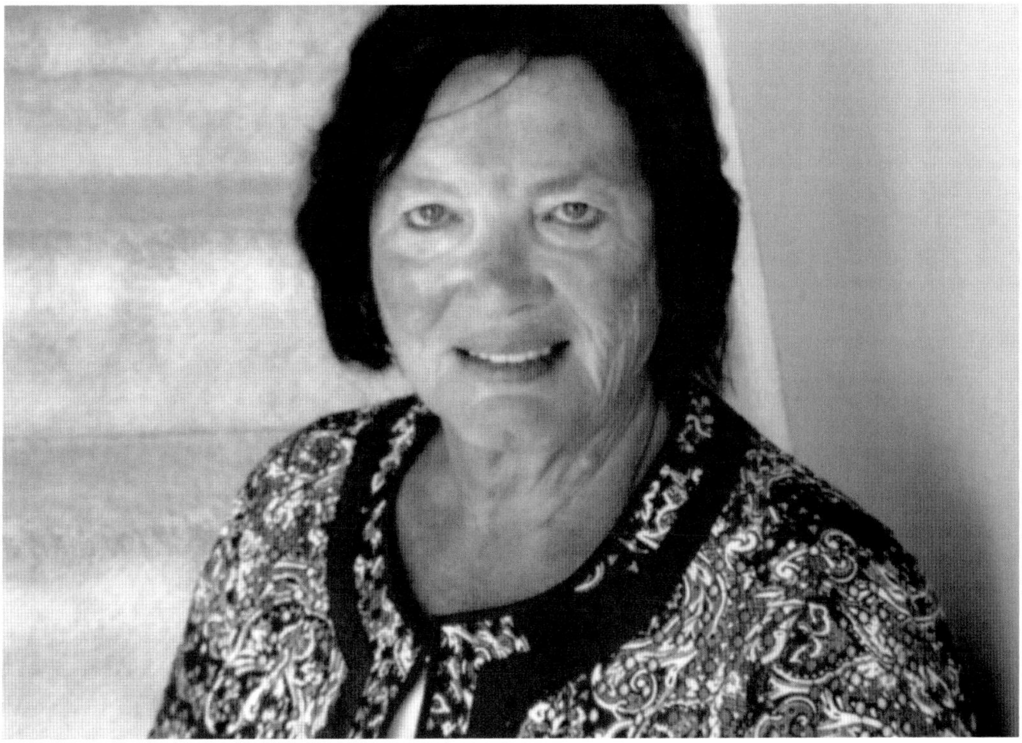

Diana B. Kreiling
Diana B. Kreiling is a former manager of public relations and volunteer services at Latrobe Area Hospital. She was recognized for her efforts with a Winner's Circle Award for Community Service in 2000. She has been a member and officer with the hospital's Aid Society since 1962. She has been involved with the chamber of commerce, the Art Center, and the United Way and is a member of the Latrobe Presbyterian Church, where she served on the Board of Elders. Kreiling encourages young people to continue the wonderful tradition of volunteerism, adding, "Community service is what makes the Latrobe area such a special place to live and raise a family." (Diana Kreiling.)

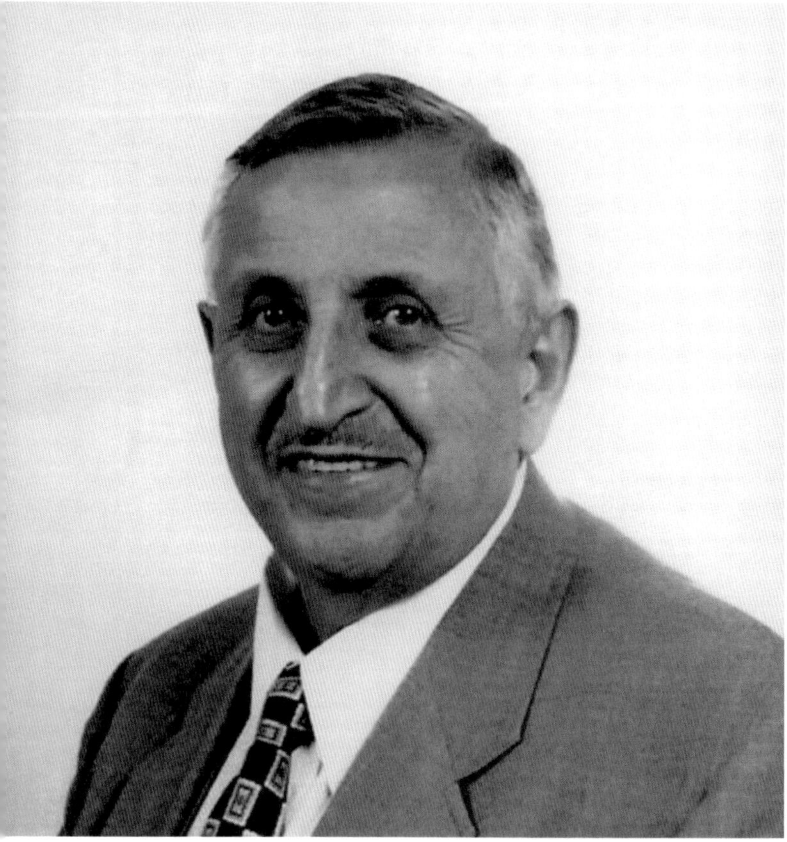

Warren V. Marckioni
Warren V. Marckioni (1936–2014) was a former mayor of Latrobe who presided over the city's sesquicentennial celebration, boasting at the time in a 2004 *Post Gazette* interview, "It's been a beautiful day in the neighborhood for a long time." Marckioni retired after working his way up the ladder at the nearby Coca-Cola bottling plant. His rough and calloused hands were testaments to his days heaving cartons of six-packs. He also served on the Latrobe Municipal Authority for more than 30 years, with 10 years as chairman, and was a founding committee member of the Latrobe Fourth of July Celebration, where he served for 20 years and was a former cochairman. (*Latrobe Bulletin.*)

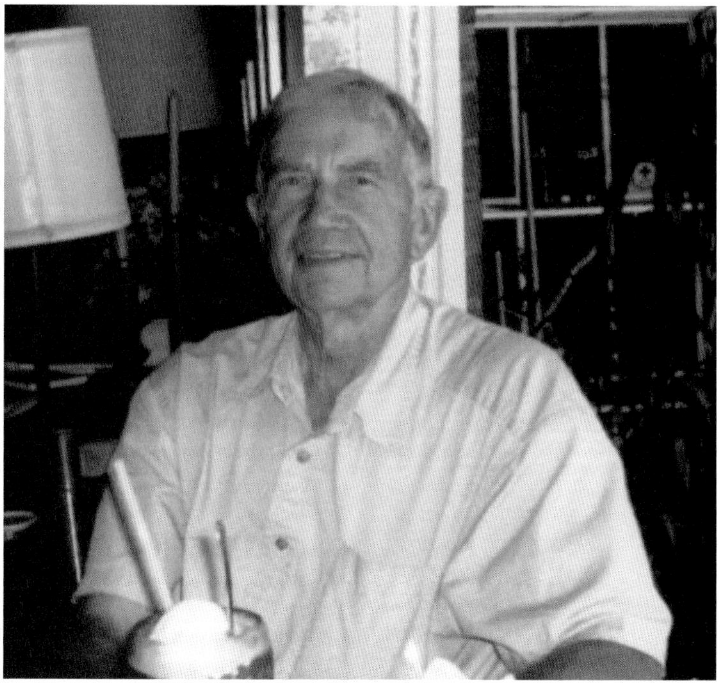

John Wandrisco
John Wandrisco is the originator of Latrobe's Mini Gardens and community vegetable gardens. Wandrisco and his team care for 62 flower gardens and 60 flower planters throughout the city, as well as the vegetable gardens that community members can rent and develop. The vegetable gardens began with 16 plots on a site at Catherine Street and Irving Avenue, near Legion Keener Park, and have grown to 29 plots at various locations throughout the city. (AC.)

Barbara Griffin

Barbara Griffin, a retired schoolteacher, was elected the first female mayor in the history of Latrobe in 2009. During her administration, she completed the 20-page application to the Pennsylvania Historical and Museum Commission for the banana split historical marker. The dedication ceremony took place on August 23, 2013, and kicked off the opening day of the first Great American Banana Split Celebration in downtown Latrobe. Mayor Griffin is shown speaking at the ceremony, where she recalled that Dr. Strickler, an optometrist and inventor of the famous triple sundae, prescribed her first pair of glasses when she was in the fifth grade. Griffin grew up in Latrobe and attended nearby Seton Hill College. (AC.)

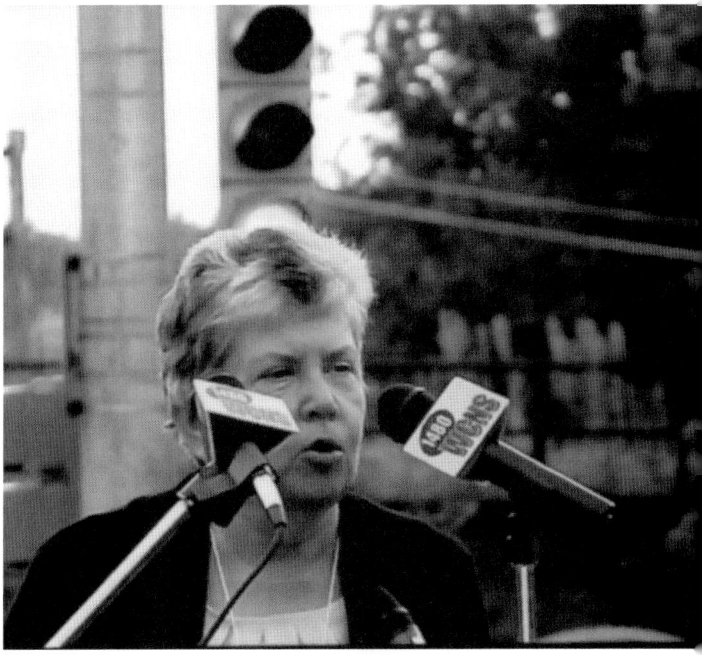

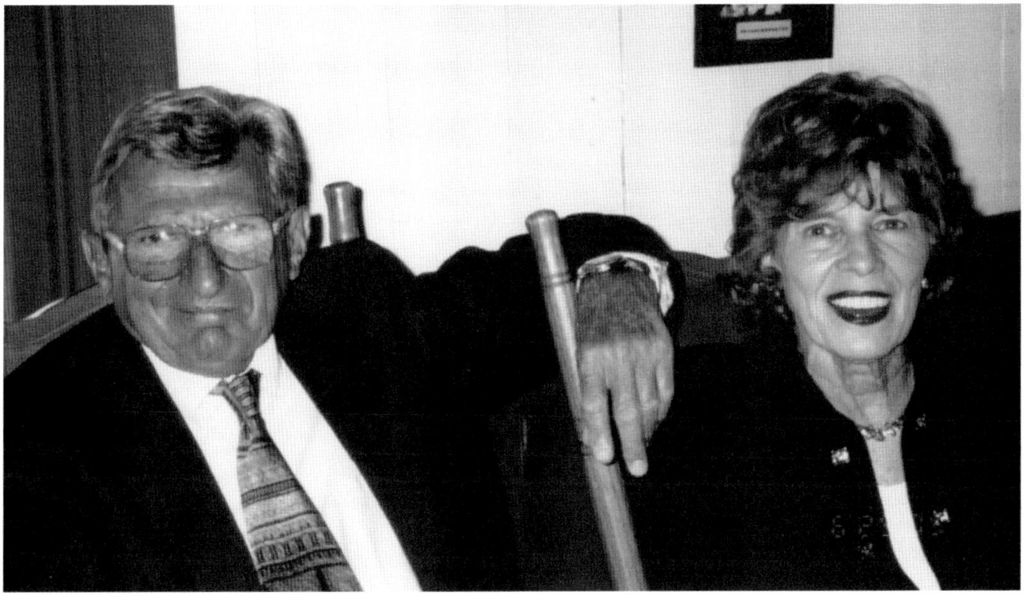

Suzanne Pohland Paterno

Sue Paterno, the former Suzanne Pohland, of Latrobe was an English literature honors student when she met Joseph Vincent Paterno, the assistant football coach at Penn State. They were married in 1962. Sue Paterno was always more than a coach's wife at Penn State. She served as a tutor to players, a host for recruiting gatherings, a counselor to concerned parents, and a prodigious fundraiser. She championed the Special Olympics, helping to organize the Pennsylvania summer games each June on the Penn State campus. The Pohland family name goes back more than a century in Latrobe, with their first lumberyard appearing in 1891. Twenty-six years later, Charles, Edward, and August Pohland established Pohland Brothers Lumber Company on Alexandria Street. It moved to East Depot Street in 1925. (AC.)

Bibiana Boerio

Bibiana Boerio was born in Latrobe and graduated in 1971 from Greensburg Central Catholic High School. She received her bachelor's degree from Seton Hill College and her master's degree from the University of Pittsburgh's Graduate School of Business. She is a retired auto executive who served as chief financial officer of Ford Motor Credit Company and managing director of Jaguar Cars, Ltd. After retiring from Ford, she fulfilled a long-held interest in federal public policy, serving as chief of staff for a member of the US House of Representatives from Pennsylvania. In September 2012, she was nominated by President Obama to fill the position of director of the US Mint and would have become the 39th director in the mint's 220-year history. However, because of her mother's health issues, she chose instead to return to Latrobe and was asked to return to her alma mater as interim president of Seton Hill University in August 2013. Boerio served for one year and oversaw several major building projects, including the Dance and Visual Arts Center, the Health and Sciences Center, the acquisition of the Verizon Building, and the renovation of Brownlee Hall. She replaced Dr. JoAnne Boyle, the university's former president, who had held the position for more than 25 years and is noted for helping to transform the small Catholic college for women into a coeducational university that hosts international luminaries and altered the landscape of the city. Sadly, in November 2013, Boerio had to announce Boyle's untimely death to the students of Seton Hill and to oversee the memorials in her honor. She spoke at the memorial Mass held in St. Joseph Chapel on campus for students, faculty, and staff. "JoAnne was at the forefront of leaders who recognized the value of a university to the economic stabilization and growth of downtowns." Regarding her tenure as interim president, Boerio said, "I was honored to have maintained the University's momentum in executing and extending JoAnne's vision." (Sean Stipp/Copyright © *Tribune-Review*, 2014, all rights reserved. Reprinted with permission.)

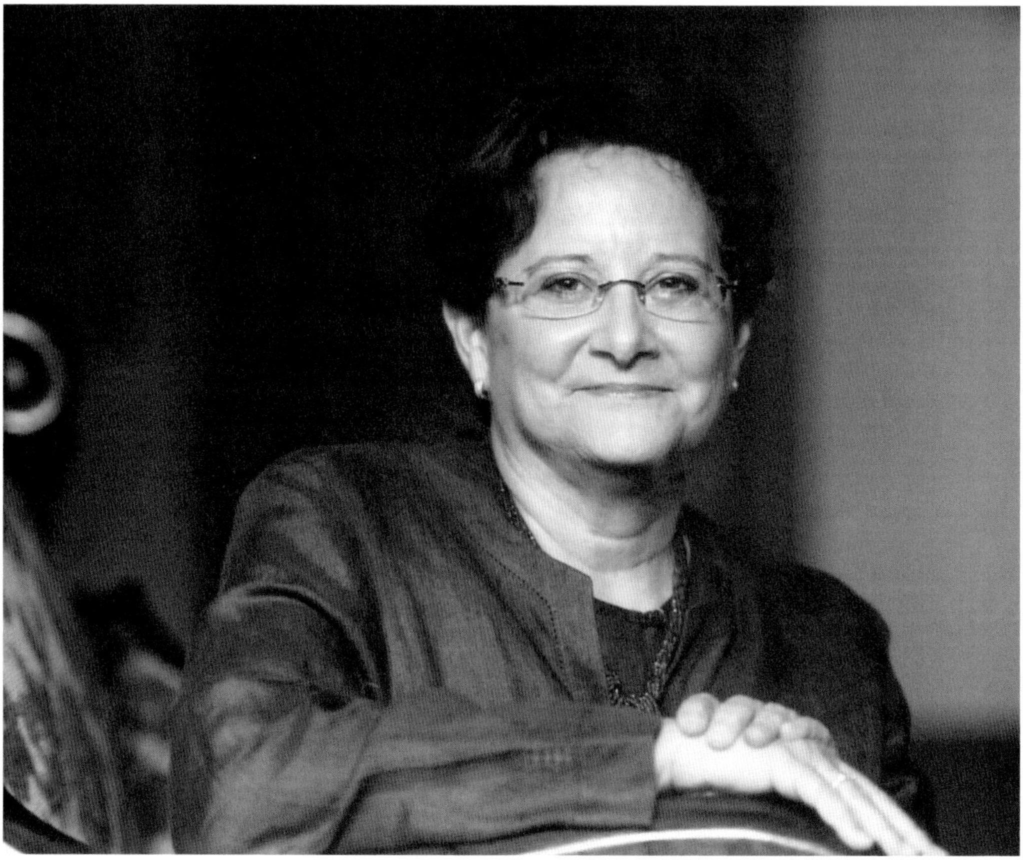

CHAPTER FOUR

Entertainment and the Arts

It is no wonder so many creative people have come from the Latrobe area; they only needed to step outside and look around for inspiration. Perhaps none was more so than Fred Rogers, who used Latrobe as the basis for his children's television program, *Mr. Rogers' Neighborhood.* Rogers often spoke about his childhood rides on Latrobe streetcars and how this experience led to the familiar red trolley that transports viewers to his whimsical "Neighborhood of Make-Believe." The Latrobe of Rogers's youth was one of industry and growth, but once this foundation had been laid, the next era of success began with individuals who stretched their imaginations and flexed their creativity.

James Hayes, a native of Latrobe, moved to New York in 1981 to study fashion at Parsons School of Design. For nearly five years, he designed sportswear for Bugle Boy, Sergio, J. Crew, and Tommy Hilfiger. Then he moved to Los Angeles in 1990 with one dream—to design science fiction costumes for the movies. For Halloween that year, Hayes created a realistic Tyrannosaurus rex costume. The creation caught the attention of Jeffrey Lampert of the Walt Disney Company, in charge of production on a newly created sitcom called *Dinosaurs.* Hayes was hired to sew, and five months later, he got the top spot as designer. In 1997, he was nominated for an Emmy award for his work on the PBS children's series *The Puzzle Place.*

Chris Lightcap is a jazz composer and bassist who has played on over 60 albums to date, including four critically acclaimed albums as a bandleader. He started out on the piano at age eight, switched to violin at nine, and began to teach himself the electric bass at 14. He simultaneously played violin in the Westmoreland youth symphony and took gigs on bass guitar with local rock bands, as well as Latrobe High School's jazz and concert bands. As a senior in high school, he started to study the upright bass and, the following year, enrolled at Williams College, where he majored in music. Upon graduating in 1993, he moved to his current home in New York City, where he went on to perform, record, and tour with such artists as Regina Carter, Paquito D'Rivera, John Scofield, Marc Ribot, and John Medeski. His most recent CD is entitled *Epicenter,* inspired by his adopted city, though he has never forgotten Latrobe.

There are many outlets in the Latrobe area through which residents can pursue or enjoy art, music, and entertainment, including the St. Vincent Summer Theatre, now in its 45th season, and the Latrobe Art Center, started by Nancy Rogers Crozier and the late Elizabeth Hazlett. Their vision is today a showcase for local artists and a hub of activity, encouraging everyone to share in the creative process. Latrobe has been home to artists, writers, musicians, and television and radio personalities. Many of the people in this chapter are known not just locally but also worldwide. And they all have one thing in common—they call Latrobe home.

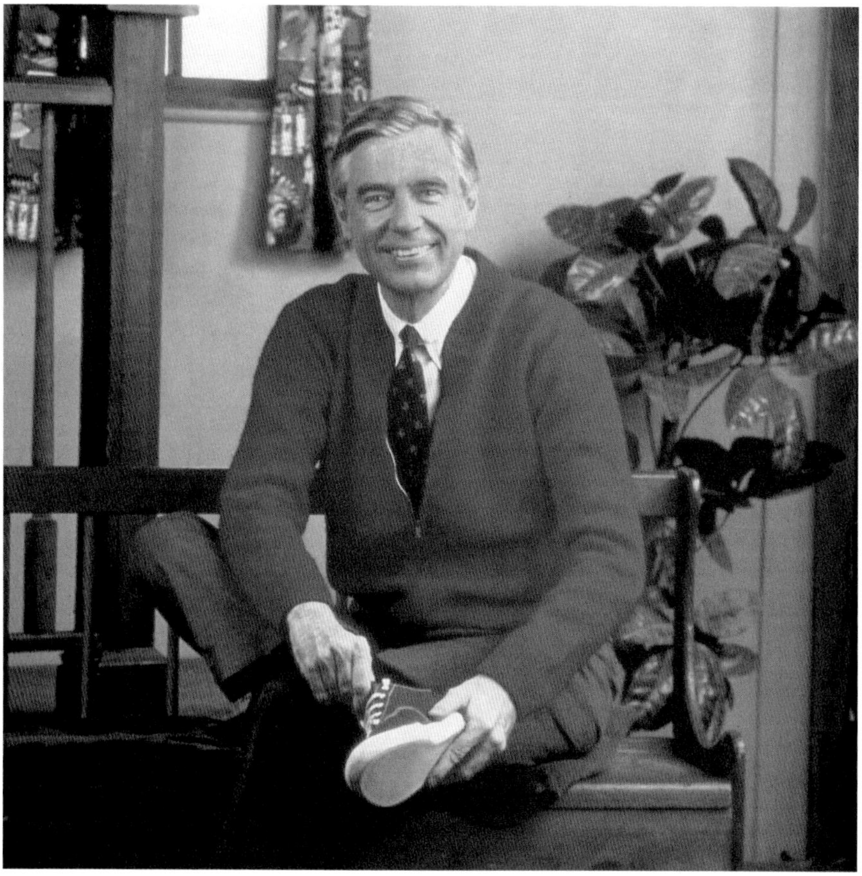

Fred McFeely Rogers

When asked about his hometown of Latrobe, Pennsylvania, in a PBS interview, Fred Rogers (1928–2003) grinned, stating, "Well, of course it's 'the garden spot of the world,' " an expression used by Lady Elaine Fairchilde, one of the regular puppet characters on his children's television program, *Mister Rogers' Neighborhood.* Rogers often made reference to his experiences growing up in Latrobe. Lady Elaine was named for his sister, Elaine Rogers Crozier, and Speedy Delivery's Mr. McFeely was named after his maternal grandfather, who patiently taught him to have a sense of self-esteem: "Freddie, you made this day a special day by being yourself." Rogers even compared himself to Daniel Striped Tiger for being the shy kid in school. He overcame his shyness in high school and went on to become a member of the National Honor Society, appeared in the all-class play, was president of the student council, and was editor of the Latrobean yearbook his senior year. He enrolled at Rollins College in Florida to study music composition and, following graduation, planned to enter the seminary and become a minister until he saw his first television show in his parents' home in 1951. Disappointed with what he saw, Rogers had an idea that he could accomplish his mission to help people in an entirely new way, using television as an instrument to nurture and educate. He landed a job in New York City as an assistant floor manager for NBC, and when the first public television station was formed in Pittsburgh, WQED-TV, Rogers came back home to help launch the station and produce programs. He worked on a local program, *The Children's Corner,* for several years and then began the national broadcast of *Mister Rogers' Neighborhood* in 1968. It ran for almost 1,000 episodes. The rest is history, as Rogers became one of America's most recognized personalities and won a plethora of awards and recognitions: four Emmys, a star on Hollywood's Walk of Fame, and the Presidential Medal of Freedom, the nation's highest civilian honor. (Copyright © The Fred Rogers Company, used with permission.)

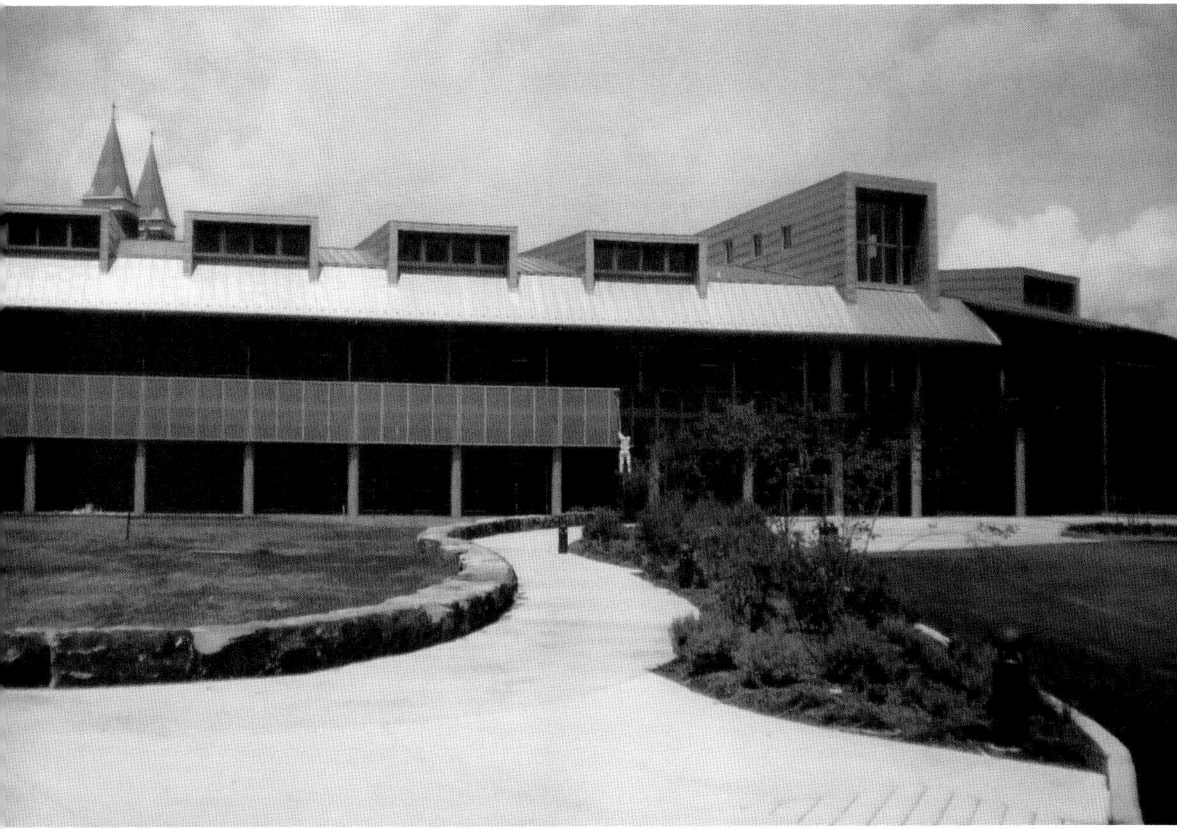

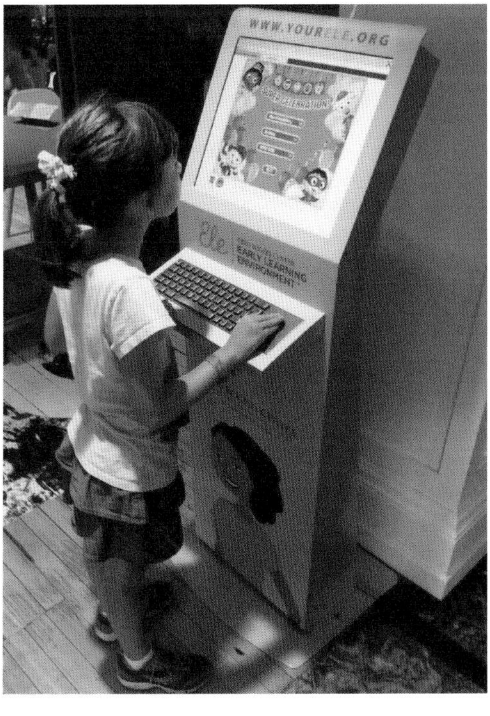

Fred Rogers Center

Staying true to the vision of Fred Rogers and emulating the guiding principles of his life's work, the mission of the Fred Rogers Center at St. Vincent College is "to advance the fields of early learning and children's media by acting as a catalyst for communication, collaboration, and creative change." As a national and international resource for addressing emerging issues affecting children from birth to age five, the center continues Rogers's commitment to building bridges between early learning and children's media. The center resonates with Rogers's own belief in the positive potential of television and new media for supporting healthy young children. Pictured at left is Chloe Comm, of Greensburg, as she interacts with a Fred Rogers Center "Ele" (Early Learning Environment) kiosk at the Pittsburgh Children's Museum. (Above, Emily Uhrin/Fred Rogers Center for Early Learning & Children's Media; left, AC.)

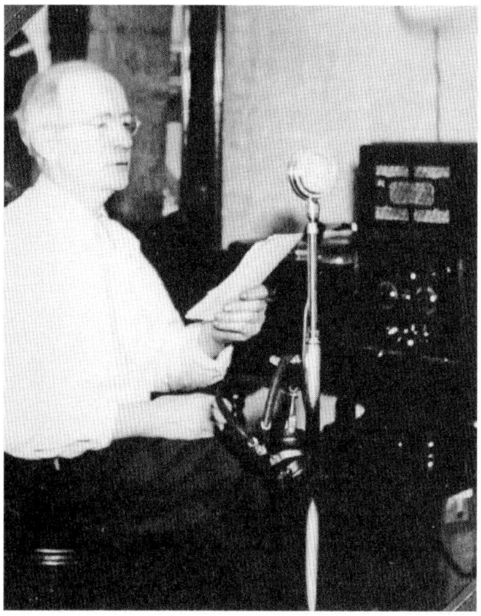

Basilio Amatucci

Basilio Amatucci (1886–1955) mans the microphone of WERS, the first radio station in Latrobe. Broadcasting from his Thompson Street home every Sunday afternoon, he played records and presented live country and western groups from 1938 to 1941. Locals, like Carl Mattioli in the *Latrobe Historical Gazette* (Spring 2011), remember his Italian accent as he announced, "I'm gonna play a nice-a tune. If-a you no like, I like!" (LAHS.)

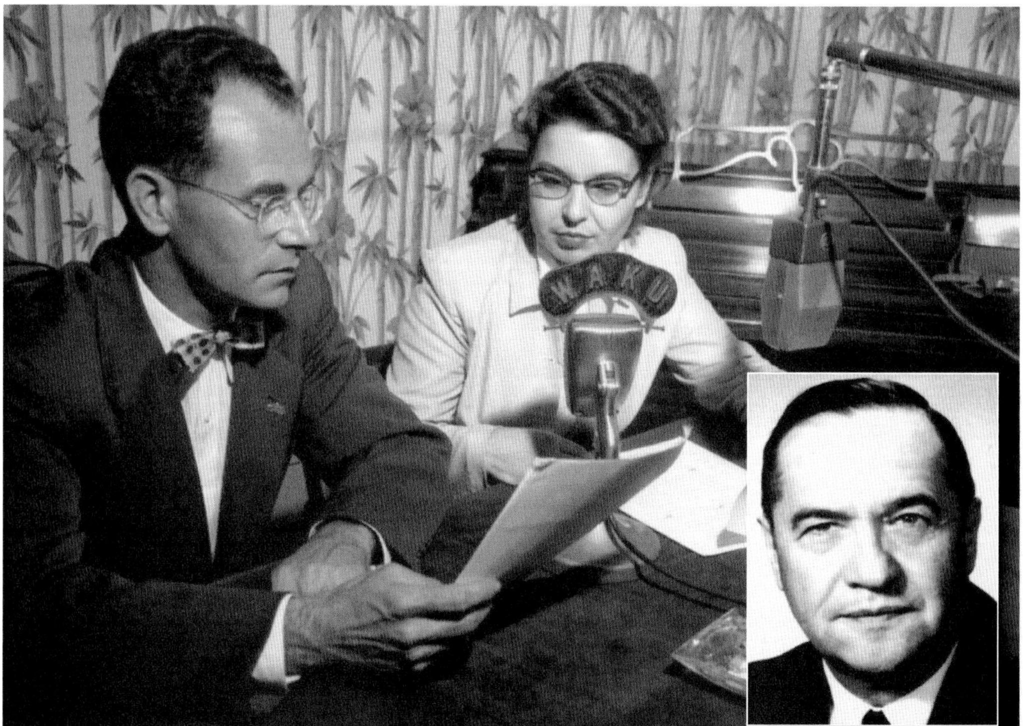

William K. Ulerich

William K. Ulerich (1910–2000) founded the WAKU radio studio on Main Street in Latrobe on December 12, 1951, making it the second AM station to come on the air in Westmoreland County. The last three call letters of "WAKU" were Ulerich's mother's initials, Anna Keener Ulerich, a former grade school principal in the Latrobe schools. In 1959, WAKU was acquired by Rosenblum Stations, and the call letters were then changed to WSHH, later acquired by a Pittsburgh FM station that still uses them today. Pictured are unidentified on-air WAKU personalities in the 1950s and William K. Ulerich (inset). (Above, FF; inset LAHS.)

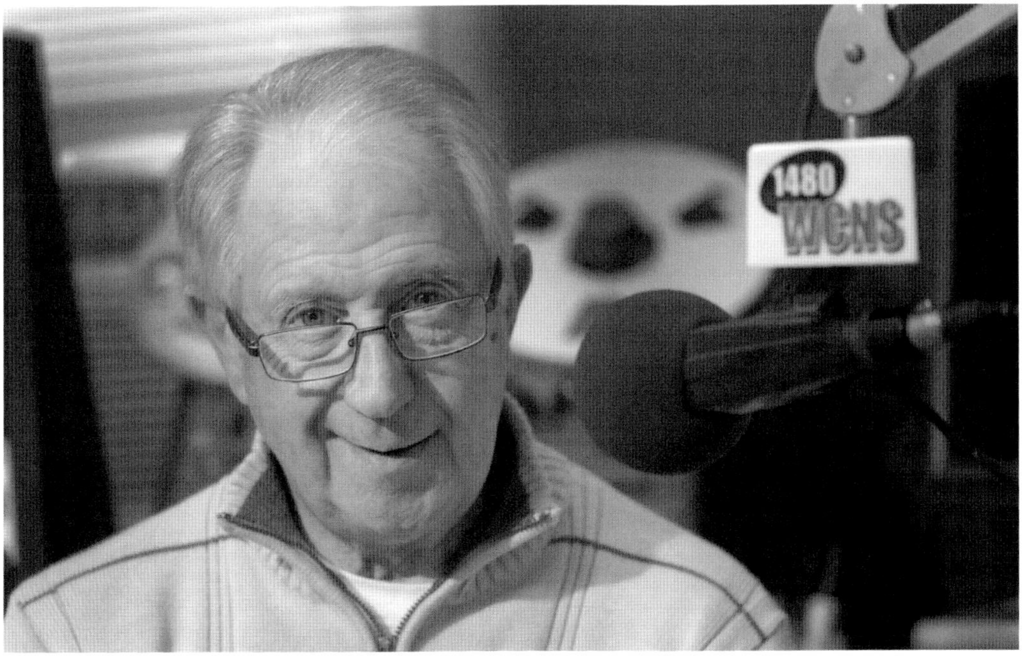

John L. Longo

John L. Longo and his wife, Dawna, were the owner/operators of Latrobe's Hometown Radio Station WCNS for 25 years before they retired and sold the station in 2014. John Longo, who started working as a disc jockey at WCNS in 1959 for $1 an hour, was honored with the Pennsylvania Association of Broadcasters' 2000 Broadcaster of the Year and the Pittsburgh Radio and Television club's Art Stein Award for exemplary service to the industry. Now under new ownership, Latrobe's Hometown Radio Station WCNS is still going strong, broadcasting the news, "America's Best Music," Pittsburgh Pirates baseball, and a variety of local topic conversations on *Saturday Talk Block*, as well as covering live events like the Westmoreland Air Show and Greater Latrobe High School sports. (Evan Sanders/Copyright © *Tribune-Review*, 2014, all rights reserved. Reprinted with permission.)

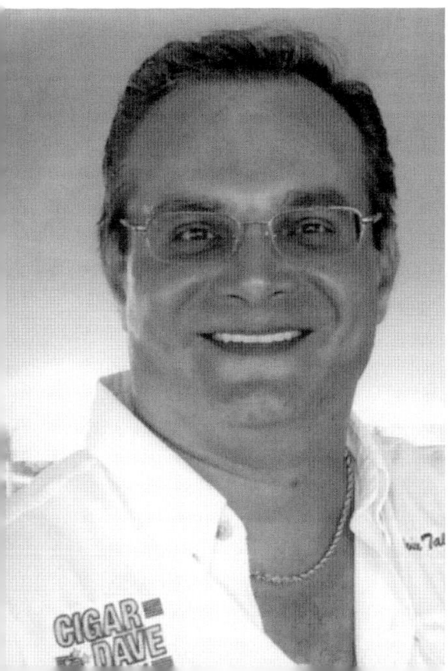

Ed Weigle

Ed Weigle is a 1985 graduate of Greater Latrobe High School. He attended Point Park College and became a radio disc jockey. He was greatly influenced by his close friend and mentor the late Pittsburgh radio legend and rock and roll pioneer Porky Chedwick. For more than 30 years, Weigle has remained one of America's most prolific voice actors. His unmistakable sound has brought to life tens of thousands of commercials, concert promotions, and film narrations showcased worldwide. (Ed Weigle.)

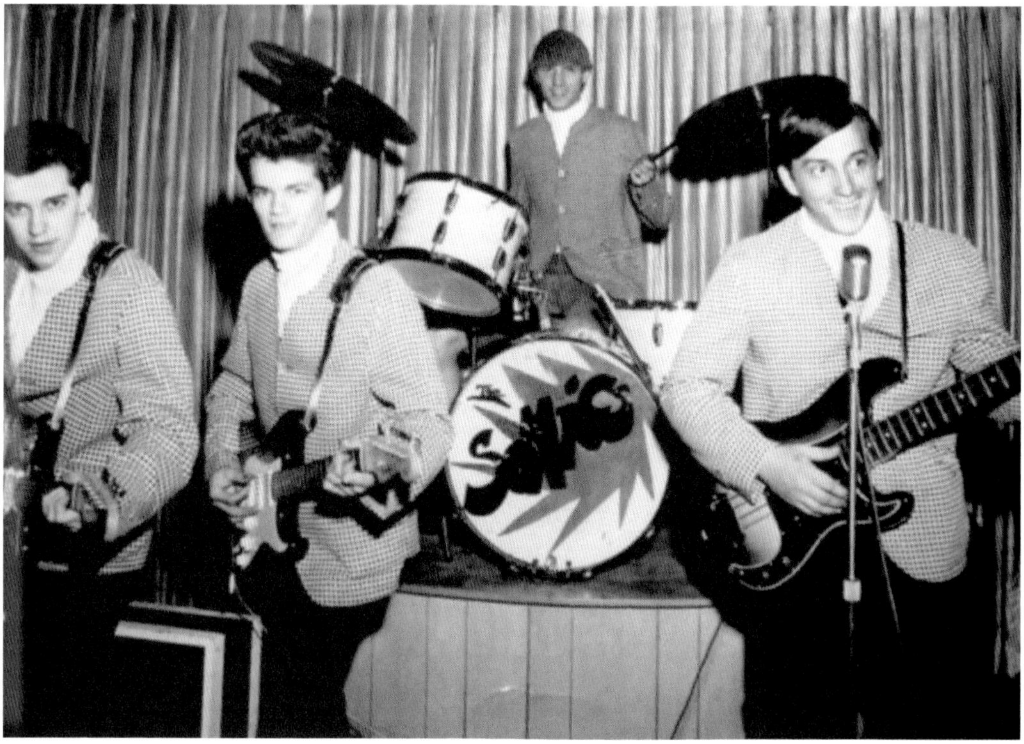

Harry C. Lattanzio

Harry C. Lattanzio was born and grew up in Hillside, a village in Derry Township. In 1941, he opened Skateland, later called Harry's Danceland, in downtown Latrobe at 201 Depot Street. Lattanzio was often called "the Dick Clark of western Pennsylvania" for his headliners, which included the Glenn Miller Orchestra, Frankie Avalon, Dionne Warwick, Conway Twitty, Chubby Checker, Paul Anka, Fabian, and more. Pictured is Harry's Danceland's house band, the Sonics. The band members are, from left to right, Bill Rhodes (lead guitar), Lou Penzera (rhythm guitar), Ron Horak (drums), and Latrobe's Mike Vale/Vucish (bass guitar). (Cathi Rhodes.)

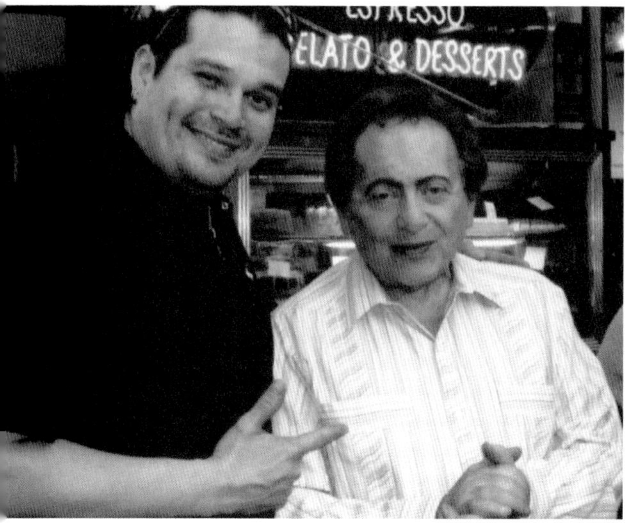

Jackie Mason

Jackie Mason was born Yakov (Jacob) Moshe Maza on June 9, 1931, into a family of rabbis—his father, grandfather, and three older brothers all having chosen that profession. After receiving a bachelor's of arts from the City College of New York, Mason himself briefly became a student rabbi in Latrobe. Deciding that his true love was comedy, he cut two albums and made numerous appearances as a stand-up comedian on television, including frequent guest spots on *The Ed Sullivan Show.* Mason also acted in films such as *The Jerk* (1979), *History of the World, Part I* (1981), and *Caddyshack II* (1988). He is pictured in 2003 with Magick Balay, a fellow New York City entertainer and magician. (Magick Balay.)

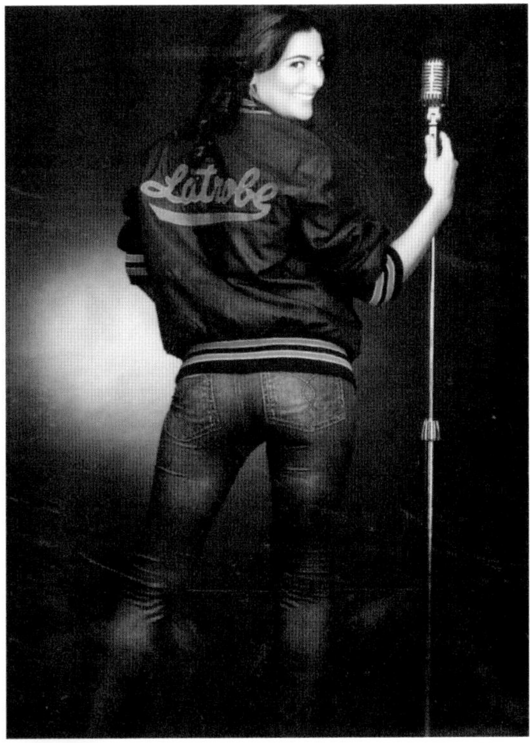

Natalie Shugars

Natalie Shugars hails from Latrobe. She is a singer and model who got her start in the professional entertainment industry at the age of 17. She holds an extensive résumé as a vivacious live performer, singer, dancer, songwriter, model, and actress. She discovered modeling as a career in the Carolinas and has appeared in numerous magazines. Being from Latrobe, home of the Steelers' training camp, Shugars cofounded the Black 'N' Gold Girls, a Pittsburgh sports fan club for women who assist with and attend many charitable events all over the city. In 2008, she was the first woman to write and record a Steeler fight song. The song, "I Love Black 'n' Gold," hit the radio waves during the 2008 Super Bowl season for the Steelers. Today, Shugars continues her journey as a spokeswoman for a Pittsburgh-based business and dental practice. (Dennis Keim/Natalie Shugars.)

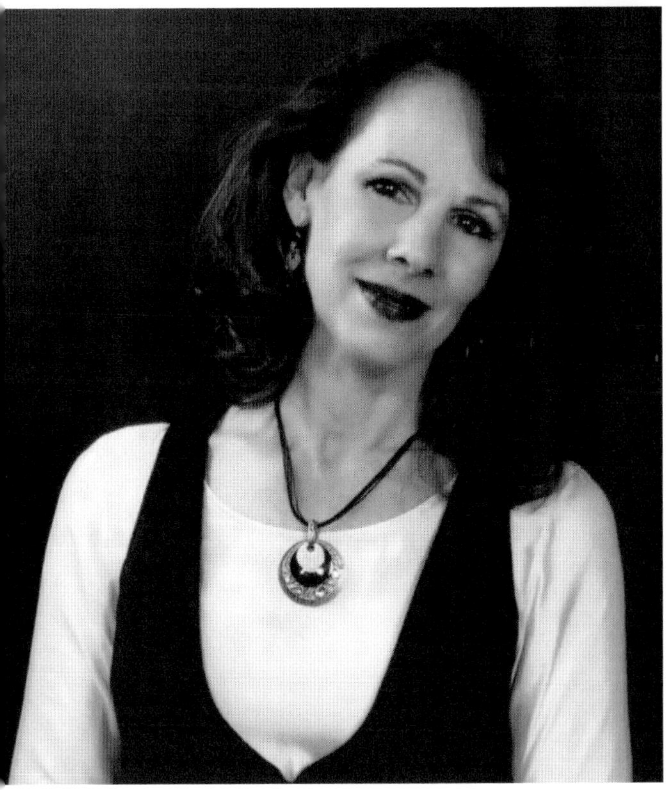

Irene Kelley

Irene Kelley's signature mix of bluegrass, country, and Americana appeals to music lovers across all genres. A native of Latrobe, Kelley discovered her flair for songwriting as a teenager and soon found her way to Nashville, where her songs were quickly noticed and recorded by Carl Jackson, Ricky Skaggs, and Sharon White. While recording an album for MCA and independently releasing two more records and touring worldwide, Irene raised two daughters and scored cuts with Alan Jackson, Trisha Yearwood, Loretta Lynn, and others. Her new full-length bluegrass album, *Pennsylvania Coal*, produced by multi–Grammy award winner Mark Fain, was released in 2013. (Stacie Huckeba/Irene Kelley.)

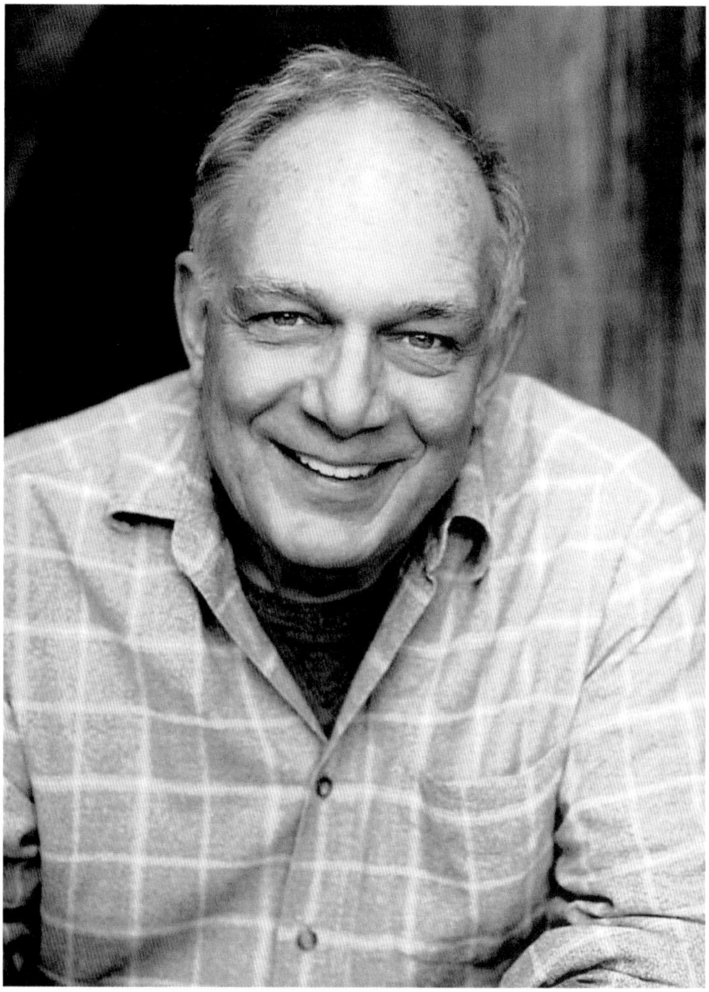

David Allen Downs

The son of a local steelworker, David Allen Downs was born on February 25, 1946, in Whitney, Pennsylvania, and graduated from Latrobe High School, where he was a popular and involved student. He participated in annual theatrical productions there and was also a key member of the Latrobe track team, establishing a long-standing school record in the high hurdles and becoming a high scorer for the 1964 county meet. He won a number of awards, including the school honor for dramatics, the Harvard Book Award for high scholarship, and a college scholarship from the Latrobe Steel Company. Downs attended Allegheny College and Loyola University of Chicago for coursework in English literature. He participated in theater-department productions at Loyola and received a master's degree in 1970. Downs then relocated to Bloomsburg, Pennsylvania, to study under the celebrated Alvina Krause, a former teacher of acting at Northwestern University. Combining his long enthusiasm for the theater, his demonstrated talents, and the lessons he learned from Krause, he applied for a faculty position at Northwestern University. He was hired as an instructor there in 1973 and began teaching the high-energy style of acting for which he became well known. Some of his former students include David Schwimmer, Zach Braff, John Logan (screenwriter: *Skyfall* and *Hugo*; Tony award–winning playwright: *Red*), Bruce Norris (Pulitzer prize for *Clybourne Park*), Anna Gunn (actress: *Breaking Bad*), and Denis O'Hare (*American Horror Story*, *True Blood*, Tony award: *Take Me Out*). Downs is now retired and lives in Los Angeles, where his involvement in the theater continues. (David Allen Downs.)

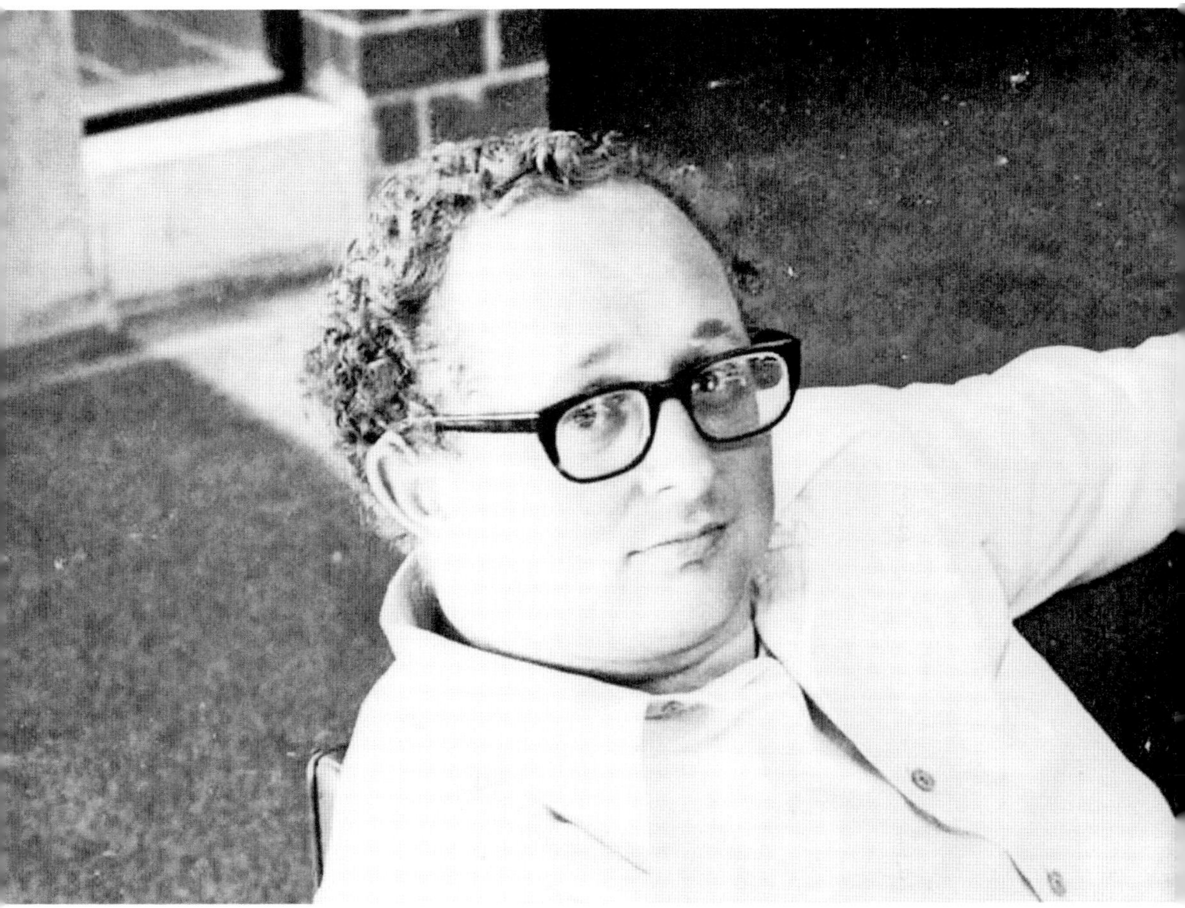

Tom Devereux

Fr. Tom Devereux (1932–2008) was a Benedictine monk who founded the St. Vincent Summer Theatre. He attended St. Vincent Preparatory School, earned a bachelor of arts degree in 1952 from St. Vincent College, and graduated from St. Vincent Seminary in 1959. In 1969, he was named producer of St. Vincent Summer Theatre. For more than 40 years, he shaped and molded the theater there and directed and produced hundreds of shows, including *Fiddler on the Roof*, *West Side Story*, and *Arsenic and Old Lace*. He also worked with hundreds of actors and actresses, including Stuart Pankin, well known from television and films, and Joy Pankin, who performed with the theater in its early days. (Colleen Reilly/St. Vincent Summer Theatre.)

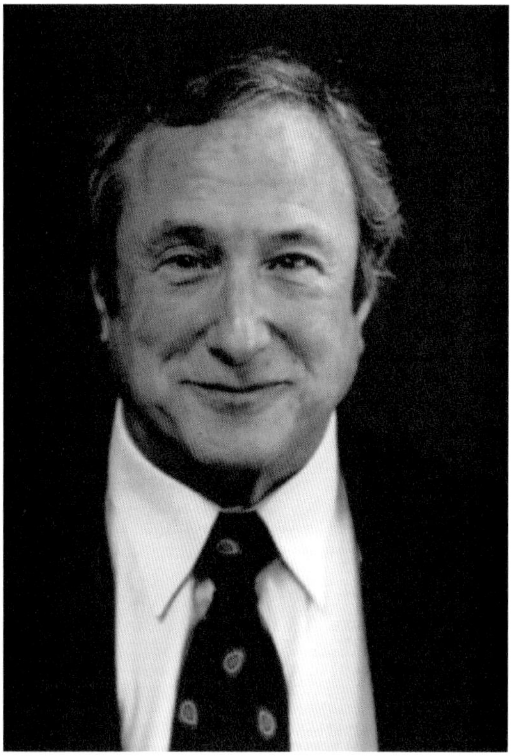

Stuart Pankin

Stuart Pankin, while not a native of Latrobe, is recognized locally for his many appearances as an actor at the St. Vincent Summer Theatre. Early in his career, Pankin frequently performed there, and he still returns often. Born in Philadelphia, he was an anchor on HBO's *Not Necessarily the News*, played Earl Sinclair on the TV sitcom *Dinosaurs*, and was the father on the sitcom *Nearly Departed*. His film roles include *Honey, We Shrunk Ourselves* as the brother of Wayne Szalinski, and he costarred as a bossy, self-important lawman in the horror/comedy film *Arachnophobia*. (Colleen Reilly/St. Vincent Summer Theatre.)

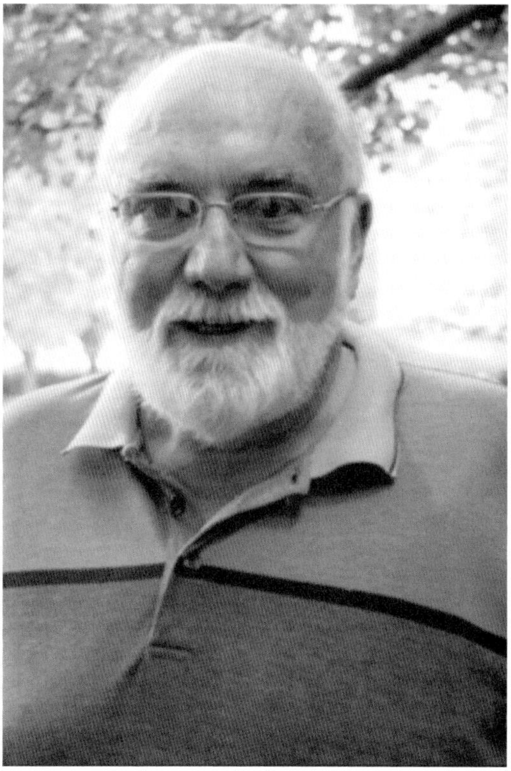

Joe Reilly

Joe Reilly (1944–2009) was a very popular St. Vincent Theatre director and producer and lecturer in the college's department of communication and fine arts. He also taught film and theater classes, directed numerous student theater productions, and was an active member of the Westmoreland County cultural and educational community. Reilly attended St. Vincent College and Seminary, as well as Penn State University, and for 40 years, he directed more than 150 shows for the St. Vincent Theatre in collaboration with the late Fr. Tom Devereux. (Colleen Reilly/St. Vincent Summer Theatre.)

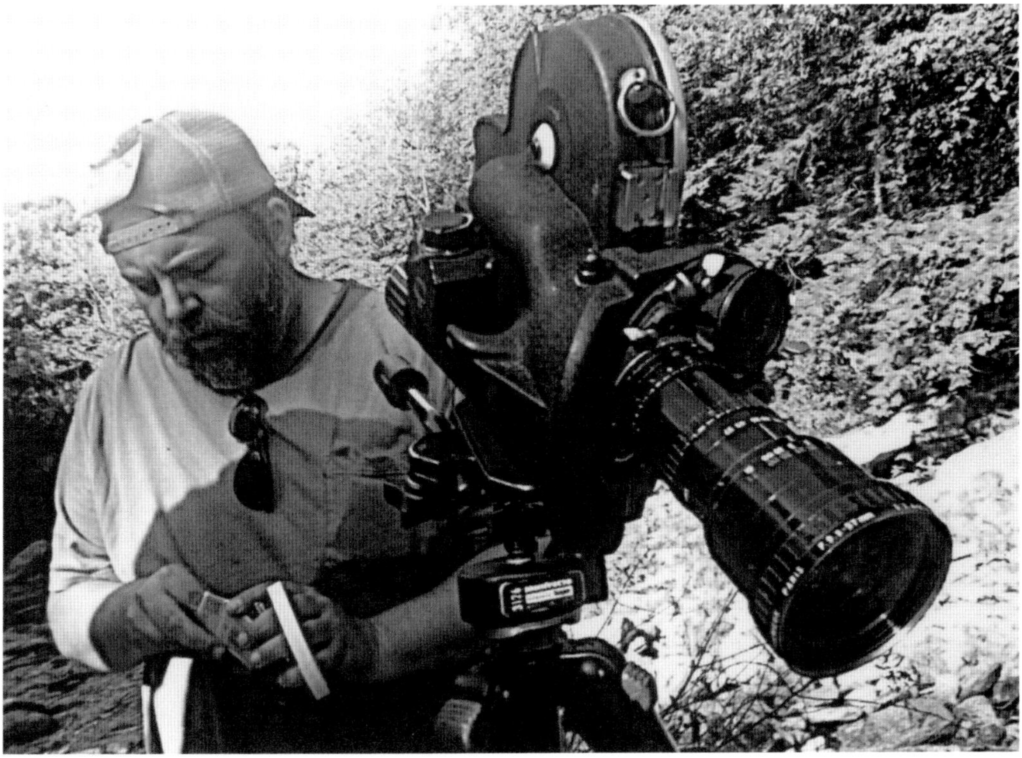

Mike Bonello
Mike Bonello is a filmmaker, educator, musician, and producer. Raised in Latrobe, he studied writing at Penn State University. He founded Rickety Records in 1994 and is the bass player for Dirty Faces, a local punk rock band he helped form in 1997. Bonello works full time at Pittsburgh Filmmakers in Oakland, where he is operations manager and adjunct faculty, teaching introductory film and video production and experimental film workshops. He has exhibited films at the Museum of Modern Art in New York and at the Mattress Factory and Warhol Museum in Pittsburgh. (Mike Bonello.)

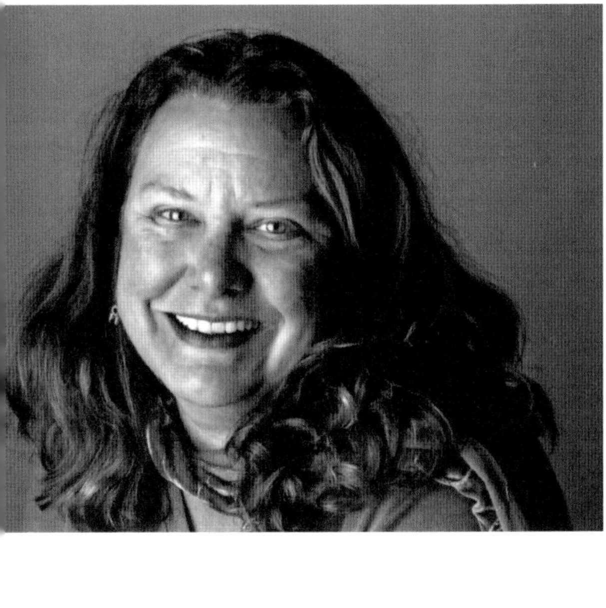

Megan McDonald
Megan McDonald, a successful children's author, was born in Pittsburgh on February 28, 1959, but prior to her career as a writer, she worked as a children's librarian at Adams Memorial Library in Latrobe. It was there she read aloud her first picture book, *Is This a House For Hermit Crab?*, which was published in 1990. McDonald credits her time at Adams, along with many other life experiences growing up in western Pennsylvania, as most influential when writing children's literature. She spoke with Latrobe-area elementary students during an author visit in 1999. Today, the students are especially fond of her popular *Judy Moody and Stink* series of books. (Michele McDonald/ Megan McDonald.)

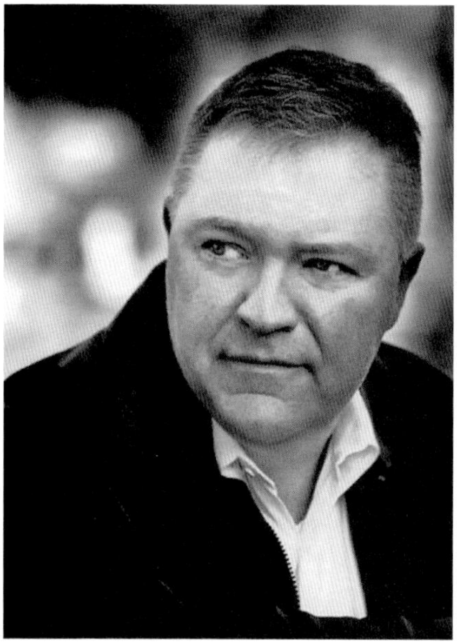

F.J. Lennon

F.J. Lennon is a novelist, screenwriter, and digital media producer, designer, and writer. He is the author of three books in a trilogy that follow the turbulent life of rogue ghost hunter Kane Pryce and has been actively employed in multiple industries, including computer games and apps, interactive television, advertising, and toys. He is a graduate of Latrobe High School and a 1986 magna cum laude graduate of St. Vincent College. He currently lives in the Washington, DC, area with his wife and two daughters. (F.J. Lennon.)

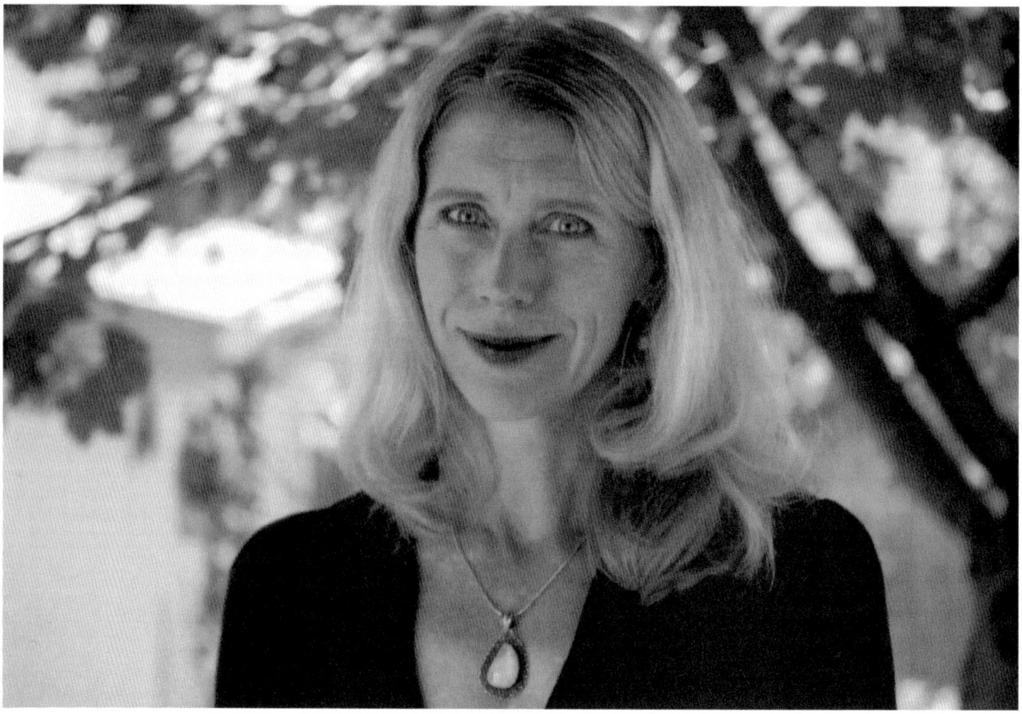

Ann Lightcap Bruno

Ann Lightcap Bruno, a native of Latrobe, is an English teacher, writer, and dean at the Wheeler School in Providence, Rhode Island. Her stories and essays have appeared in such publications as *Memoir, Painted Bride Quarterly, Vestal Review, Sweet, Elimae, Alimentum*, and *Talking Writing*. A graduate of Brown University and Boston College, Bruno first began writing as a child after visiting the Carnegie Museum of Natural History in Pittsburgh, jotting down names of interesting animals and exhibits and writing poems with the new words she discovered there. (Ann Lightcap Bruno.)

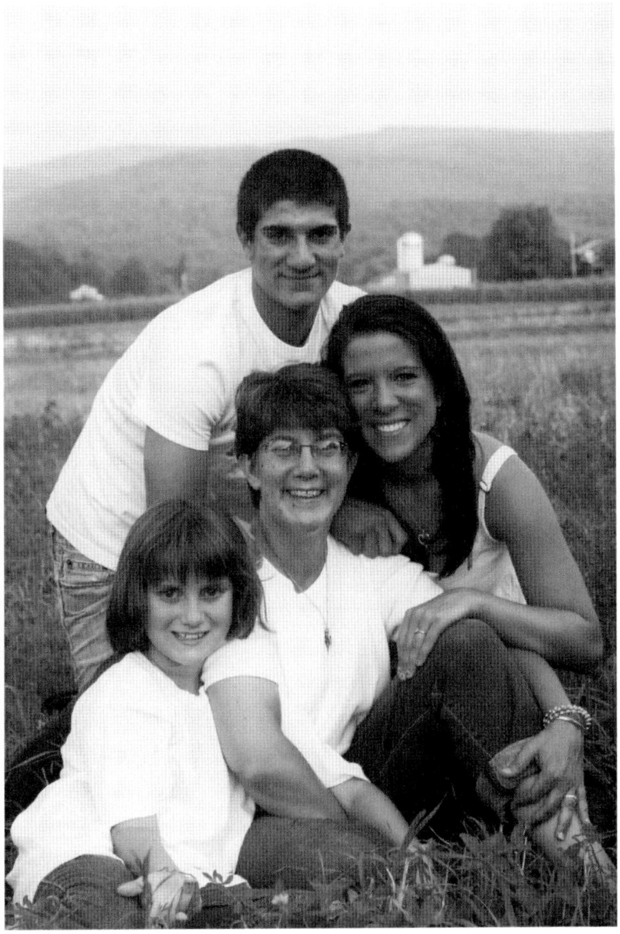

Julie Anne Bisi

Julie Anne Bisi grew up and currently resides in Latrobe. Certified in elementary education with a master's degree in elementary and middle school mathematics, she has a passion for children's literature and sees tremendous value in using stories across the curriculum. She is the author of *The House on Baker Hill*, a children's picture book about a Victorian house in Latrobe, and is the cofounder of the Absolute Value of One, a service learning program for students. She is an adjunct instructor in the Mathematics Department of Westmoreland County Community College and the manager of the Home Care Department at the Arc of Westmoreland. Bisi, pictured with her three children—Anna (13), Megan (22), and Ryan (20)—is also on the city council and a member of the Adams Memorial Library board of directors. (Julie Anne Bisi.)

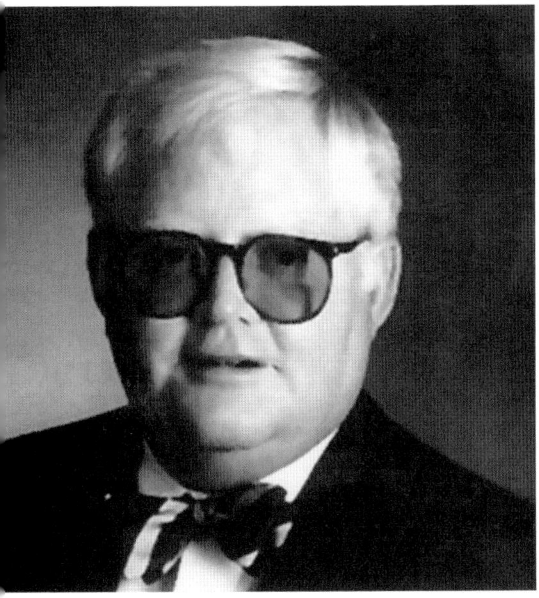

Dennis P. McIlnay

Dennis P. McIlnay is a native of Latrobe and the author of five books, three of which are regional history books on Pennsylvania. He holds a bachelor of arts degree in English from St. Vincent College, a master's degree in higher education administration from Penn State University, and a doctorate in higher education administration from Seton Hall University. He is professor emeritus of management at St. Francis University in Loretto, Pennsylvania, where he earned a number of awards, including the Distinguished Professor Award from the Alumni Association. McIlnay retired from St. Francis in December 2009 and lives with his wife, Kathy, in Hollidaysburg near Altoona, where he is president of Seven Oaks Press, a regional publishing company. (Dennis P. McIlnay.)

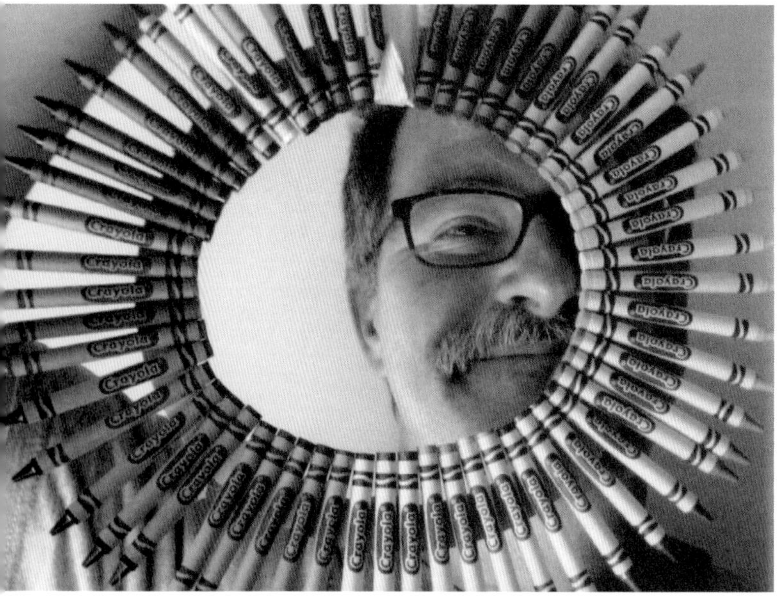

Chris Rodell

Chris Rodell's biography reads, "I'm a Latrobe, Pa., writer who'll work for anyone who pays me. I've written for some of the best magazines in America and been rejected by the rest." His book, *Use All The Crayons! The Colorful Guide to Simple Human Happiness* was released in April 2012 and includes a foreword by his neighbor Arnold Palmer. In his book, Rodell shares simple ideas for living a more colorful life. (Chris Rodell.)

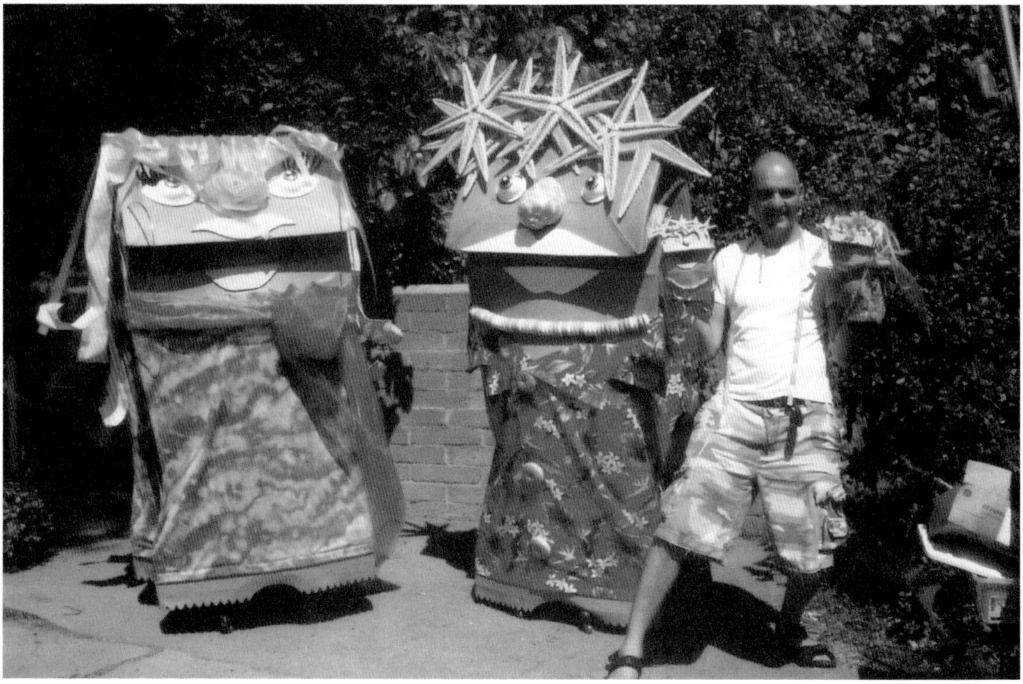

James Hayes

James Hayes, an Emmy-nominated designer, has been creating and building specialty costumes for motion pictures, television programs, the stage, and national ad campaigns since 1990. Many will recognize his paper bag puppets for Fandango.com. A native of Latrobe, Hayes fondly remembers being recommended for the Pennsylvania Governor's School for the Arts as a junior at Greater Latrobe High School by his acting teacher, Jim Mikula. "The experience enlightened me," Hayes recalled, "and opened my eyes to the possibility that I could follow my dream and have a career in the arts." Today, he is living that dream in Los Angeles, surrounded by foam, fleece, and feathers. (James Hayes.)

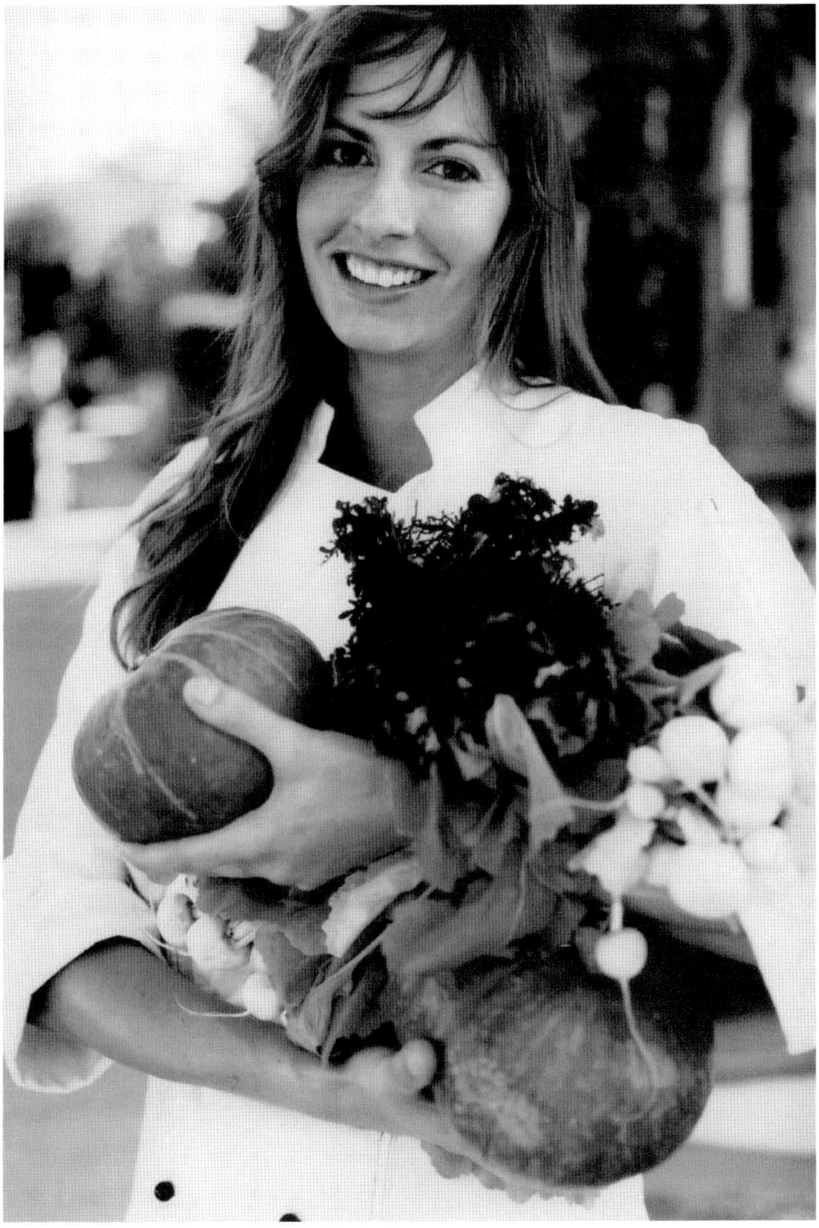

Jill Snyder

Jill Snyder, born in Latrobe, is a culinary artist who was featured on *Top Chef* (2006). She attended Mountain View Elementary School and graduated from Greater Latrobe High School in 1998. Her culinary interests were sparked at an early age when she began helping on her uncle's farm, picking berries and baking cookies to sell at the local farmers' market. She didn't plan on becoming a chef, but she counts her decision to attend culinary school as one of her best moves. She currently has her own personal chef business in Los Angeles. Of her time in school and growing up in Latrobe, Snyder wrote, "I loved art class, elementary through high school, and recall all of my teachers being great and unique. I remember the sense of pride that students had for Latrobe, especially supporting sports and the arts." (Jill Snyder.)

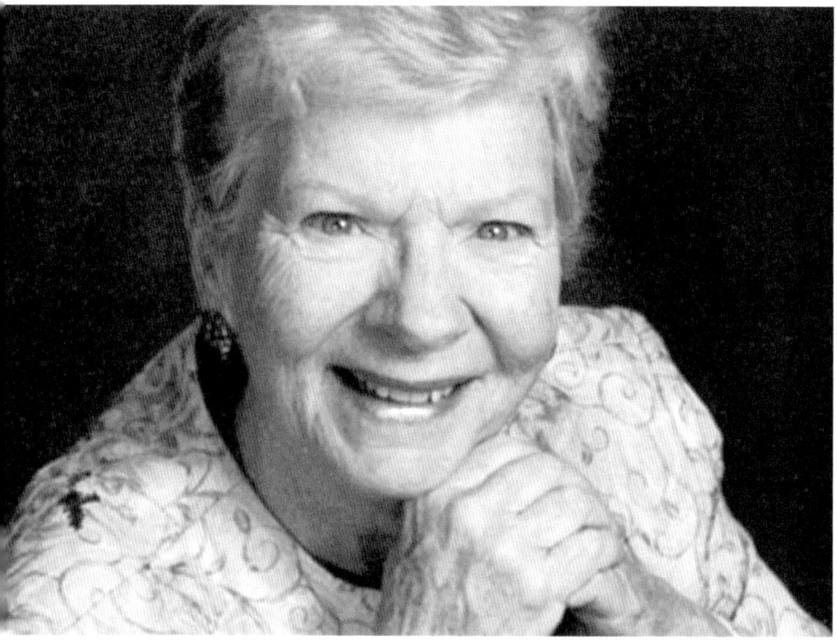

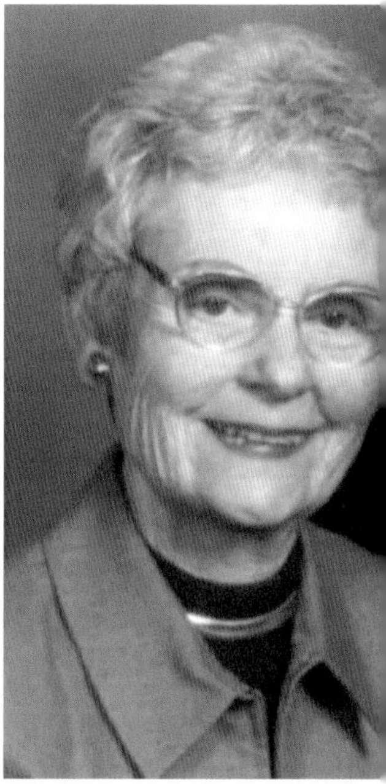

Nancy Rogers Crozier and Elizabeth Hazlett

Nancy Rogers Crozier (above, left) and Elizabeth Hazlett (above, right) are the cofounders of the Latrobe Art Center. Crozier (Fred Rogers's sister) and the late Elizabeth Hazlett wanted a place in the heart of downtown Latrobe where local talent could exhibit work. The nonprofit organization opened its doors on June 15, 2002. After more than a decade, the Latrobe Art Center has become a hub of activity by reaching out to the community and encouraging everyone to share in the creative process. The center is known for its education programs, community involvement, quality artwork, and the Neighborhood Café. In 2012, the center provided educational programs to nearly 3,000 children. Pictured below are finalists in the art center's banana split song contest, held during the first Great American Banana Split Celebration in 2013. (Above, both, Latrobe Art Center; below AC.)

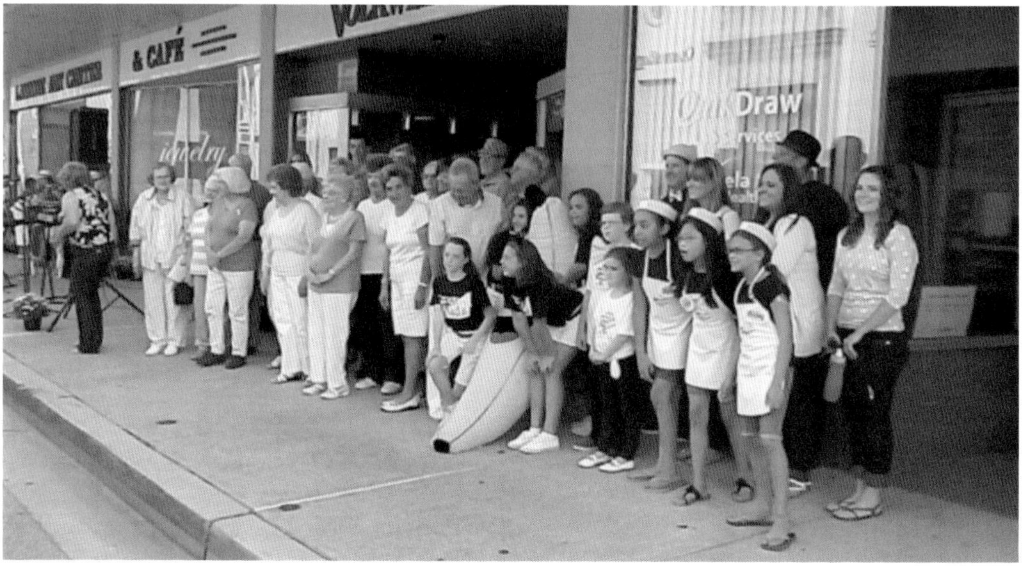

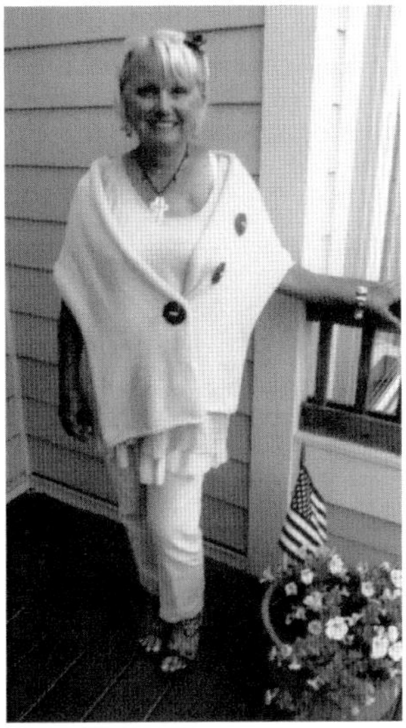

Doreen Currie

Doreen Currie is a fourth-generation native of Latrobe who still resides on a portion of her great-grandparents' farm. She enjoys the beauty of gardens, rolling hillsides, forests, and country landscapes of the area and loves painting them. She studied graphic art and design at Seton Hill College and describes her painting style as impressionistic. "I am most interested in describing feeling in the painting rather than a perfect rendition. I think that one remembers a painting because of how it makes you feel, rather than what it describes." Her paintings are on display in Pittsburgh-area galleries and the Latrobe Art Center, as well as in many corporate and private collections. (Doreen Currie.)

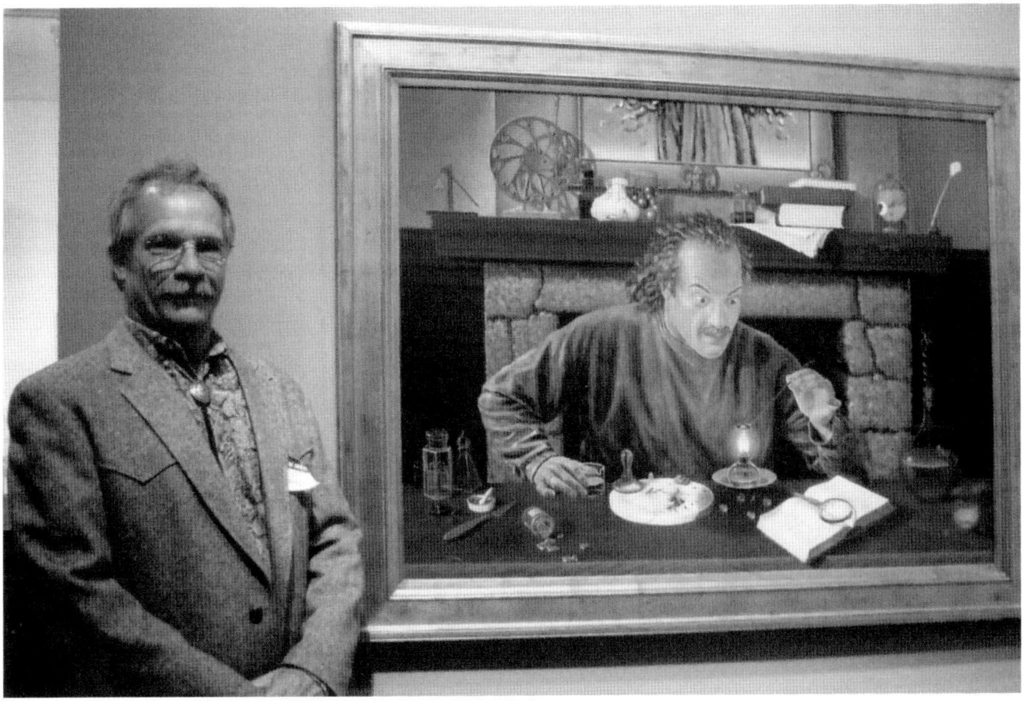

Paul McMillan

While not a Latrobe native, artist Paul McMillan won Best of Show at the 2011 Westmoreland Art Nationals in Youngwood, Pennsylvania and twice won the People's Choice Award at Twin Lakes' Westmoreland Art and Heritage Festival in Greensburg, Pennsylvania. In 2013, his work was added to the Greater Latrobe School District Special Art Collection. Reflecting on this experience, McMillan wrote, "In 1996, I was runner-up in the Texas Sesquicentennial Artist of the Year contest. Biggest is not best and so I say very heartfully, the award I treasure the most was being included in the Greater Latrobe Art Collection, where the true value of art is integral to education and where a practice of bringing art to the educational process is a long standing tradition." (Paul McMillan.)

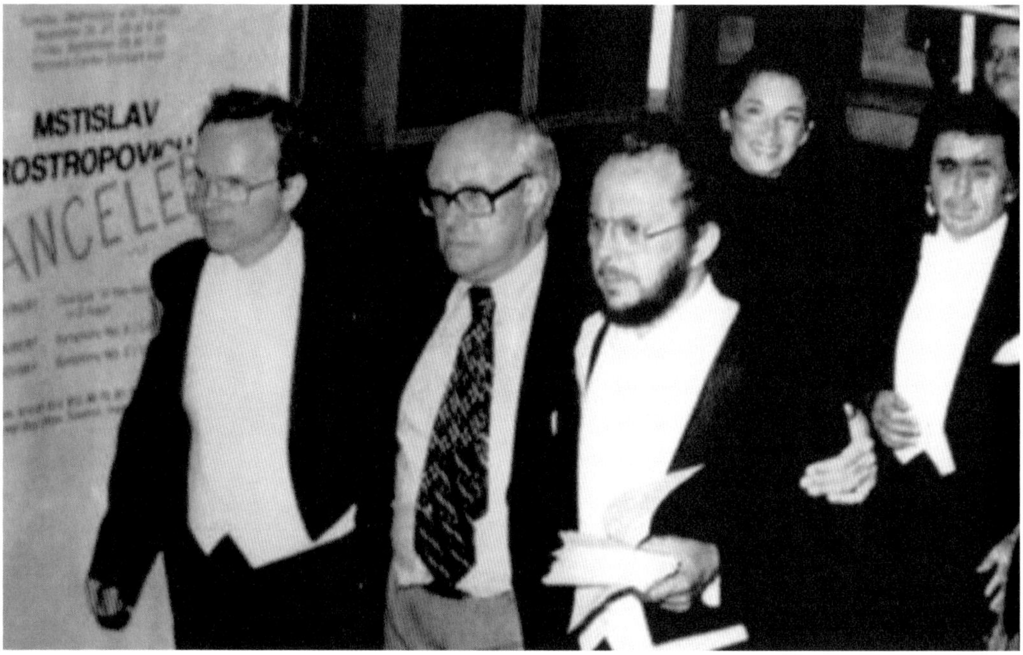

Frederick Zenone

Frederick Zenone (1936–2010) was born on January 26, 1936, in Latrobe. He was studying music at Indiana University of Pennsylvania when he switched from trumpet to cello. He spent 30 years as a cellist with the National Symphony Orchestra and exerted a greater influence on the musical world as an advocate for the rights of musicians. In the picture, Zenone, right, is among the leaders of a 1978 musicians' strike against the National Symphony Orchestra. He is shown with William Foster, left, and maestro Mstislav Rostropovich, center. (Laura Ross/International Conference of Symphony and Opera Musicians Archives.)

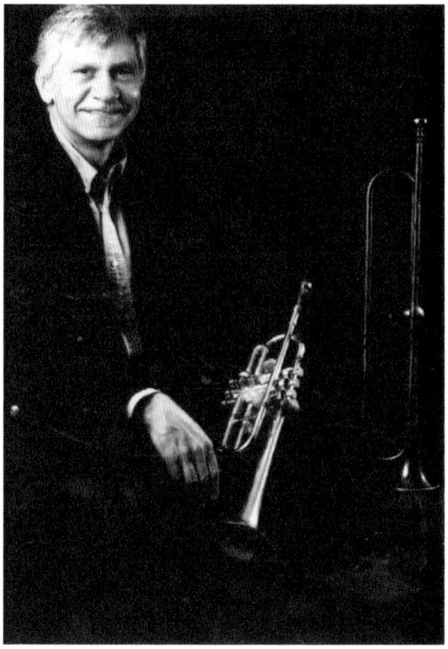

Dennis Ferry

Dennis Ferry was born in Latrobe and began his musical education with his father, Tony Ferri, a big-band trumpeter. He obtained a bachelor of fine arts in music from Carnegie Mellon University and a master's of music from Catholic University. He was the principal trumpet of the Orchestre de la Suisse Romande in Geneva from October 1977 until January 2009. Since then, Ferry moved to the Washington, DC, area and has been very active in the Washington National Opera, the Kennedy Center Opera House Orchestra, the National Symphony Orchestra, and the Baltimore Symphony Orchestra, among others. (Dennis Ferry.)

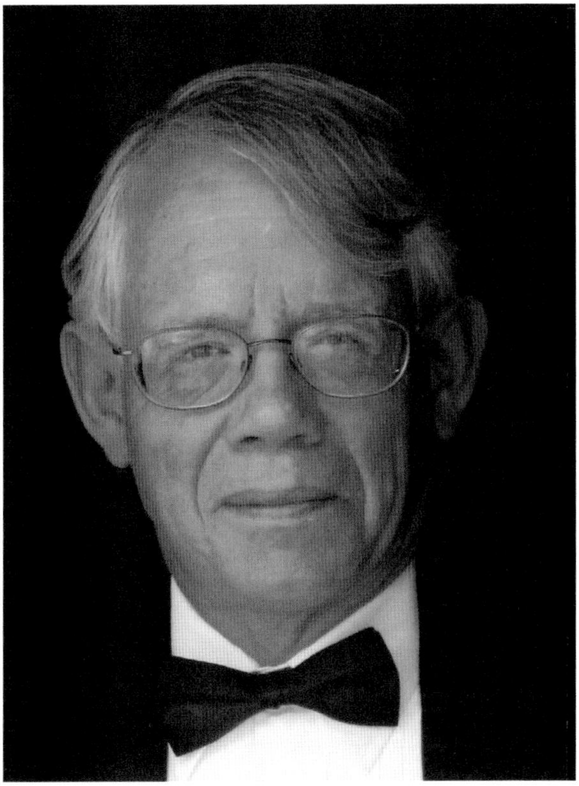

Harold Stover

Harold Stover is a native of Latrobe and a graduate of the Juilliard School in New York. From 1968 to 2013, he served as organist and director of music at churches in New York City and Portland, Maine. He presently pursues an active career as a freelance organist and composer, as director of the Portland-based chamber chorus Renaissance Voices, and on the faculty of the Portland Conservatory of Music. His career as an organ recitalist spans 45 years and includes appearances at St. Patrick's Cathedral in New York, the National Cathedral in Washington, Westminster Abbey in London, and many other distinguished venues. The *New York Times* called his performances "a succession of listening pleasures." (Harold Stover.)

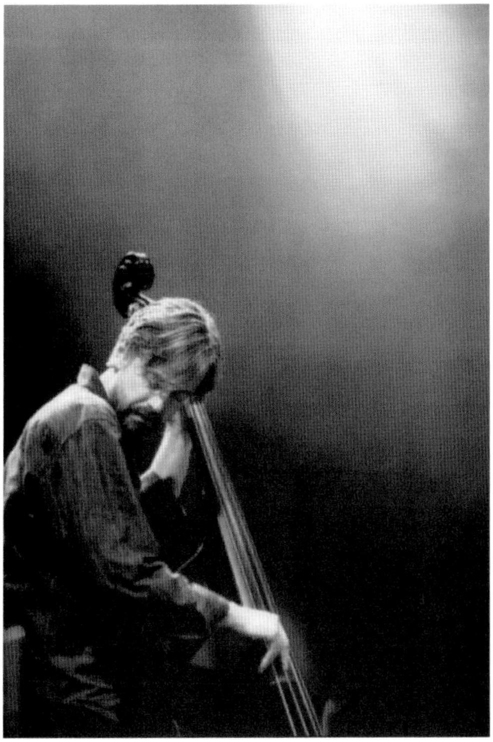

Chris Lightcap

Chris Lightcap was born and raised in Latrobe. He played violin and piano before taking up the electric bass at 14. As a senior in high school, he started to study the upright bass and, the following year, enrolled at Williams College, where he studied bass, composition, and improvisation. As a bandleader, he has released four critically acclaimed albums of original music, including *Lay-Up* (2000), *Bigmouth* (2003), *Deluxe* (2010), and *Epicenter* (2014). In 2011, Chamber Music America awarded Lightcap a New Jazz Works commission grant. The result was *Lost and Found New York*, which premiered at the 2012 Earshot Festival and was featured on NPR's *Jazzset with Dee Dee Bridgewater.* (Petra Cvelbar/ Chris Lightcap.)

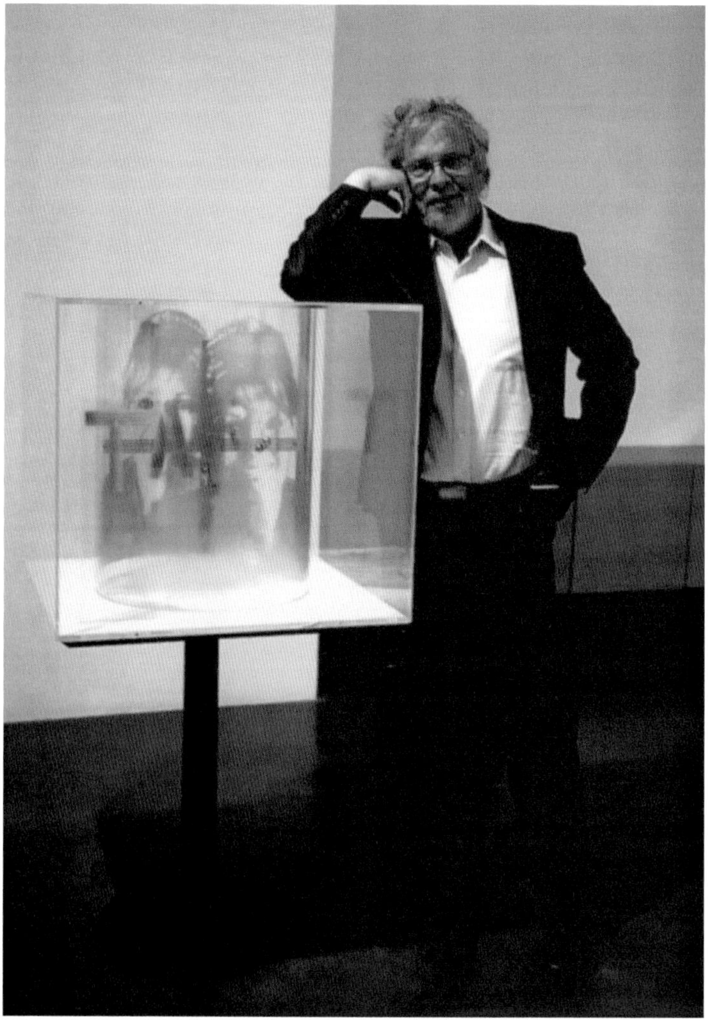

Daniel Lentz

Daniel Lentz, born in Latrobe on March 10, 1942, is a classical electronic music composer. He attended St. Vincent College for his bachelor's degree, Ohio University for his master's of fine arts, Brandeis University, and Stockholm University as a Fulbright grantee. He achieved notability as a musician while a student at Brandeis for his National Defense Education Act Fellowship, and he was awarded a fellowship in composition at Tanglewood in the summer of 1966, followed by a Fulbright fellowship in electronic music in 1967–1968, which he completed in Stockholm, Sweden. In 1972, Lentz won the Gaudeamus International Composers Award, and since then, he has won a number of other awards and grants, including six National Endowment for the Arts grants. He taught at UC–Santa Barbara, Antioch College, Arizona State University–West, and UCLA. He was the founding director of the performance ensembles the California Time Machine, the San Andreas Fault, and the Daniel Lentz Group, and to this day, he has a regular commission-based composition practice. Lentz is pictured with one of his "Illuminated Manuscripts," which have been featured in *Source* and *Esquire* magazines and have been shown at museums and art galleries in New Mexico and California. The three-dimensional works feature suspended elements, abstractly representing actual musical scores that inspired each work. Lentz explained that viewing the artwork with the music being played adds a fourth dimension to the experience. (Daniel Lentz.)

CHAPTER FIVE

Sports and Medicine

The term "sports medicine" was first used in 1961 to describe the modern practice in the prevention and treatment of sports injuries, but in the Greater Latrobe area, sports and medicine go back quite a bit further. Many of Latrobe's early sports legends became doctors who served the community. Legend John Brallier, once thought to be the first professional football player, became an orthodontist and served the city until retiring in the 1950s. Brallier's teammate on the first all-pro football team was Dr. James Edward Blair, a skilled surgeon. John Mazero was a quarterback with the Latrobe High School Wildcats from 1946 to 1947 and was recognized much later for a distinguished career as a hometown physician. Dr. Walter S. Hazlett Jr. also attended Latrobe schools, where he participated in basketball, track, and volleyball and then served in World War II; upon being injured and awarded the Purple Heart, he returned home to practice family medicine. Kevin Guskiewicz played high school football and tennis in Latrobe and is the leading expert in the field of sports-related brain injuries. He has been honored for devising a simple but effective way to make contact sports much safer for young athletes. Of course, not all of the region's doctors and nurses were athletes first, but it is interesting to note how many were. Golf legend Arnold Palmer is by far the most famous professional athlete from Latrobe. He was named "Athlete of the Decade" for the 1960s in a national Associated Press poll and amassed 92 championships in professional competitions of national or international stature. Although victories and championship triumphs are awe-inspiring, his achievements away from the golf course—including his charity work and business ventures—have earned him even more respect in the region. Palmer hosts the annual Latrobe Classic, a fundraiser to generate money for the Arnold Palmer Medical Center, which comprises the Arnold Palmer Hospital for Children and Winnie Palmer Hospital for Women and Babies. In July 2002, University of Pittsburgh Medical Center (UPMC) and Latrobe Area Hospital (LAH) announced that the new UPMC Cancer Center in Latrobe would bear his name.

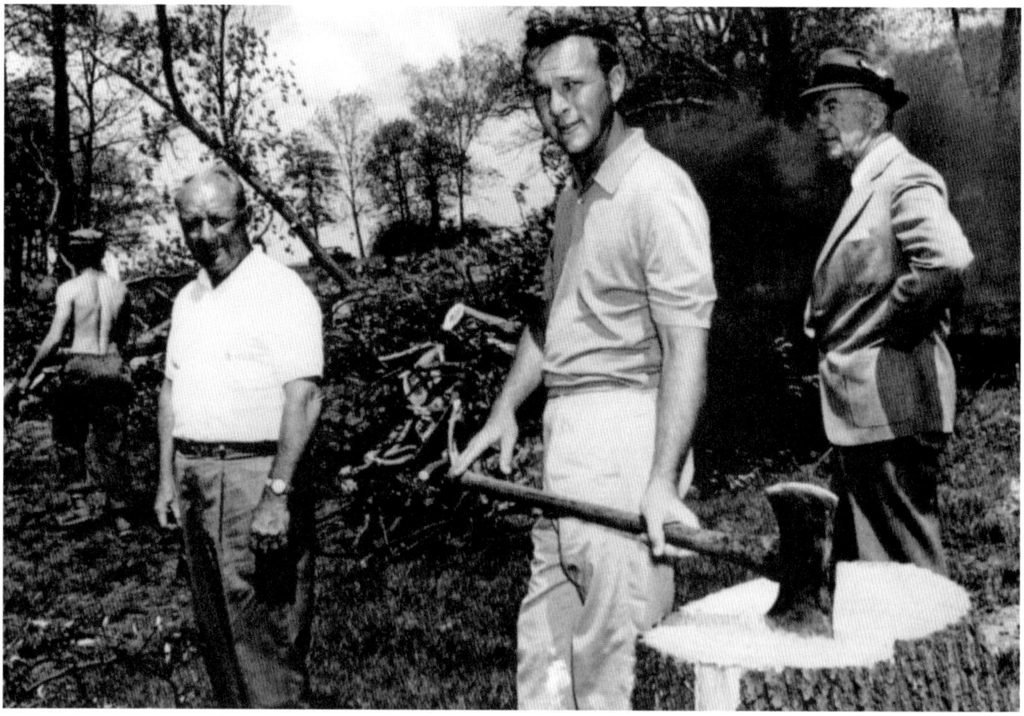

Deacon Palmer

As a teenager, Milfred J. "Deacon" Palmer (1904–1976), along with other men employed by the Latrobe Steel Company, was put to work helping with the construction of a new golf course and country club. He taught himself to play golf, and when the country club could no longer afford a groundskeeper and a pro, he was given both jobs. By the end of his tenure at Latrobe Country Club, Palmer had increased people's respect of the game through his old-fashioned values and hard work. Pictured in 1964 clearing brush during the building of the back nine at Latrobe Country Club, from left to right, are Deacon Palmer, his son Arnold, and Harry S. Saxman Sr., past president of Latrobe Steel and Latrobe Country Club. (LAHS.)

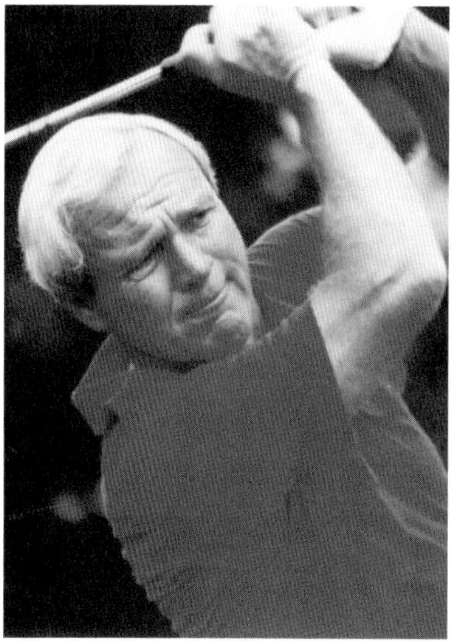

Arnold Palmer

Arnold Daniel Palmer was born on September 10, 1929, in Latrobe and still calls it home. The son of a country club groundskeeper, he began swinging his first set of golf clubs, cut to fit his small size by his father, when he was four years old. In high school, he dominated the game in western Pennsylvania, winning five amateur championships. He went on to Wake Forest College, where he became No. 1 man on the golf team. Professionally, Palmer was first to win the Masters Tournament four times and is generally regarded as one of the greatest players in the history of the game, having won 92 tournaments during his career. He is a man with a down-to-earth common touch that has made him one of the most popular and accessible public figures with his army of fans in Latrobe and around the world. (LAHS.)

Arnie's Army

In April 2014, the Golf Channel premiered *Arnie*, a three-night documentary film. It featured more than 100 notable personalities who shared their experiences with Arnold Palmer, including Harry Frye, former staff photographer for the *Latrobe Bulletin*. Frye, a Latrobe native, managed to get more than a few pictures of Palmer over the years, including the one shown below of Arnie teeing off at Oakmont Country Club with his "army" of fans lined several people deep against the gallery rope at the 1960 US Open. Palmer first visited Oakmont as a 12-year-old golfer, accompanied by Latrobe Country Club president Harry Saxman. The name "Arnie's Army" originated at the 1958 Masters, when soldiers from a nearby army base attended, and nearly all supported Palmer with homemade placards held high. In addition to his achievements on the golf course, the Golf Channel documentary also examined Palmer's many other successes as a business executive; prominent advertising spokesman; skilled aviator; golf course designer; and devoted husband, father, and grandfather. (FF.)

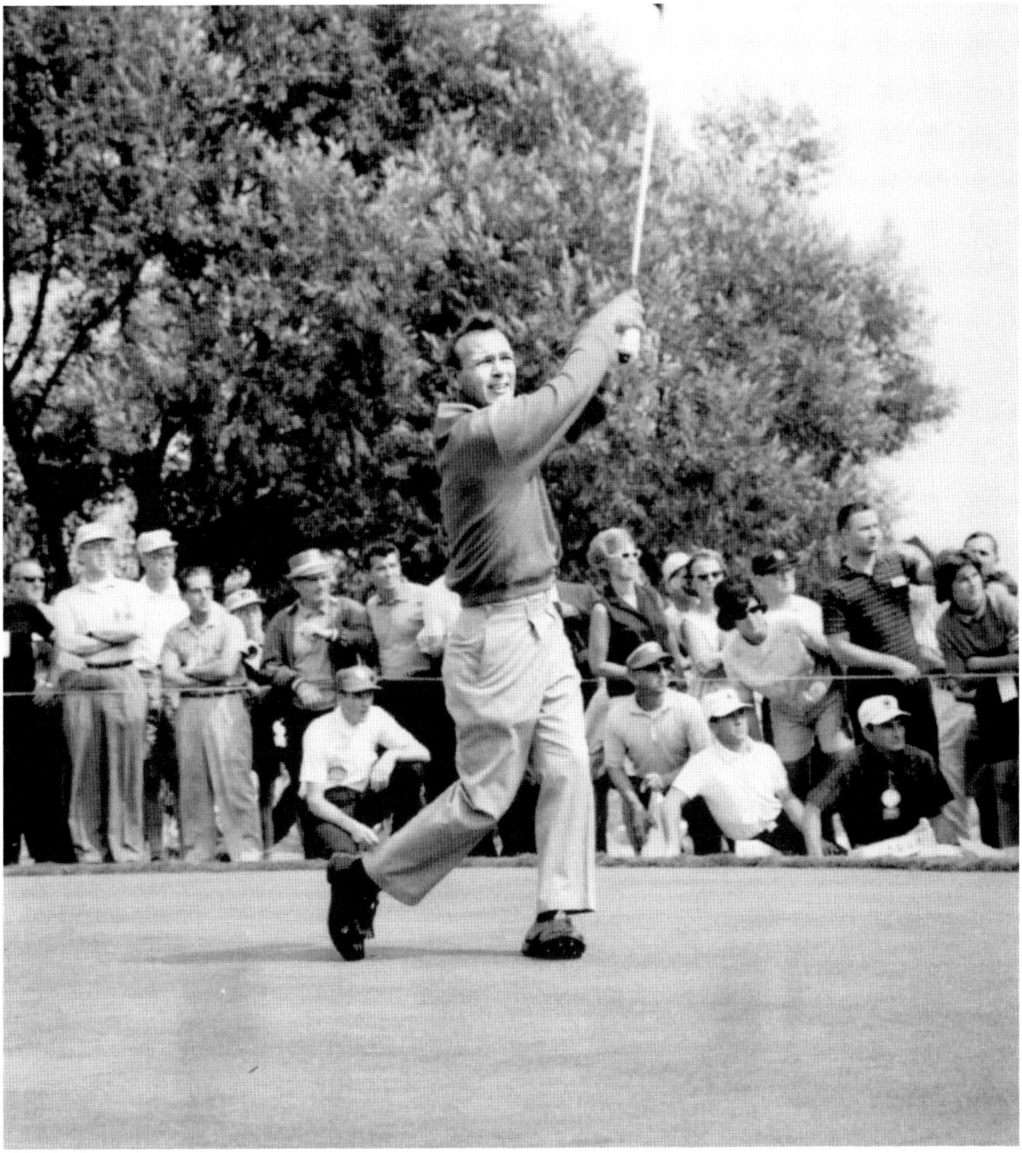

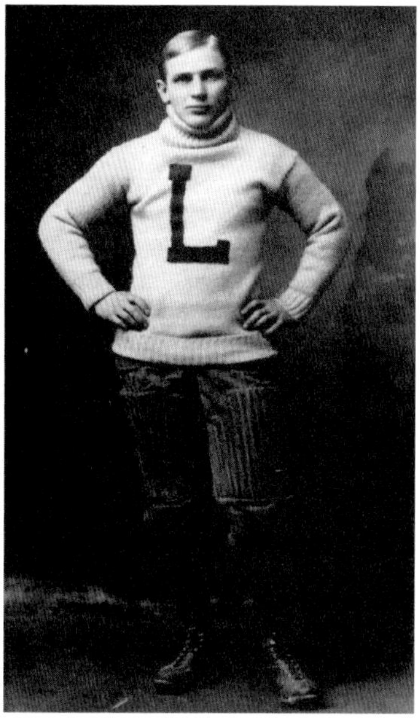

John Kinport Brallier

John Kinport "Sal" Brallier (1876–1960) is nationally acknowledged as one of the first professional football players. He was born at Cherry Tree, Pennsylvania, north of Indiana, Pennsylvania, on December 27, 1876, the son of a physician and his wife. At 18, he played quarterback for the Indiana Normal School football team and planned to attend Washington and Jefferson College when the Latrobe YMCA football team offered to pay him $10 and "some cakes [expenses]" to lead its team against Jeanette, Pennsylvania, on September 3, 1895. Brallier, a strapping five feet, six inches and 125 pounds and referred to as "Little Brallier" in newsprint, led Latrobe to a 12-0 victory. When he died on September 17, 1960, at age 83, he was the last surviving member of the Latrobe football team. (LAHS.)

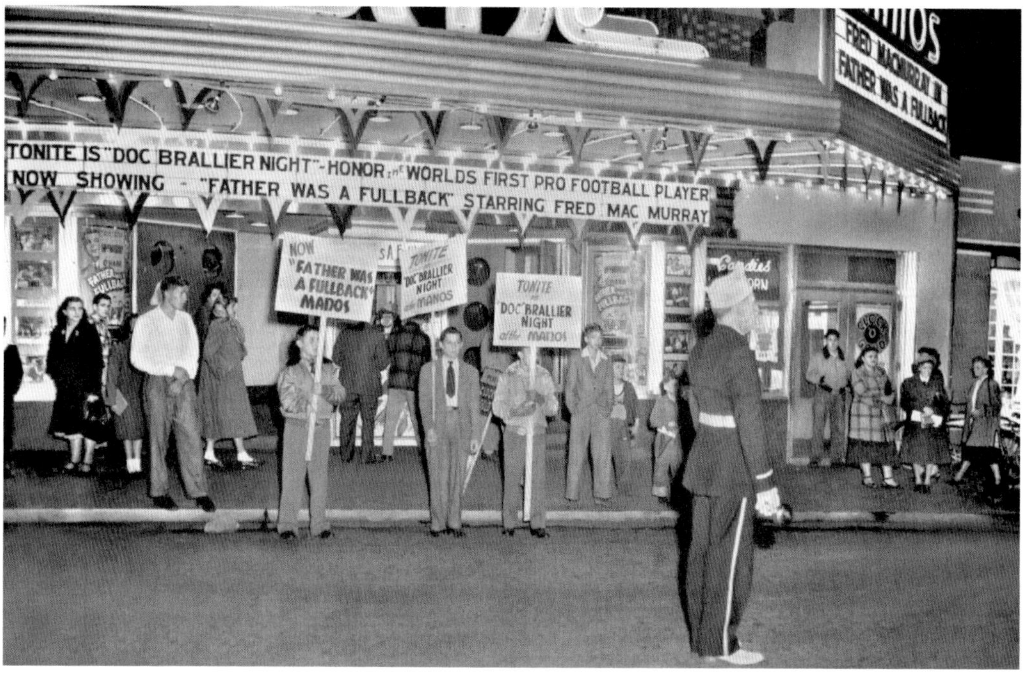

Doc Brallier Night

Brallier went on to practice dentistry and served the community during a 20-year tenure as a school director, from which he retired at the end of 1931. In the early 1950s, Latrobe was recognized by the National Football League as the birthplace of professional football, and Dr. Brallier was given lifetime passes for all National Football League games. Brallier was escorted via limousine in a parade through downtown Latrobe to the Manos Theater. It was a special night of honor for "Doc" Brallier, with a showing of *Father Was a Fullback*, starring Fred MacMurry. The marquee read, "Tonite is 'Doc Brallier Night.' In Honor of the World's First Pro Football Player." (FF.)

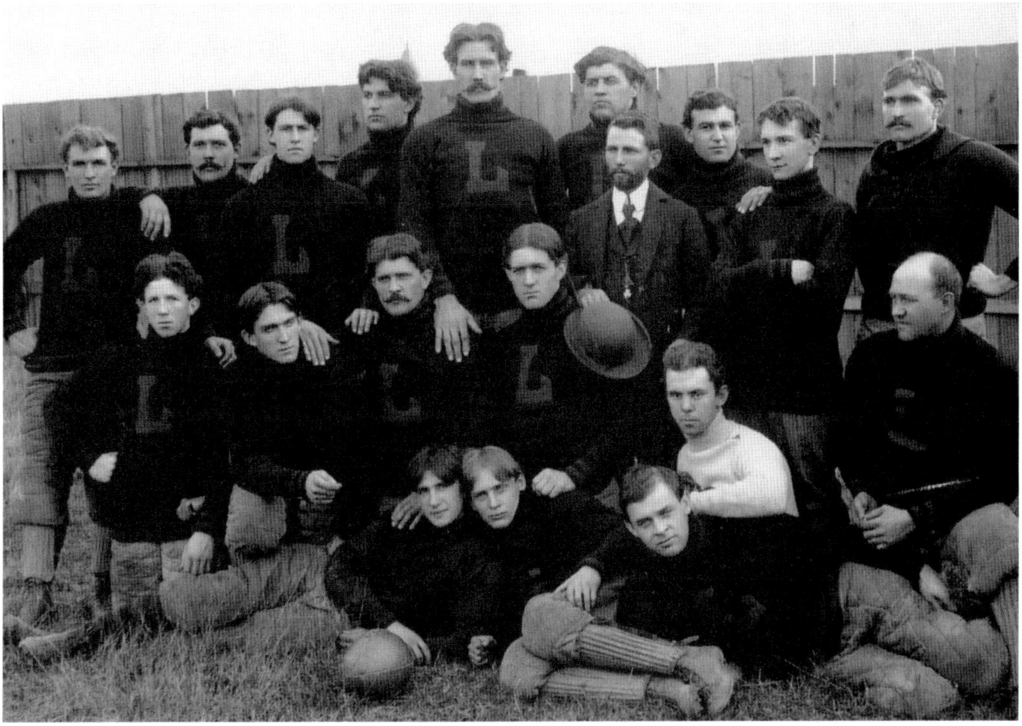

First All-Pro Football Team

The National Football Hall of Fame recognizes the Latrobe Athletics Association's 1897 team as the first all-professional team. Although the team had played wearing the Latrobe colors of orange and maroon for the two previous seasons, it went all-professional the third year, signing a number of college players from the East Coast and as far west as Iowa. The team finished 10-2-1. Standing (center) in suit and tie with hat in hand is team manager Dave Berry. From left to right are (first row) Edward Wood, John Brallier, Walter Howard, and Jack Gass; (second row, kneeling) Charles Shumaker, Walter Okeson, Harry "Cap" Ryan, George Flickenger, and Marcus Saxman; (third row, standing) Alex Laird, Bill Hammer, Charles McDyre, Ed Abbaticchio, Dave Campbell, John Johnston, Sam Johnston, James Edward Blair, and Russell Aukerman, coach. (LAHS.)

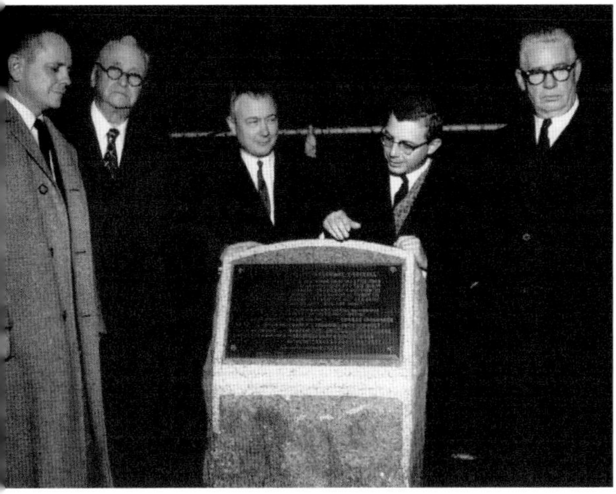

Gridiron Tribute

Dignitaries dedicate a monument, located at the entrance to Memorial Stadium, honoring the birthplace of professional football on October 28, 1960. John Brallier Jr., son of "Doc" Brallier, stands at left. Also present, from left to right, are John Schmidt, an early player; Victor B. Stader, burgess of Latrobe; E. Kay Myers, president of Latrobe Rotary Club; and Arthur J. Rooney Sr., "The Chief" and president of the Pittsburgh Steelers. (LAHS.)

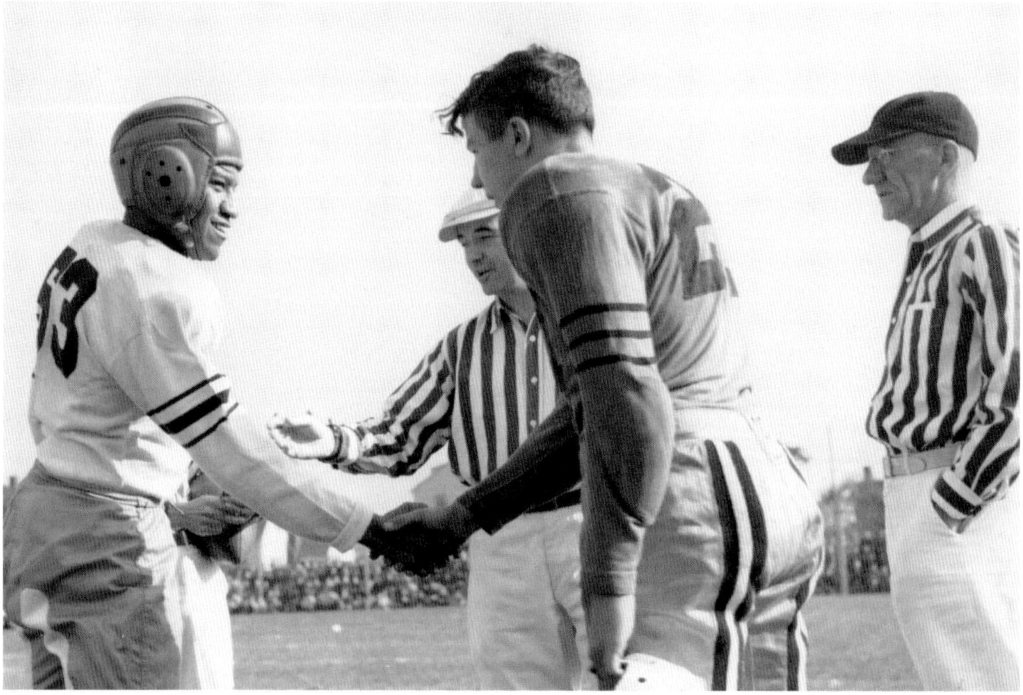

John R. Mazero

Dr. John R. "Bob" Mazero was a quarterback with Latrobe High School from 1946 to 1947. He became a hometown physician and was recognized by US representative John P. Murtha in 1996 as "the kind of doctor our parents used to call at home on a Saturday night if one of the kids had a fever." After studying medicine in Washington, DC; Cleveland; and Pittsburgh, Mazero came back home and devoted his life to making sure Latrobe had one of the best community hospitals in the country by advancing its role in creating an educational environment for physicians. In recognition of this legacy, the Dr. John R. Mazero Science Education Center at St. Vincent was named in his honor. Pictured are Abie House (left) and Bob Mazero shaking hands before the big game between Greensburg and Latrobe in 1947. (Bob Mazero.)

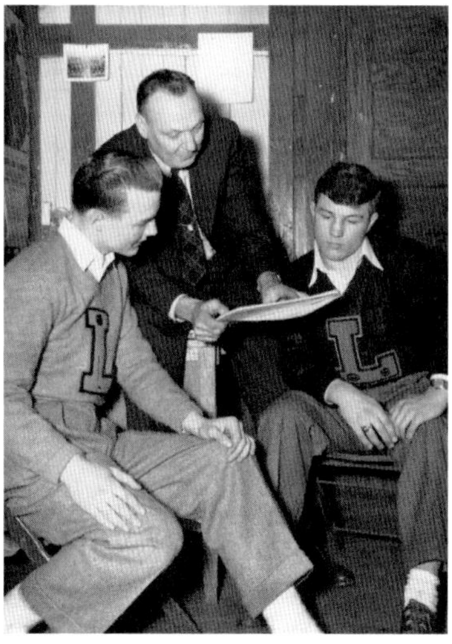

Raymond V. Wild

Raymond "Ray" V. Wild (1899–1981) coached football at Latrobe High School from 1928 until his retirement in 1964. Wild and athletics were "synonymous," according to the book *Historic Latrobe: A Glance or Two at Earlier Times* (1985). In addition to football, he was the head basketball and track coach for many years. But it was his winning football teams, referred to as "Wild's Boys," that locals remember best, and today, Latrobe's mascot, the Wildcat, still bears his name. Reviewing the coach's playbook, from left to right, are Ken Bowman, Coach Wild, and Bob Mazero. (Bob Mazero.)

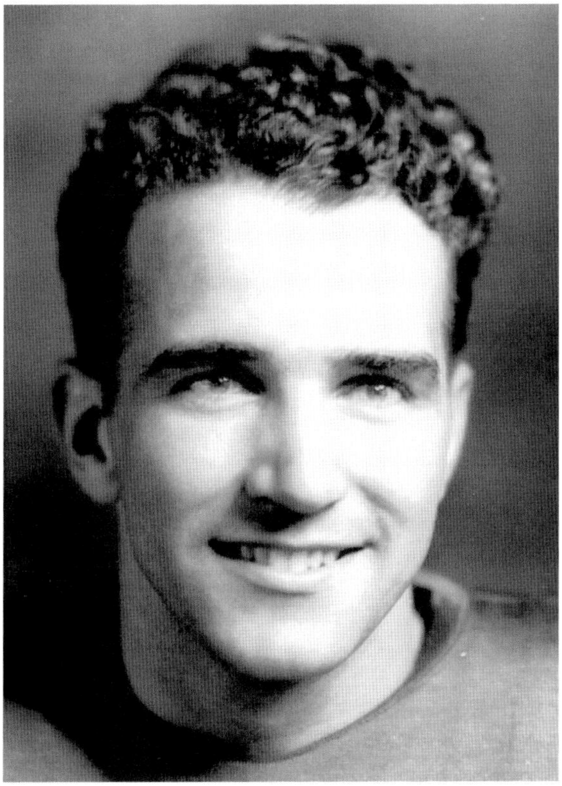

Charles Frederick Shirey

Charles Frederick "Fred" Shirey (1916–1961) was born in Latrobe and was a professional football player for the Cleveland Rams and the Green Bay Packers (1940–1941). He attended Washington and Jefferson College and the University of Nebraska, where he played right tackle and was an integral part of Husker football from 1934 to 1937. He is one of only 20 Huskers ever to be named to three First-Team All-Conference Teams. Shirey was drafted by the Philadelphia Eagles in the fifth round (32nd overall) of the 1938 NFL Draft but chose instead to teach at Beatrice High School in Nebraska. In 1976, he was inducted into the Nebraska Football Hall of Fame. (Marc Boehm, executive associate athletic director, University of Nebraska Athletic Department.)

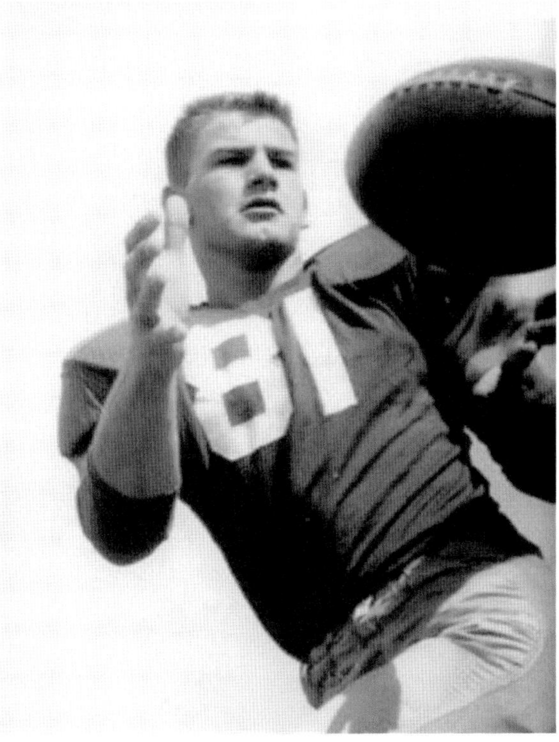

Walter Martin Corey

Walter Martin Corey, the youngest of 16 children in his family of Pennsylvania millworkers, was born in Latrobe on May 9, 1938. He is a former professional football linebacker and played college football for the University of Miami. In 1960, Corey came to the American Football League's Dallas Texans as an undrafted linebacker and went on to star for the Texans and the Kansas City Chiefs, with whom he was an AFL All-Star in 1963. Corey later held assistant coaching positions with several teams, including the Buffalo Bills under head coach Marv Levy, where he was defensive coordinator for four consecutive AFC Championship teams from 1990 to 1993. He was also the defensive line coach in New Orleans during the Mike Ditka era, 1997–1999. (AC.)

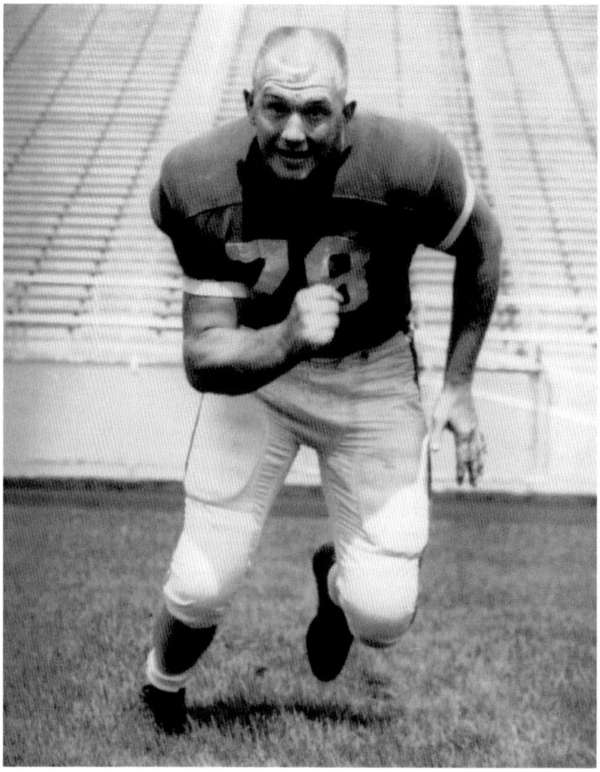

Andrew Ralph Stynchula

Andrew Ralph "Andy" Stynchula (1939–1985) was born in Greenawald, Pennsylvania, a coal mining town in Berks County. He attended Latrobe High School, where he played football and broke long-standing Western Pennsylvania Interscholastic Athletic League track and field records in discus and shot put (1956). In college, he played defensive tackle at Penn State University and was the first recipient of the Red Worrell Memorial Award, given at that time to an offensive or defensive player for "exemplary conduct, loyalty, interest, attitude, and improvement." Stynchula was drafted in the third round (28th overall) of the 1960 NFL Draft by the Washington Redskins. He played defensive lineman from 1960 to 1968 with the Washington Redskins, New York Giants, Baltimore Colts, and Dallas Cowboys. Sadly, he died in a car accident while on vacation in the Bahamas at age 46. (Tanya Stynchula.)

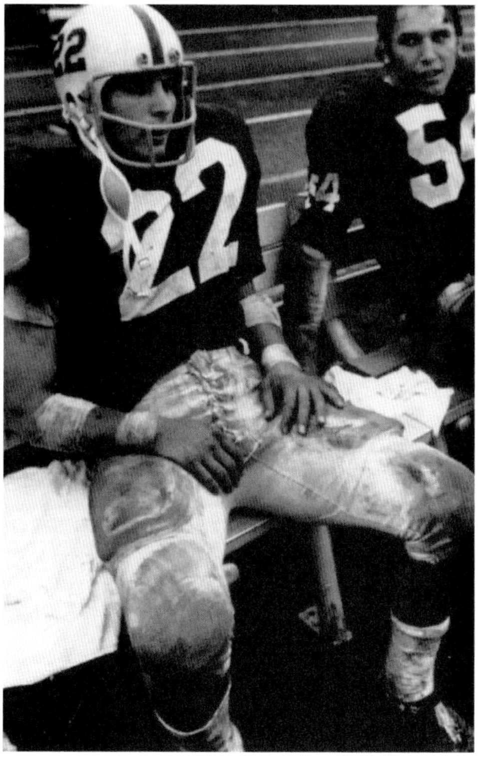

Mark Markovich

Mark Markovich was born in Latrobe on November 7, 1952, and drafted by the San Diego Chargers in the second round (43rd overall) of the 1974 NFL Draft. He attended Penn State University, where he served as cocaptain of the football team and was a friend and college roommate with John Cappelletti, the 1973 Heisman Trophy winner, whose acceptance speech about his 11-year-old brother's (Joey) battle with leukemia is well remembered for bringing tears to the eyes of everyone in attendance. Markovich said afterward, "The bond that he felt with his brother Joey and the inspiration he provided him just came out in a fashion that was so innocent—so wonderful and so touching—that we just sat there in awe." Markovich followed his days at Penn State with playing for the Chargers (1974–1977) for a total of 41 National Football League games. Pictured are Cappelletti (left) and Markovich enjoying a breather during the Nittany Lions' 12-0 season in 1973. (*Centre Daily Times*/State College, Pennsylvania.)

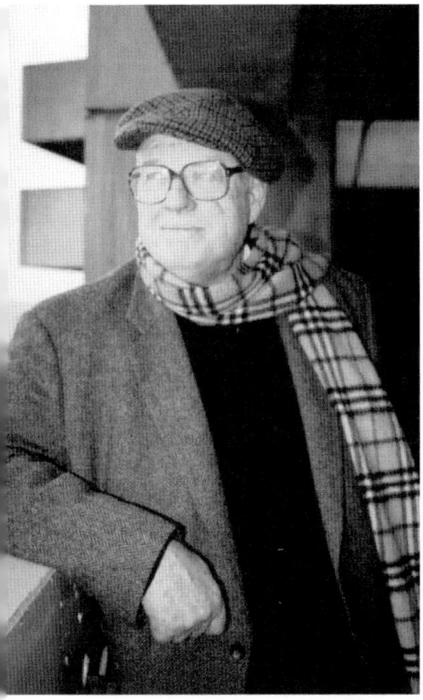

Art Rooney Jr.

Art Rooney Jr. is the second son of Arthur J. Rooney Sr., "The Chief," founder of the Pittsburgh Steelers Football Club. Art Jr. and his four brothers grew up on the North Side of Pittsburgh. All were educated in the Catholic schools and graduated from North Catholic High School. Art Jr. graduated from St. Vincent College in Latrobe with a degree in history. After completing his military service with the US Marine Corps Reserves, he began work within the Steelers organization. In 1966, he approached Oland "Dodo" Canterna, the college's athletic director at the time, about bringing the Steelers to Latrobe for training camp. According to an article in the July 28, 2006, *Tribune-Review*, Canterna penned a letter to the school's leaders "stressing the benefits of hosting Steelers training camp amid the pastoral Laurel Mountains of Westmoreland County," and the monks at St. Vincent, some of whom were fervent Steelers fans, "readily agreed to the Rooney brothers' request." (Art Rooney Jr.)

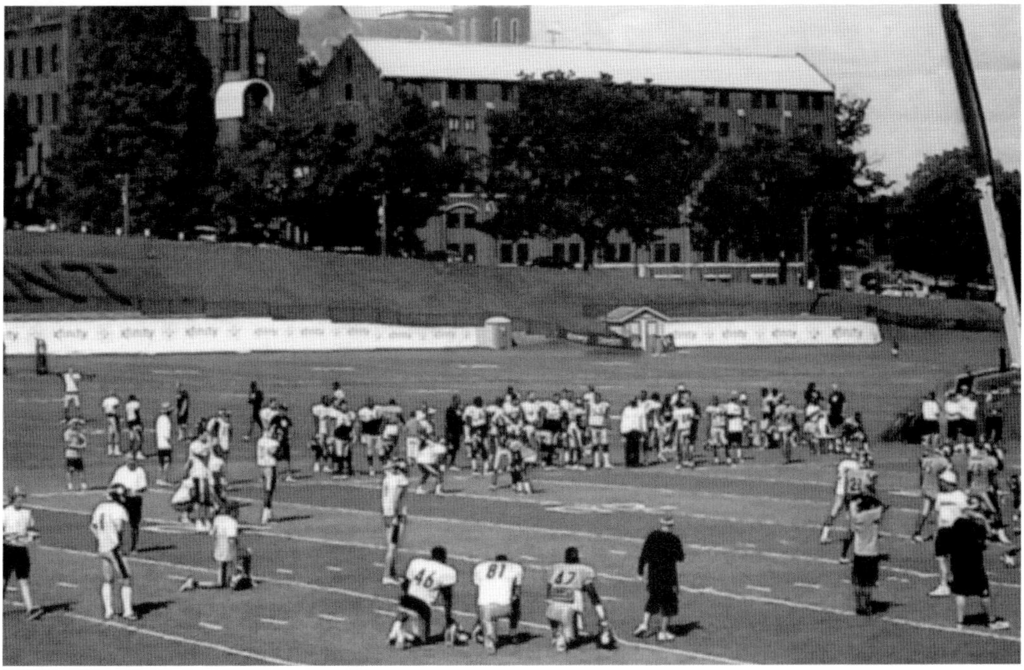

Steelers' Training Camp

The Pittsburgh Steelers have held their annual summer training camp at St. Vincent College in Latrobe since 1967. The Steelers' training camp is free and open to the public. During camp each summer, the Steelers also hold an annual "Friday Night Lights" practice at Memorial Stadium in downtown Latrobe. The evening open house–style event allows fans the opportunity to get Steelers' autographs and meet the football players close up before practice begins. (AC.)

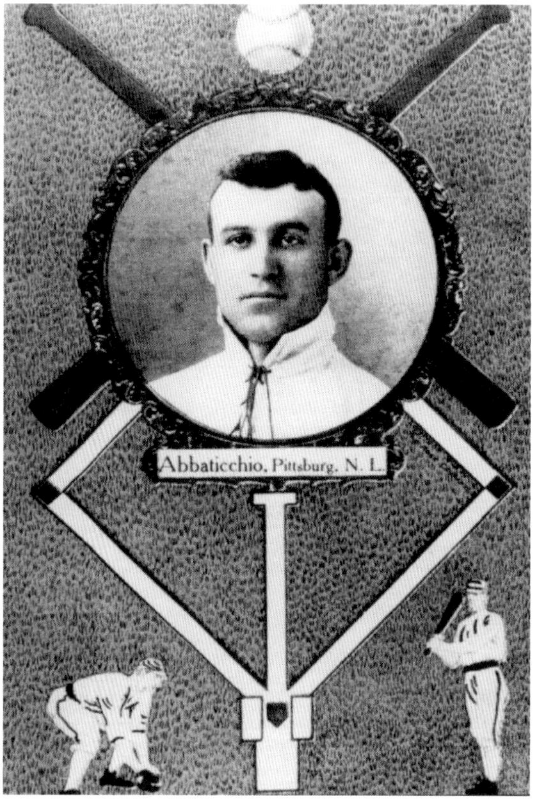

Edward James Abbaticchio
Born in Latrobe, Edward James "Batty" Abbaticchio (1877–1957) was the first Italian American professional baseball player. He was on the Pittsburgh Pirates 1909 World Series championship team with the great Honus Wagner. Abbaticchio was also on the first all-pro football team in 1897, making him perhaps the first two-sport professional. (LAHS.)

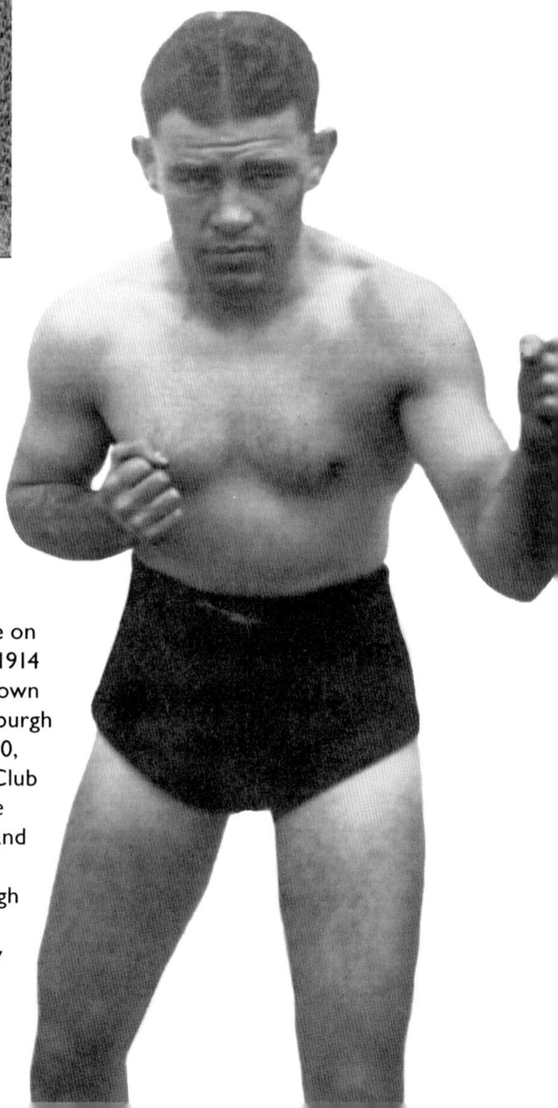

Frankie Daley
Frankie Daley (1899–unknown) was born in Latrobe on February 2, 1899. He was a lightweight boxer from 1914 to 1917 and a featherweight earlier in his career. Known as the "Millionaire Boxer" of Latrobe and the "Pittsburgh Flash," Daley fought in a total of 87 bouts, winning 50, and achieving 13 knockouts. At a National Athletic Club match in Philadelphia on January 2, 1912, the *Gazette Times* reported that Daley proved entirely too fast and furious for the hometown favorite Bobby Scanlon. "Bobby never had a chance to set himself long enough to get in his deadly right-hand wallop. Daley, from the handshake to the finish, kept Scanlon continually on the defensive." (AC.)

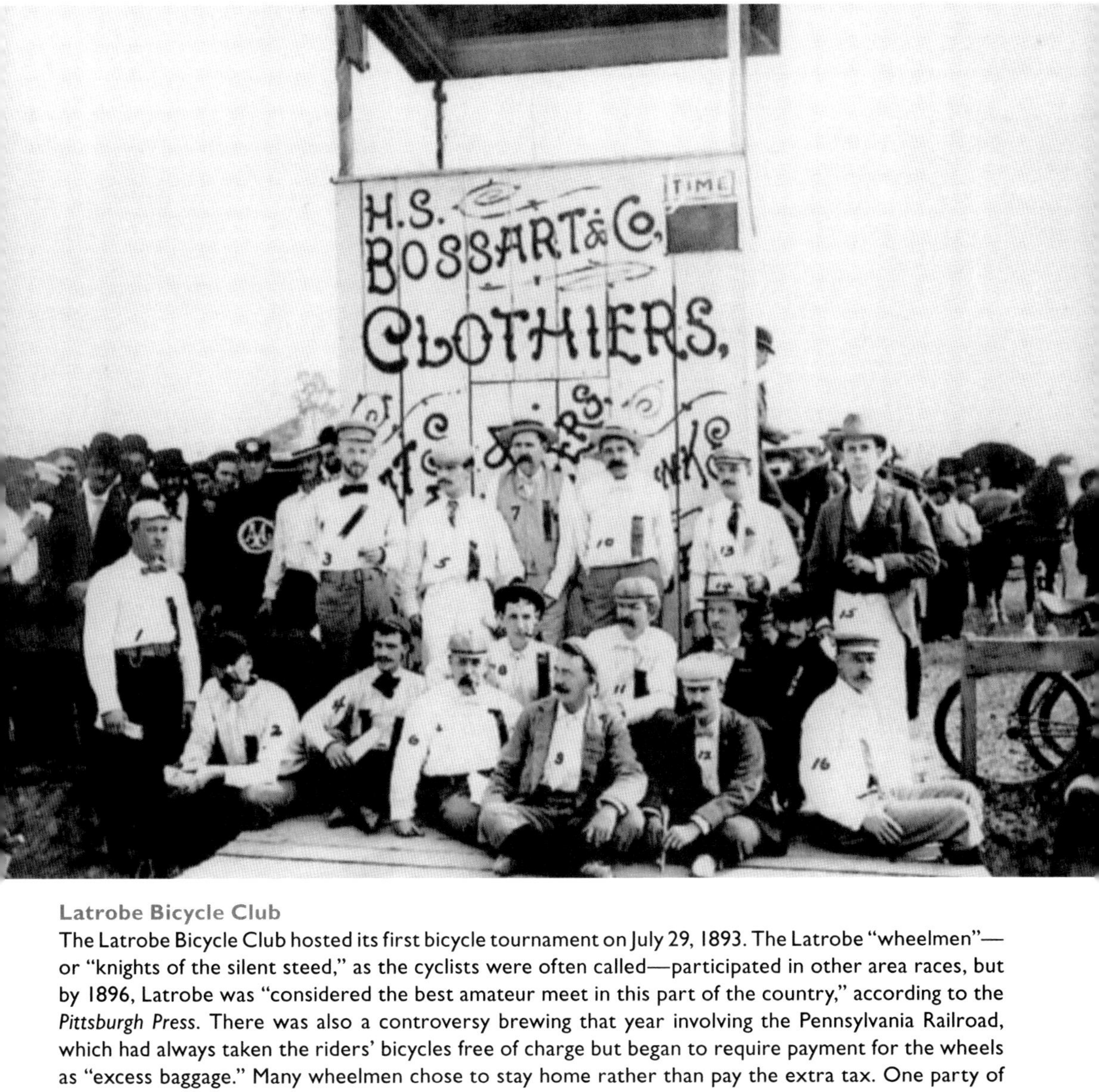

Latrobe Bicycle Club

The Latrobe Bicycle Club hosted its first bicycle tournament on July 29, 1893. The Latrobe "wheelmen"—or "knights of the silent steed," as the cyclists were often called—participated in other area races, but by 1896, Latrobe was "considered the best amateur meet in this part of the country," according to the *Pittsburgh Press*. There was also a controversy brewing that year involving the Pennsylvania Railroad, which had always taken the riders' bicycles free of charge but began to require payment for the wheels as "excess baggage." Many wheelmen chose to stay home rather than pay the extra tax. One party of Pittsburghers, however, would not be deterred and made plans to ride to Latrobe on their bicycles. They departed on Friday afternoon before the Saturday race in order to be there for all the fun. In the photograph, the Latrobe team poses on race day in 1896. Identified Latrobe Bicycle Club team members are, by number, (first row) Dan Crowe (6); (second row) Harry Hoffman (8), George H. Adams (11), and ? Aertsen (16); (third row) M.W. Saxman (1), John Howard (3), and Dr. Blackburn (7). (LAHS.)

Zach Jackson

Zach Jackson, born on May 13, 1983, in Latrobe, played baseball throughout his school career and loved visiting major-league parks with his father. The six-foot-five "lefty" pitcher attended Texas A&M University in 2000. He was drafted first in the first-year player draft by the Toronto Blue Jays in 2004, after completing his junior year at Texas A&M. He was traded and played for the Milwaukee Brewers, the Cleveland Indians, the Toronto Blue Jays, and the Texas Rangers. Of the multiple trades, Jackson stated in an interview with the Cleveland *Plain Dealer*, "A change of scenery never hurt." He is currently a minor-league player with the Washington Nationals, pitching relief for the Syracuse Chiefs in Syracuse, New York. (AC.)

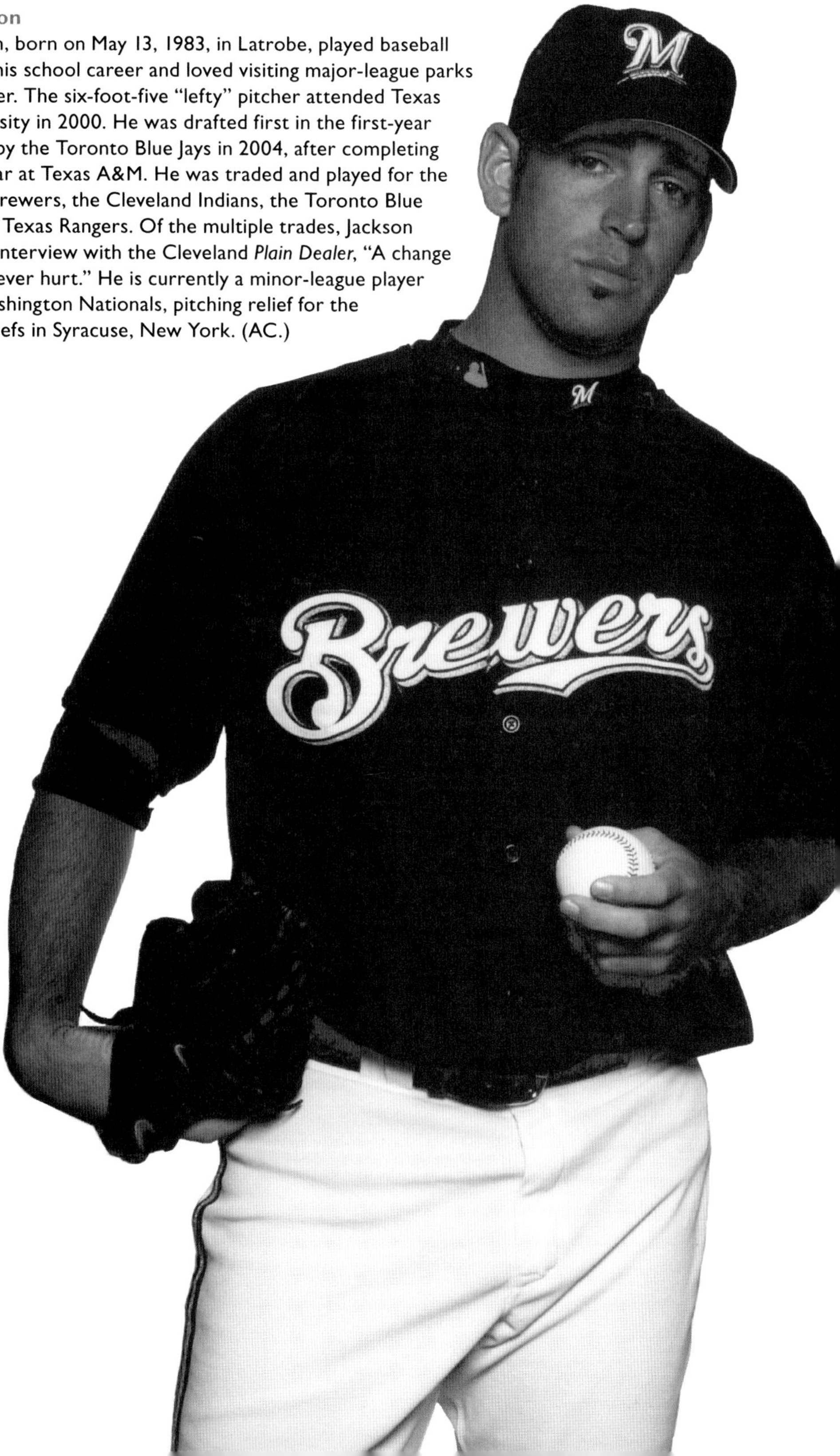

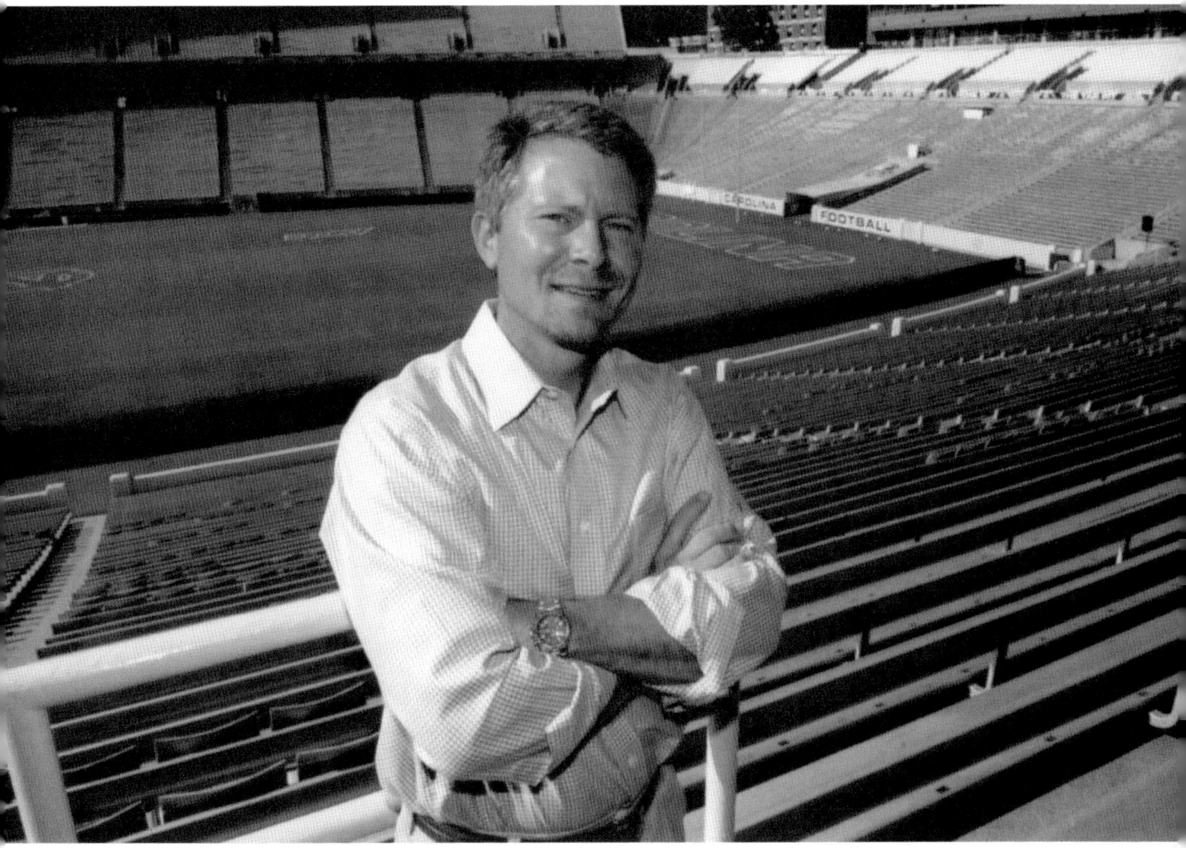

Kevin Guskiewicz

Dr. Kevin Guskiewicz, originally from Latrobe, where he played high school football and tennis, knows well the agonies and frustrations related to sports-related brain injuries. He first became concerned about concussions when he was an athletic trainer with the Pittsburgh Steelers and has been studying the brain injury for all of his 16-plus years at the University of North Carolina at Chapel Hill. Guskiewicz has a doctorate in sports medicine and in 2011 became $500,000 richer thanks to the John D. and Catherine T. MacArthur Foundation. He was one of 22 distinguished individuals to receive the no-strings-attached award, informally called the "genius grant," because he figured out how a $5 stopwatch and a $45 piece of foam cushion could make it much safer for athletes to stay on the playing field or remain on the sidelines until cleared. (Kevin Guskiewicz.)

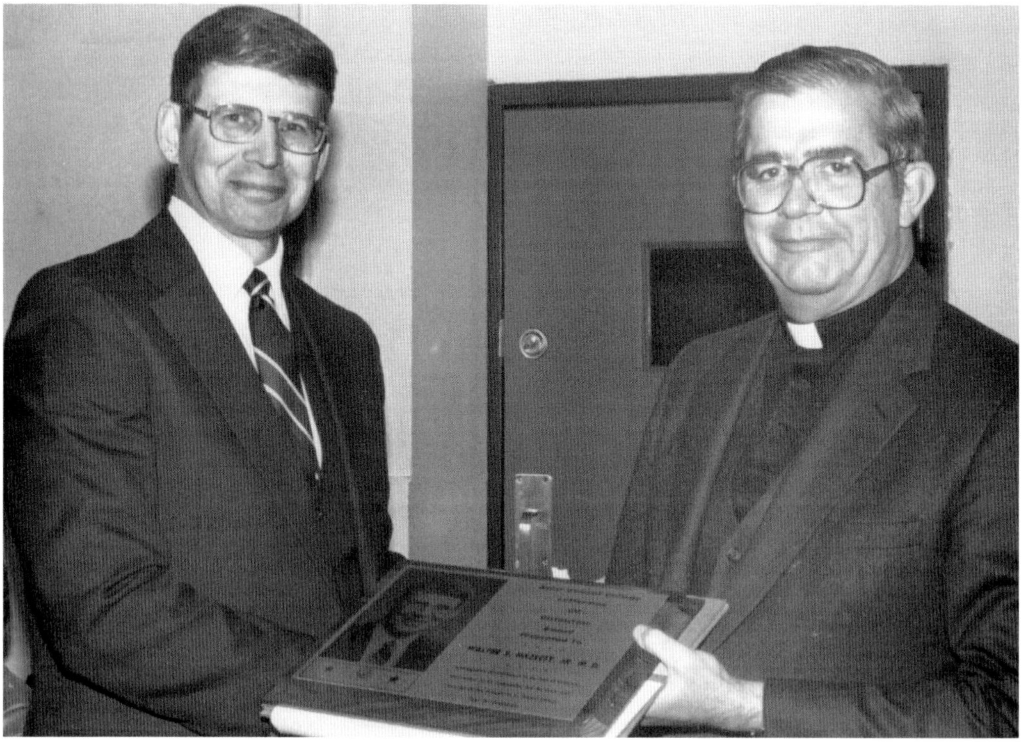

Walter S. Hazlett Jr.

Dr. Walter S. Hazlett Jr. (1925–2006) was born on June 6, 1925, in Latrobe and attended Latrobe schools, where he participated in basketball, track, and volleyball. He served in the European theater in Patton's Third Army and fought in eastern France at Metz and in Germany on the Saar River, where he was wounded and received the Purple Heart. He returned to civilian life in 1944 and attended St. Vincent College as a pre-med student. He then received his medical degree in 1952 from Temple University School of Medicine and served his internship at Conemaugh Memorial Hospital in Johnstown. He began the Family Practice of Medicine in Latrobe in 1953. Pictured is Hazlett (left) receiving a St. Vincent College Letterman of Distinction award from Rev. Cecil Dietrich, OSB, in 1982. (LAHS.)

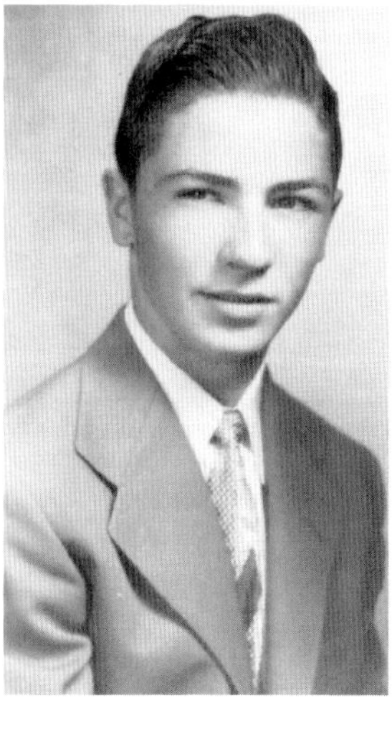

Patrick H. Hughes

Dr. Patrick Hughes (1934–2010) was born in Latrobe, the son of Michael F. Hughes, an Irish immigrant and onetime owner of Mike Hughes Men's and Boys' Shop in Latrobe. Dr. Hughes graduated from Latrobe High School in 1952, entered the University of Pittsburgh on a tennis scholarship, and stayed through medical school. He also earned a master's degree in public health from Columbia University. He was an early contributor to removing the stigma from drug addiction and traveled throughout Europe and Asia gathering data as a senior medical officer for the World Health Organization. Hughes put this knowledge to practice on the streets of Chicago and in his book, *Behind the Wall of Respect: Community Experiments in Heroin Addiction Control.* According to the April 12, 2010, *Tampa Bay Times*, his siblings called him "James Bond" for his handsome good looks and athletic ability, and for the fact that he "hobnobbed with the Black Panthers, weaved his way through opium dens in Burma, Thailand, and Indonesia, and lived for years on a sailboat after which he sailed across the Atlantic." (Kathy Molina.)

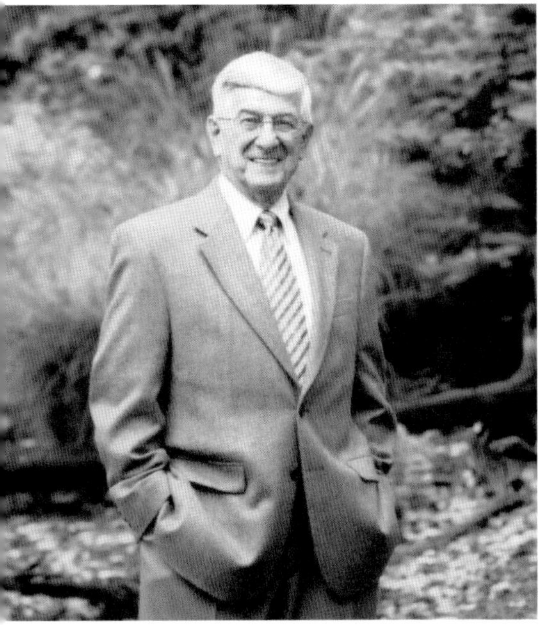

Joseph A. Mosso Sr.

Joseph A. Mosso Sr. was born on January 16, 1932, in Latrobe. He owned Mosso's Pharmacy in the city for 40 years before retiring in 1996. In 2009, he won the John W. Dargavel Medal, presented by the National Community Pharmacists Association (NCPA), for his work in drug abuse programming, as well as his spirit of leadership and accomplishments, including serving as NCPA president and promoting a student outreach program to increase awareness of the NCPA. The *Pittsburgh Post-Gazette* featured Mosso on October 29, 2009, noting his award and reporting, "In the 1970s, Mr. Mosso founded the Committee on Drug Education in Latrobe, and in 1978 he worked with Dr. Robert Teeter and other community and education leaders to found the St. Vincent College Prevention Projects." (Lake Fong/Copyright © *Pittsburgh Post-Gazette*, 2014, all rights reserved. Reprinted with permission.)

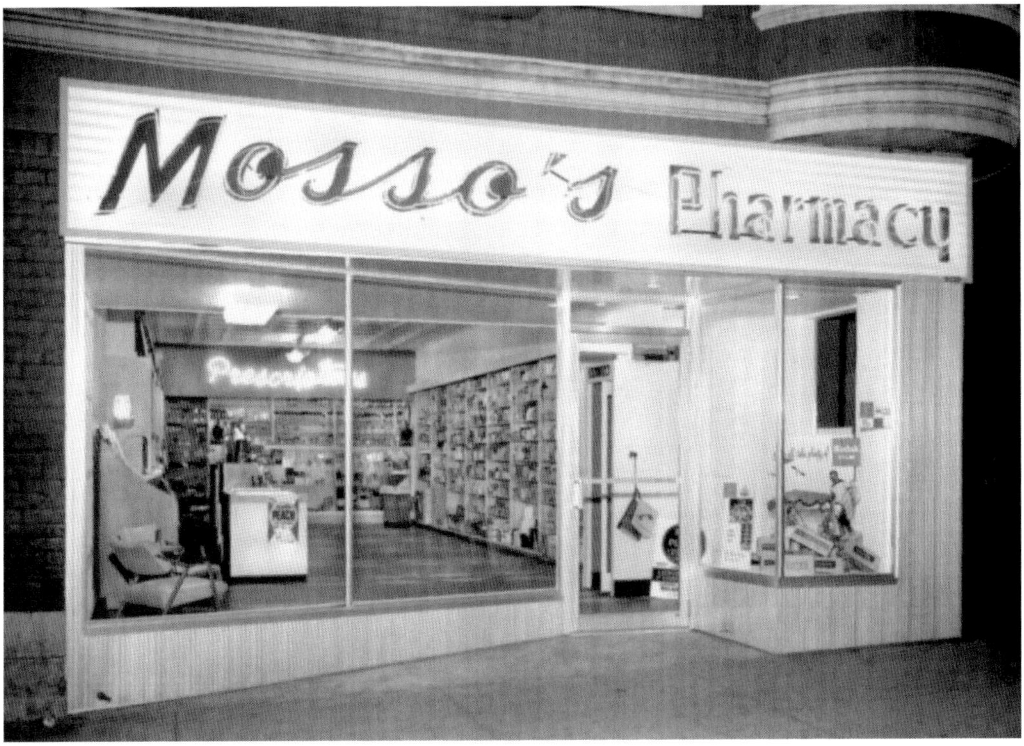

Mosso's Pharmacy

The exterior of Mosso's Pharmacy is pictured in the 1950s at twilight with its familiar neon sign aglow. Mosso's, located at the time at 1001 Ligonier Street, was the first local pharmacy to offer home delivery and 24-hour emergency service and was the first in town to carry portable oxygen canisters—which led to Joseph Jr. founding Mosso Medical Supply. (FF.)

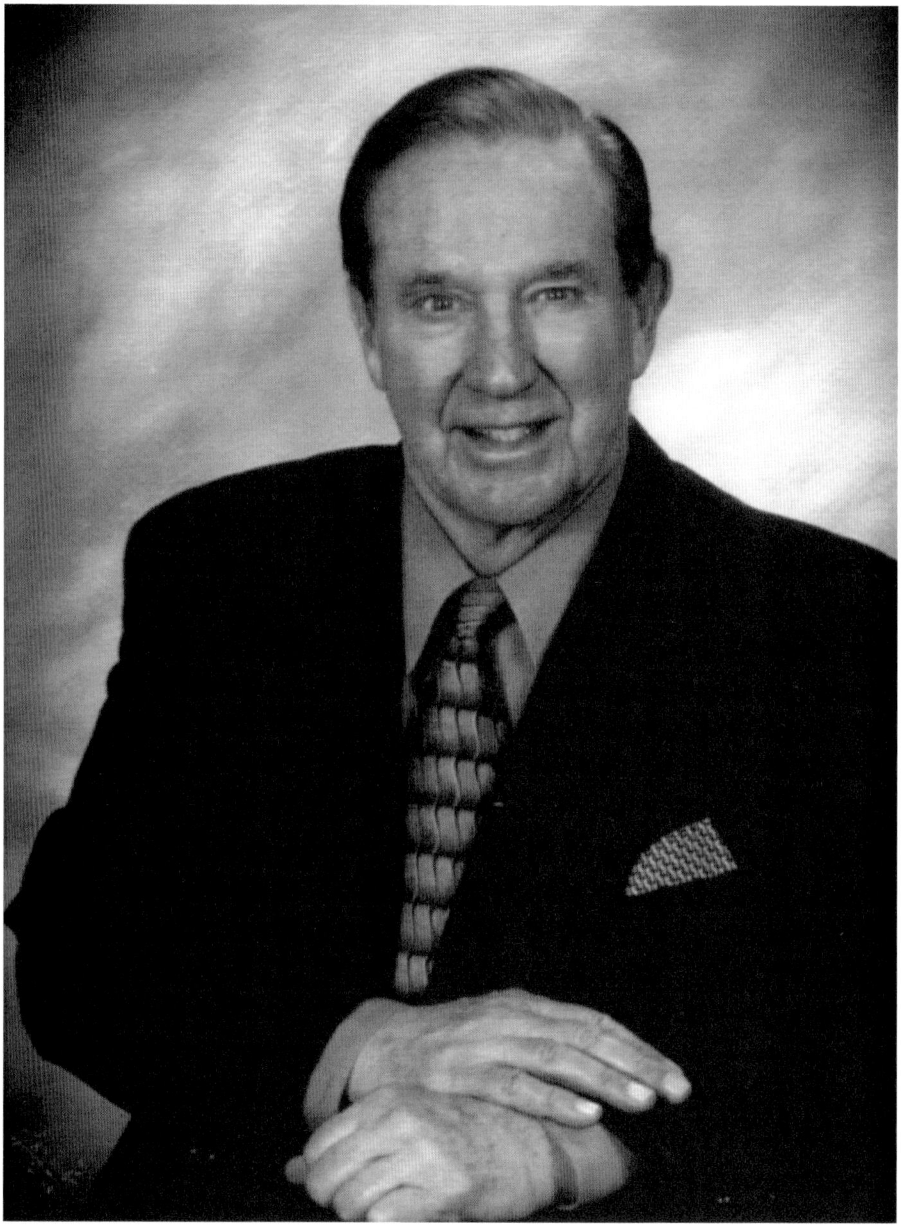

Ronald G. Cameron

Ronald G. Cameron's philosophy, "Find a need and fill it," has been his formula for achieving the American Dream. In 1970, the young pharmacist, working a rotating schedule, realized that the profession needed a real temporary service. Cameron, Latrobe born and University of Pittsburgh educated, created America's first pharmacist's registry: Cameron and Company, Inc. In 2005, Cameron, a 1957 graduate at the University of Pittsburgh, donated $50,000 to endow a pharmacy scholarship, which gives preference to students from Westmoreland County, and in 2002, he won the Distinguished Alumnus Award at Pitt. Even with all his success, Cameron still fondly recalls his start in the industry at Strickler's Drug Store in downtown Latrobe and driving the store's famous pestle and mortar–topped delivery car when Charles T. Poorman was the owner. (Cameron and Company, Inc./Ronald G. Cameron, CEO.)

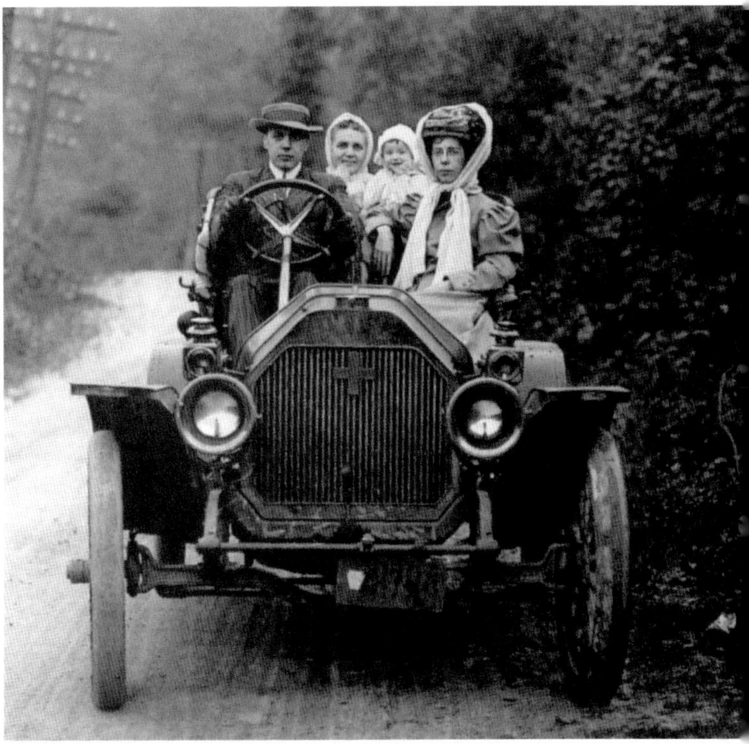

Arthur Byron Blackburn

Dr. Arthur Byron Blackburn (1884–1954), like his father before him, was a leading physician of Latrobe. Despite his extensive practice, Blackburn found the time and energy to devote to the community. He is perhaps one of the earliest known examples of a Latrobe doctor who first found success on the football field. *Old and New Westmoreland* noted, "Dr. Blackburn is particularly active in all matters connected with outdoor sports and is a great patron of the same. He is particularly well known as a football player and member of the varsity team during his college career." In the photograph, Blackburn and his family take a motor trip on the Lincoln Highway in 1913. (LAHS.)

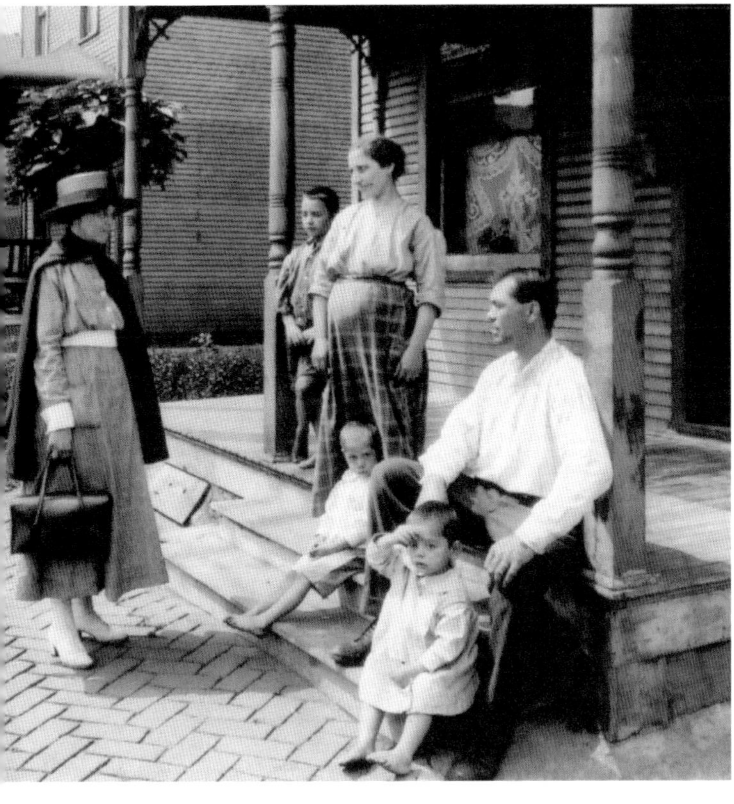

Margretha Lavold

Margretha Lavold, Latrobe's first Red Cross public health nurse from 1920 to 1946, is shown visiting a Jefferson Street family, one of many served by the program. Lavold was instrumental in establishing a well baby clinic to help ensure the health of Latrobe's younger residents. After World War I, the local chapter of the Red Cross also set up a home service to assist veterans with guidance and to help with financial problems. (LAHS.)

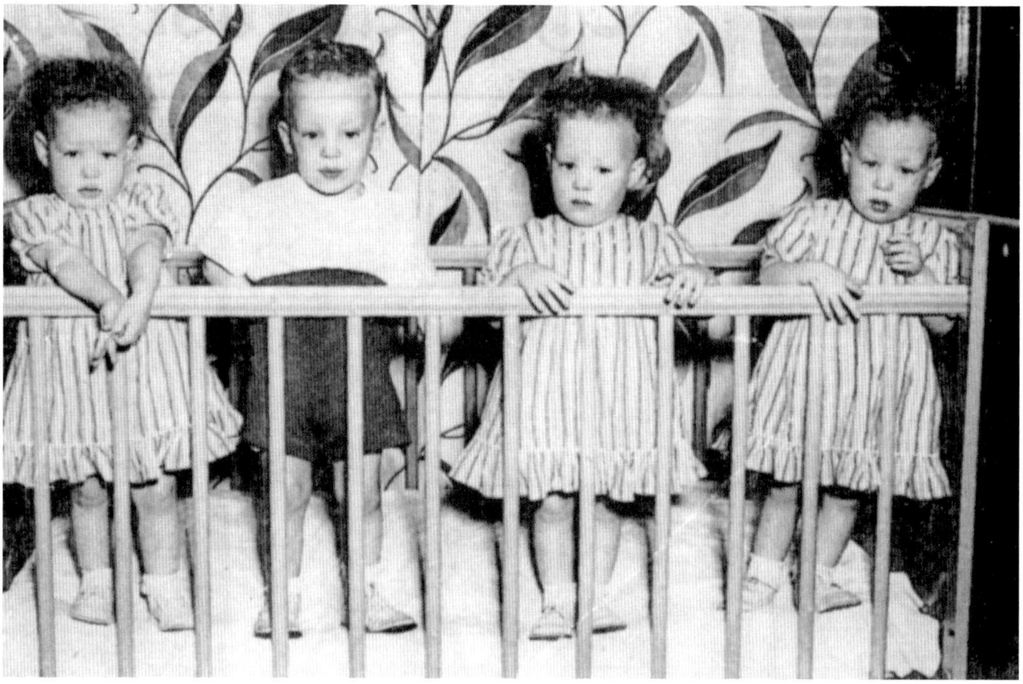

Zavada Quadruplets

The Zavada Quadruplets were born on February 15, 1948. They were the children of Andrew and Barbara Zavada of Latrobe. The quadruplets (three girls, identical, and one boy) were named Anna Mary "Annie," Bernadette, Barbara, and John. At birth, the Zavadas were given a 1-in-600,000 chance of survival, but they beat the odds thanks to the care of the staff at Latrobe Area Hospital and the prayers and warm wishes of family and friends. As they grew, the Zavadas became instant celebrities in newsprint and were featured on the *Wilkens Amateur Hour*, one of Pittsburgh's most popular radio shows. At 17 months old, they were honored guests at Kennywood Park in Pittsburgh, during the 30th annual picnic of Greek Catholic churches. (LAHS.)

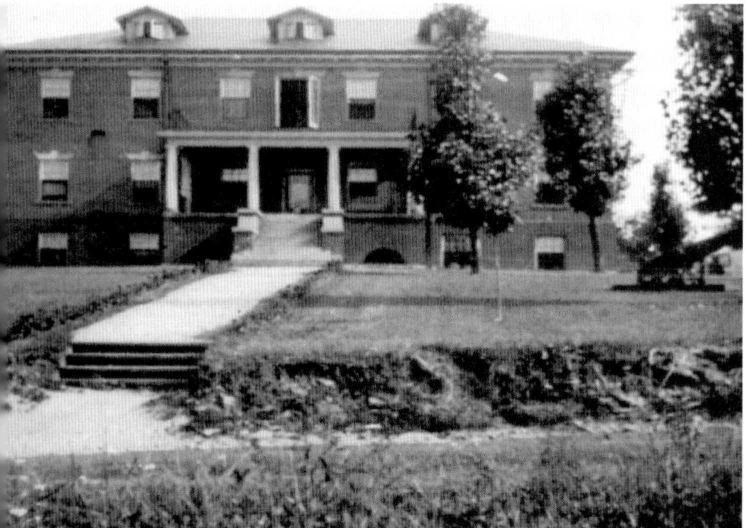

Latrobe Area Hospital

The Latrobe Area Hospital was built to serve the growing community and dominated the hill on Second Avenue. The local GAR donated the land and provided the Civil War cannons guarding the front lawn, pictured in 1909. Within eight years, the original 30-bed facility had to be expanded. Today, Excela Latrobe Area Hospital is one of the region's largest businesses, employing over 1,500 people at its main location and six community health care centers. (Steven Patterson.)

CHAPTER SIX

Education and Faith

A pageant presented at Memorial Stadium in 1954 to mark Latrobe's 100th birthday included a stirring spectacle in 16 episodes to trace the area's history and rich heritage. Episode VI, "The Three Rs—Readin', 'Ritin', and 'Rithmetic" began with the narration "As soon as these pioneers had built a church, they built a school," illustrating that education and faith were among the first tasks of early settlers in the community. Throughout its history, the Greater Latrobe area has offered educational opportunities for its youth and religious freedom for all. These fine institutions have produced many of the local legends found in other chapters, but this one is dedicated to the teachers, ministers, and other leaders who have made a memorable impact on their students and followers not because they were looking for recognition but because they cared.

Both schools and places of worship began small. Meetings were held in homes or log structures built by farmers and their families. St. Vincent Archabbey and College was founded in 1846 by Boniface Wimmer, a Benedictine monk. From modest beginnings the college grew rapidly and soon began to confer degrees in the arts and sciences. Today, the college ranks in the top tier of *US News & World Report*'s ranking of national liberal arts colleges and still lists 15 percent of the faculty as Benedictine priests and brothers.

The construction of the railroad and early industry attracted a wide variety of people to this region—often immigrants who saw education as a way to a better future. As the area grew and diversified, more places of worship and schools were added to meet the changing needs of the people. Unity Township was, in the beginning, largely agricultural but was later dotted with small mining communities. Each had its own schools and churches located every few miles. In downtown Latrobe, neighborhoods were densely populated through much of the 20th century, with an elementary school in five of its six wards. The early schools in both the borough and the township offered a very practical elementary curriculum, with emphasis on the Three Rs. Latrobe had one of the first public high schools in the area. The first class—just eight students—graduated in 1883. Until 1911, all high school courses were college preparatory. The curriculum has steadily expanded as students' goals have changed, and to the Three Rs, the district has added the Three As: "Academics, Arts, and Athletics."

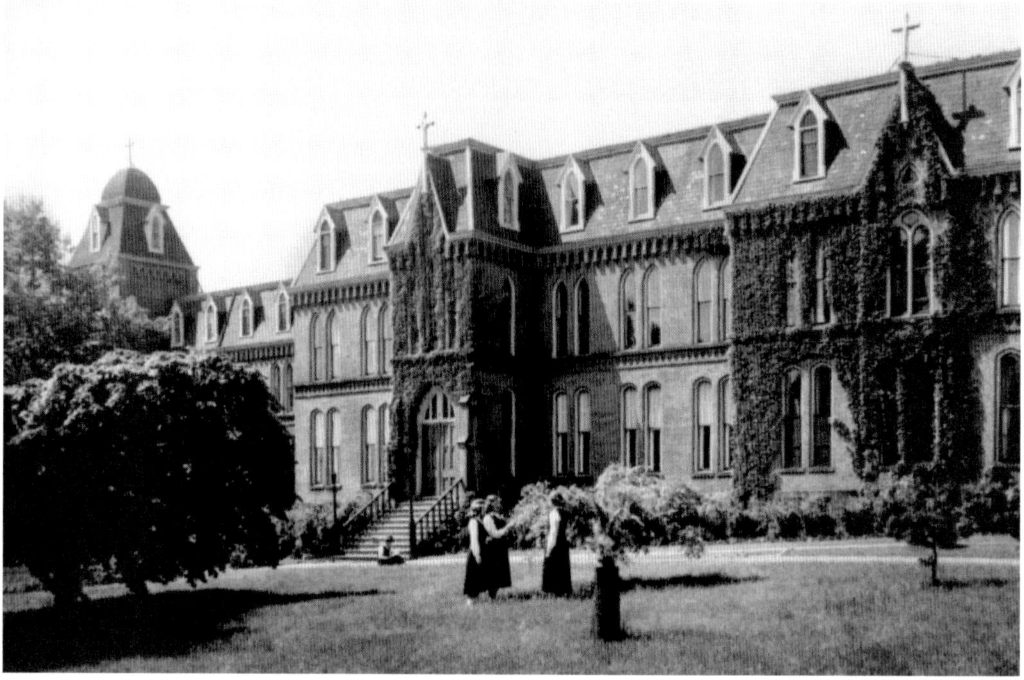

Henry Kuhn

In his *History of the Catholic Church*, the Reverend A.A. Lambing recorded, "No part of western Pennsylvania figures more prominently in the history of Catholicity than Westmoreland County, Pa." In 1787, six Catholic families left Goshenhoppen near Philadelphia and journeyed by wagon train 250 miles to settle here. The following year, the young colony received an addition of several more families from the east, including Henry Kuhn (1753–1808), who was destined to take a prominent part in the future development of the pioneer settlement. His land later became the site of St. Xavier's Academy and Convent (above), the oldest institution of the Sisters of Mercy, who came from Ireland in 1843, just as the Great Famine was taking hold. (FF.)

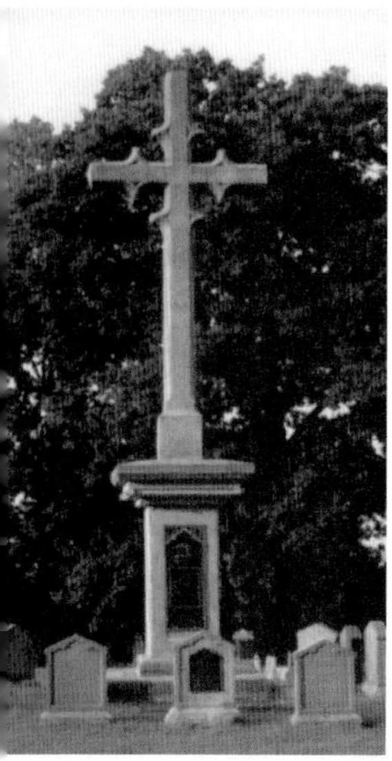

Theodore Brouwers

Fr. Theodore Brouwers (1738–1790) was a Belgian by birth and a member of the Orders of Friars Minor (OFM). Having heard of the colony that had been established in Westmoreland County and the promise given that the settlers should have a resident pastor, he chose western Pennsylvania for his mission. Brouwers arrived at the colony toward the close of 1789. At this time, a valuable tract of land in Unity Township was offered for sale. It was called Sportsman's Hall, a name given to it by a Harrisburg gentleman who had used it as a hunting ground. Brouwers purchased the tract of land in 1790 and became the first priest of the little colony. He died on October 29, 1790. His remains found a resting place under the massive stone cross (left) in the center of St. Vincent Cemetery. (Both, AC.)

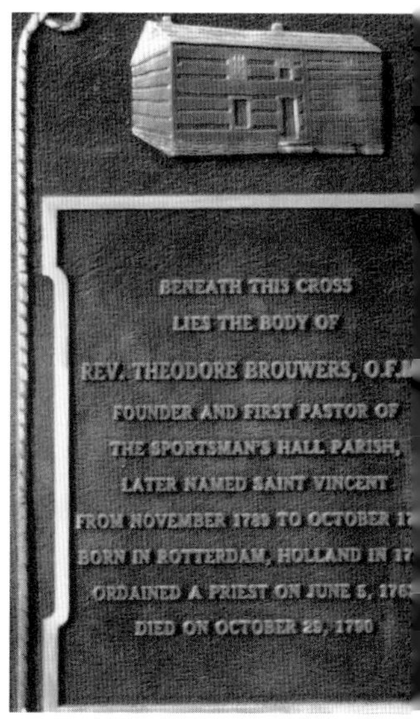

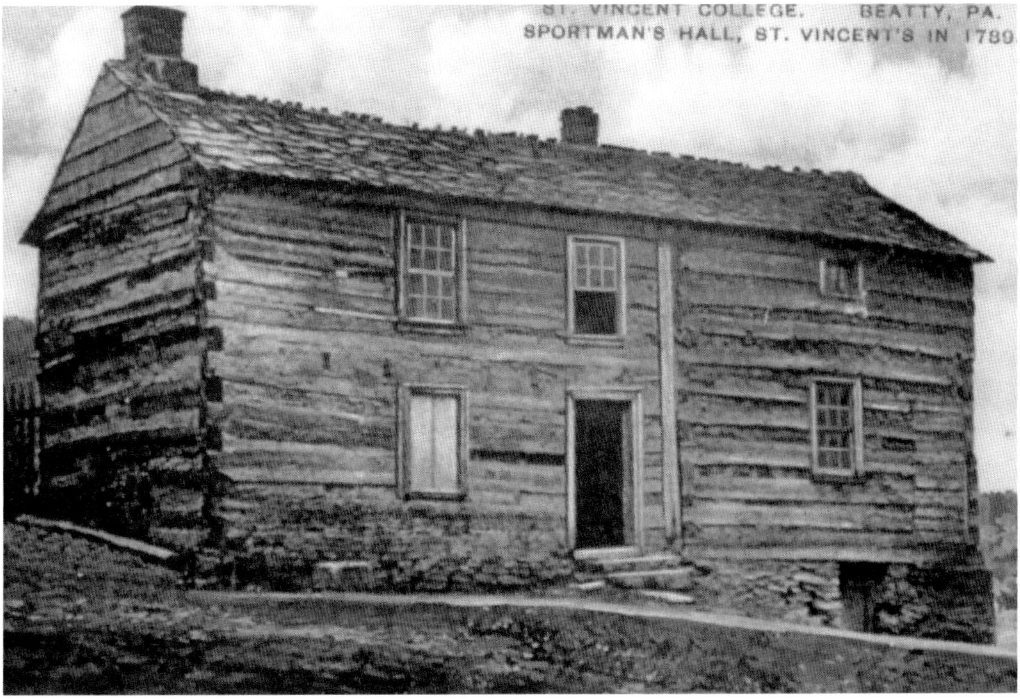

Sportsman's Hall Parish

Sportsman's Hall Parish (1790–1846) was purchased by Fr. Theodore Brouwers on April 16, 1790. A house 17 feet square and one and a half stories high was constructed on the partially cleared property, and Brouwers took up residence. During this early period, all the stations of Catholic worship in Westmoreland were supplied from Sportsman's Hall, now the Abbey of the Benedictines at St. Vincent's, making it the first Catholic parish in Pennsylvania west of the Allegheny Mountains. (St. Vincent College.)

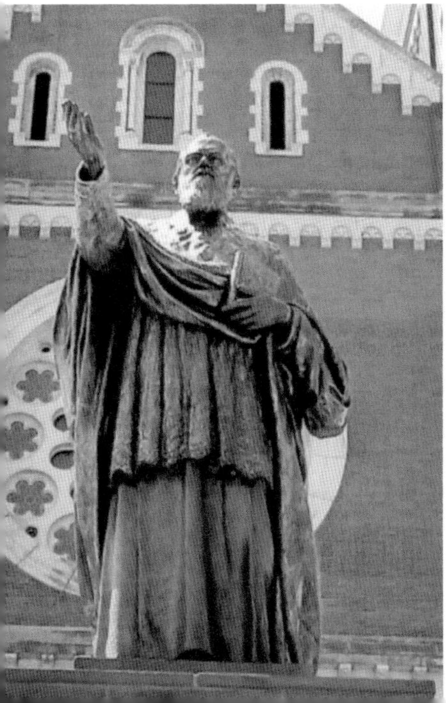

Boniface Wimmer

Archabbot Boniface Wimmer (1809–1887) was a German monk who, in 1846, founded the first Benedictine monastery in the United States, St. Vincent Archabbey in Latrobe. Born to tavern keepers in Bavaria, he believed he had a vocation to the priesthood and was ordained on August 1, 1831. He came to the United States to serve the working-class Catholic immigrants who had settled on the rural frontier. In 1846, he accepted an invitation from the first bishop of Pittsburgh, asking him to take the pastoral responsibility of St. Vincent. An active monk rather than a contemplative, Wimmer and his companions built up the small parish into a self-sufficient community that ground its own flour, raised its own crops, mined its own coal, and brewed its own beer. (LC.)

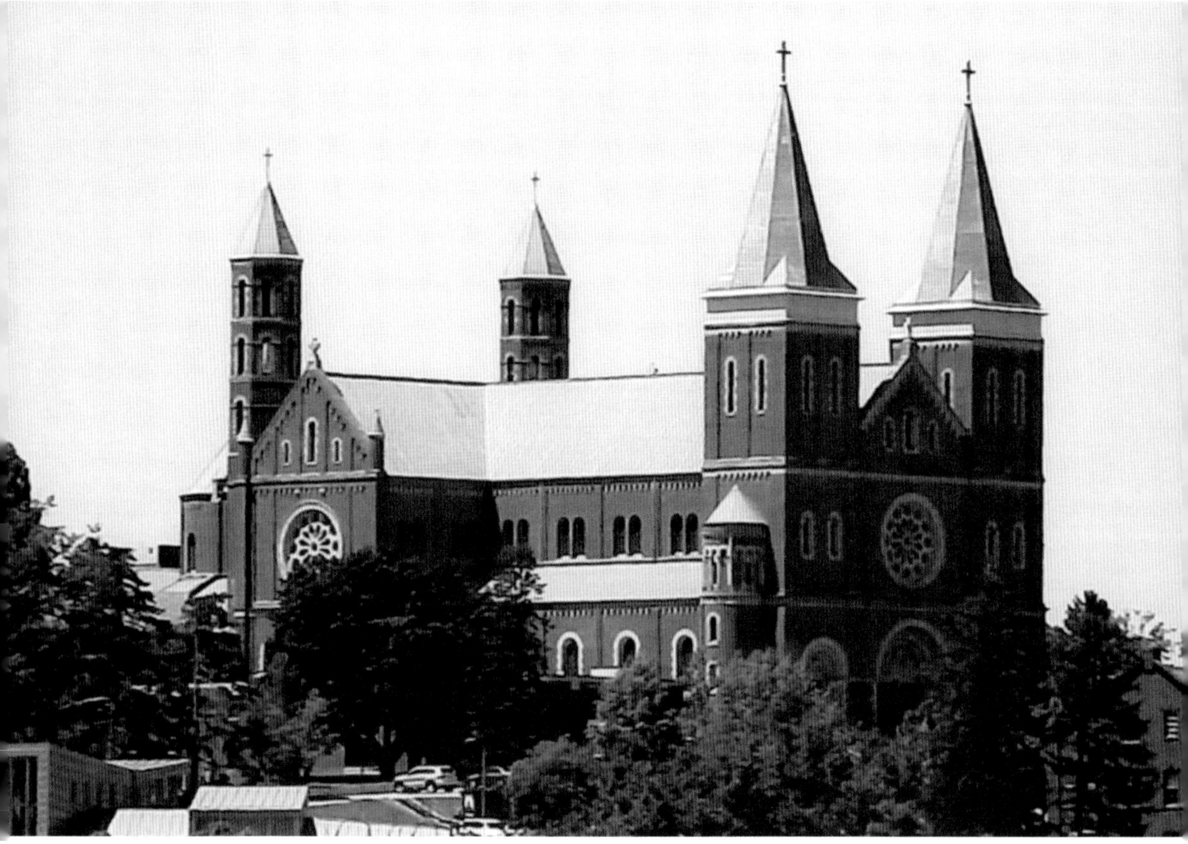

St. Vincent Basilica Parish

St. Vincent Basilica Parish was formed on April 16, 1790. With the arrival of Boniface Wimmer, the parish began a long affiliation with the Benedictine Order. Today, St. Vincent is the largest Benedictine abbey in the world. It had been Wimmer's dream to someday build a magnificent church, but construction on the basilica was not begun until 1891, four years after his death. Completed in 1905, the basilica is a symbol of the evangelization efforts of Wimmer and the early Catholic settlers in the area. St. Vincent serves as a college and seminary, as well as a monastery for almost 200 Benedictine monks. (LC.)

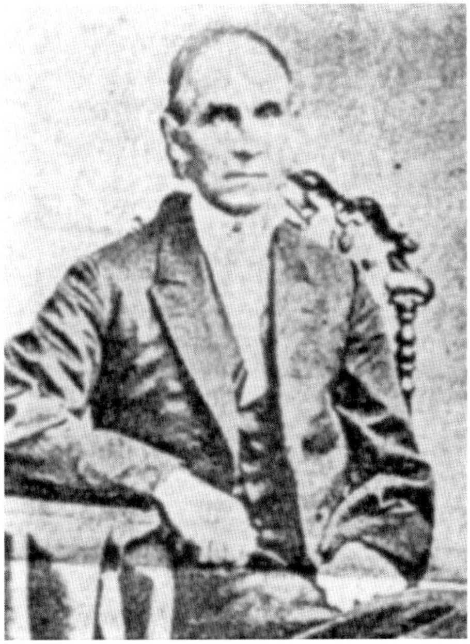

Noah H. Gillette

Noah H. Gillette (1849–1868), a Presbyterian minister, was traveling through Westmoreland County in 1833 on his way west when, according to *A History of Latrobe Presbyterian Church 1852 to 1994*, by Walter S. Hazlett Jr., "he was injured when his horse stumbled and fell on his leg." Gillette was cared for by the people of the area, who persuaded him to stay. After serving in a variety of short-term pastoral duties in the area, he was installed as permanent pastor at Unity Church on February 13, 1849. By 1852, the little village just over the hill from Unity was beginning to grow. In that year, the first train of the Pennsylvania Railroad came through, and a post office was established. "Father Gillette," as he was called, convinced the people at Unity to establish a mission in the growing town, which became the present-day Latrobe Presbyterian Church. (LAHS.)

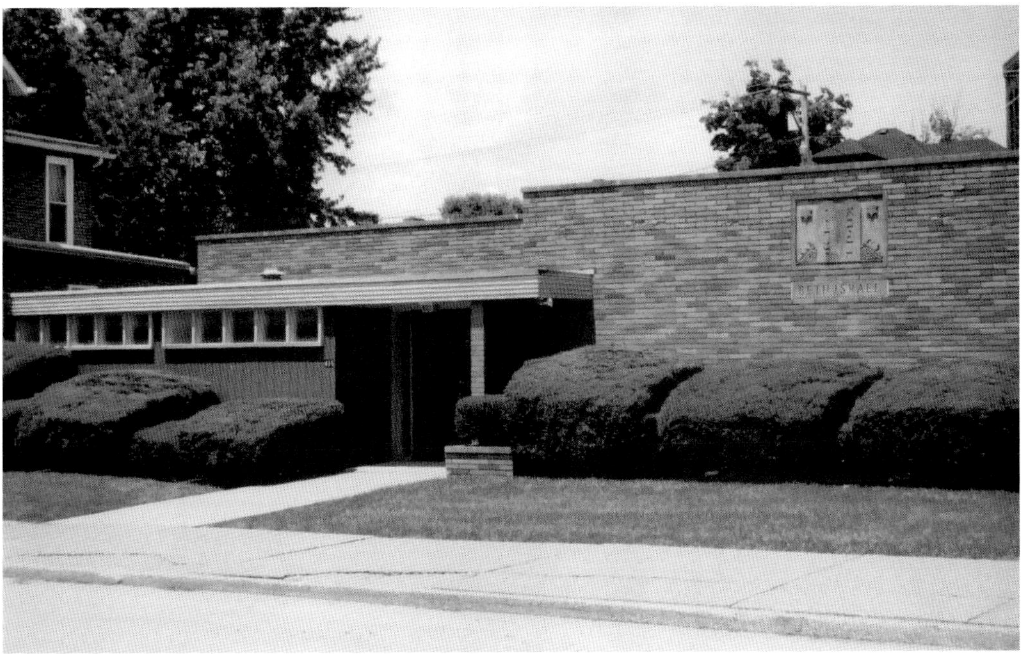

Henry Fellheimer

Henry Fellheimer, according to the history of the Beth Israel Congregation, is noted as the first recorded Jewish presence in the city of Latrobe. The history goes on to explain that though there were Jewish residents in Youngstown as early as 1846, "the Jews arriving in Latrobe settled in the First Ward area." In 1907, the first synagogue was built on Miller Street on land donated by scrap dealer Harry Tapolsky. This synagogue remained active until a new building (pictured) was erected at the present location on Weldon Street in 1954. It was here that comedian Jackie Mason was a student rabbi before resigning to dedicate his life to the entertainment industry. (AC.)

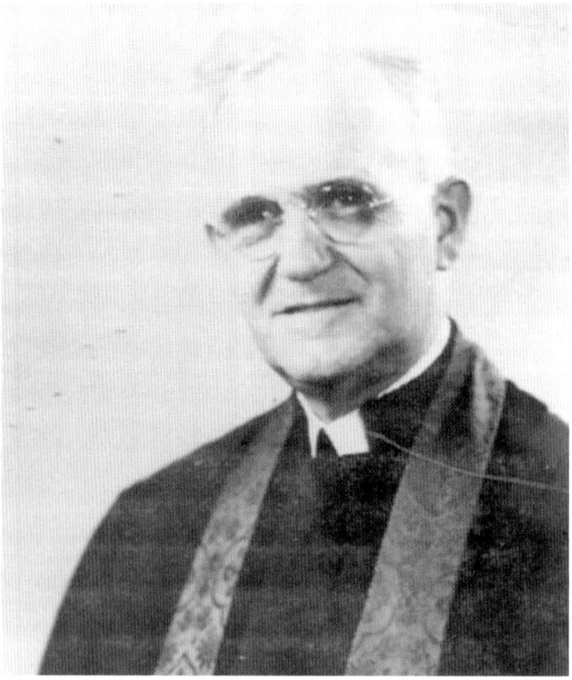

John B. Gardner

Rev. John B. Gardner came to Latrobe in 1927 to serve as minister of the Trinity Evangelical Lutheran Church. Since its founding in 1865, the church had nine pastors. Gardner's 19 years was the longest pastorate until that record was broken by the Rev. Dr. John Lewis Reiner, who was pastor for 25 years. Gardner made great advances in the education ministry of the church. Under his leadership, the congregation authorized a Building Committee to construct a school building, which was dedicated on June 1, 1930, at the beginning of the Great Depression, and offered vacation Bible school each summer as well as weekday church school. (LAHS.)

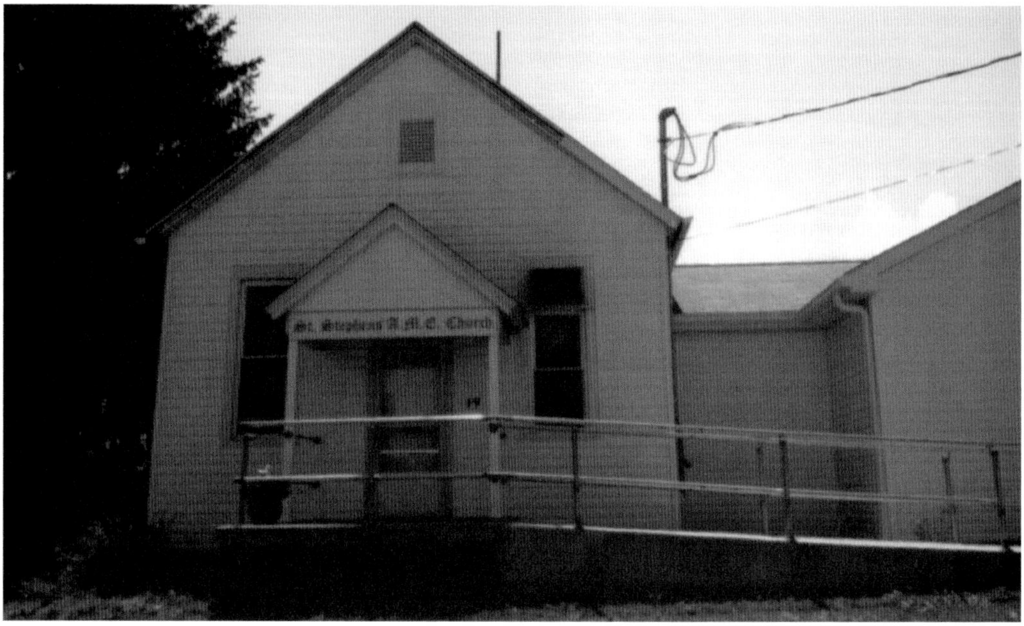

Prudence Harris

Pastor Prudence Harris used to have a favorite phrase to describe her church. "This is a church that sits between a brewery and a brook blessed by God," she often said. The affectionate phrase literally described St. Stephen's AME Church in Latrobe, The 40-by-20-foot wood-frame church used to sit between the City Brewing plant and Loyalhanna Creek. However, in 2011, city officials gave the go-ahead to City Brewing to move the Thirty-Third Street church to a nearby parcel of land to make room for its proposed $7.5-million wastewater treatment facility. (AC.)

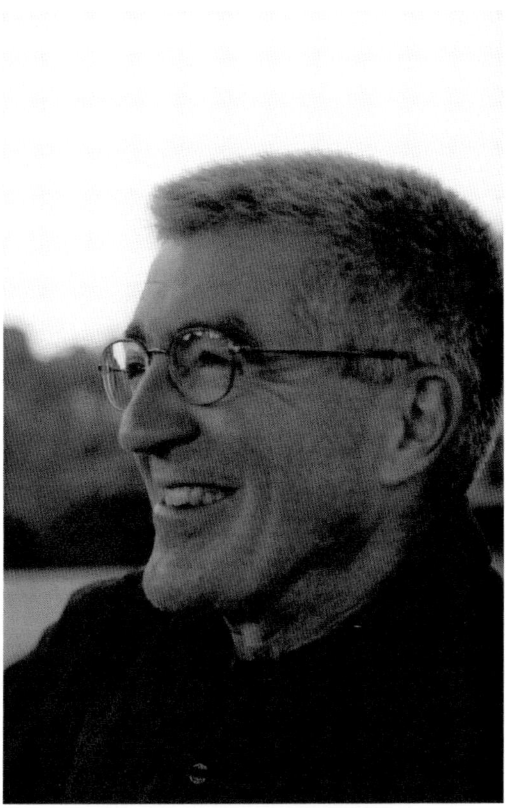

Morris P. Fiorina Jr.
Dr. Morris P. Fiorina Jr. is a professor of political science and coauthor of the book *Culture War? The Myth of a Polarized America* (2005). He grew up in Latrobe, the son of the late Morris P. "Mo" Fiorina and Helen M. Plachta (Plato) Fiorina. His father worked for Bergman's Dairy, and his mother was a longtime reporter for the *Latrobe Bulletin*. Dr. Fiorina is a graduate of Latrobe High School (1964) and earned an undergraduate degree from Allegheny College (1968) and a doctorate from the University of Rochester (1972). He taught at the California Institute of Technology and Harvard University before becoming a professor of political science at Stanford University in 1998. He is a senior fellow at Stanford's Hoover Institution and has written widely on American government and politics. (Morris P. Fiorina Jr.)

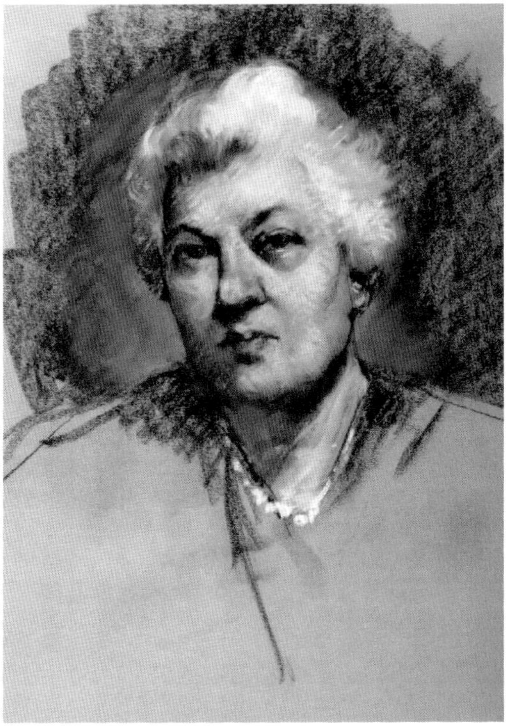

Mary Martha Himler
Mary Martha Himler (1890–1982), born in Greensburg, grew up in Latrobe and began teaching elementary school there in 1911. For 28 years, she organized loan exhibitions for Latrobe High School from the annual shows of the Associated Artists in Pittsburgh. She joined with her colleague James R. Beatty II each year to present those works as an exhibit to the student body and to the Latrobe community. The high school students then determined what works should be added to their Special Art Collection. The practice of student voting continues today, over 75 years later. Himler, herself an artist, not only helped create the unique art collection but also contributed to it—four of her works and her portrait (left) by Angelo DeVincenzo are included in the collection. (Center for Student Creativity.)

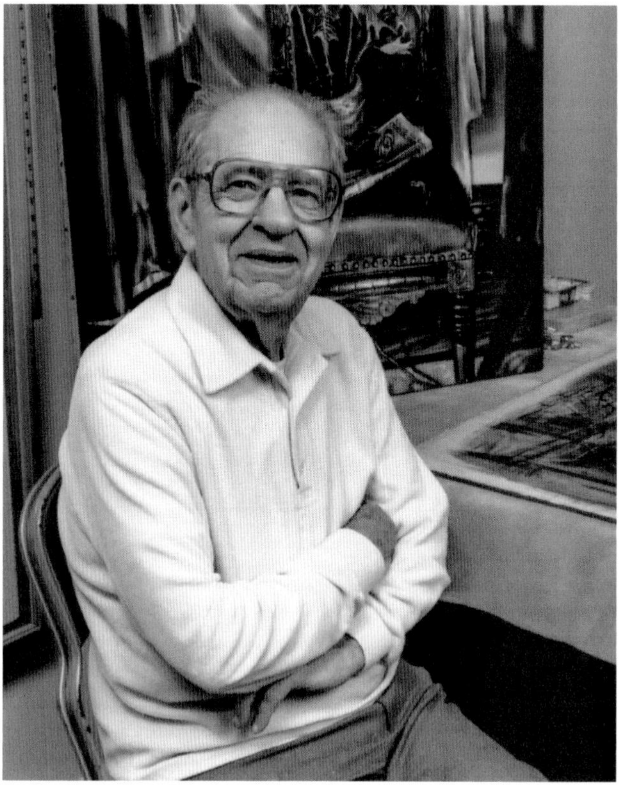

James R. Beatty II

James R. "Jim" Beatty II (1903–1992) taught social studies for more than 40 years in Latrobe and founded the Latrobe One Hundred Friends of Art. The group was organized in 1938 to promote the Latrobe High School art collection and help the students to purchase their selections. Like his colleague Mary Martha Himler, Beatty was a member of the Pittsburgh and Greensburg Art Club and also has a painting in the collection. His *Greywing Manor* was added in 1951. It features an impressionist's view of a house owned by the Steele family of New Alexandria, Pennsylvania. Beatty once said that one of the proudest moments of his life was when the students voted to add his painting. (Jonathan Nakles Photography.)

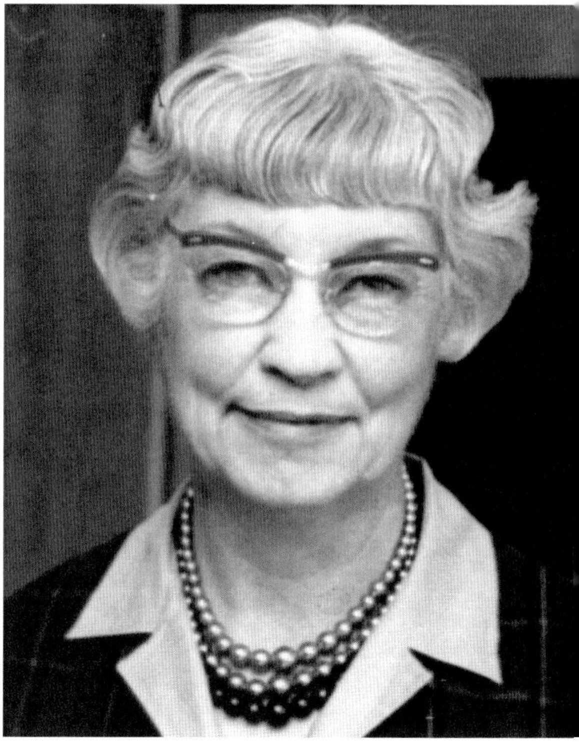

Virginia A. Daniels

Virginia A. "Slugger" Daniels (1907–1996) taught biology at Latrobe High School for decades and was the founder of the day camp program for the recreation board. Although known for her amusing storytelling, Daniels took her day camp director duties very seriously. She received training in Washington, DC, and at Camp Audubon in Connecticut. When Latrobe was looking for a slogan, Daniels won the contest and $100 for her motto "Latrobe—A Label of Distinction." She used her winnings to buy a projector used at the day camps. Daniels studied at Boyds School, Latrobe High School, the University of Pittsburgh, and Columbia University. In addition to her teaching duties, she coached dramatics, handled publications, took charge of the school library, and advised the Girls' Club. She also enjoyed playing the piano and wrote the Ligonier High School alma mater. (LAHS.)

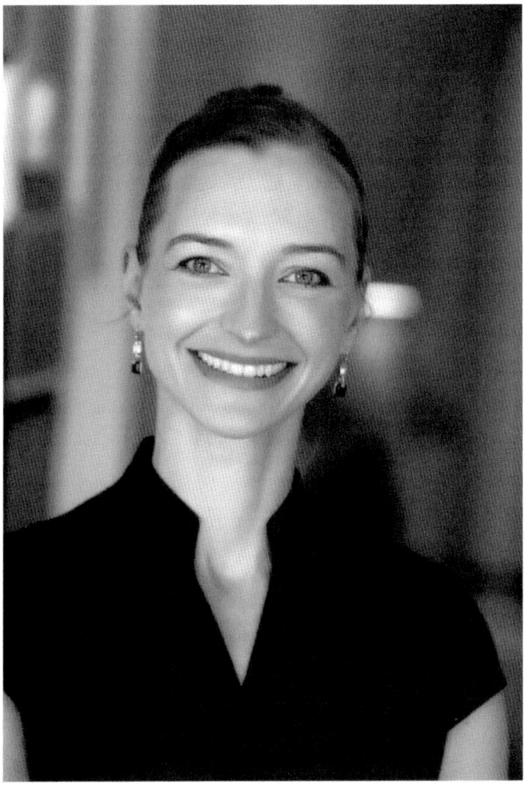

Rebecca Snyder
Rebecca Snyder, 2009 Pennsylvania State Teacher of the Year, chairs the Language Arts Department and teaches English at Greater Latrobe Senior High School. A 16-year veteran of the classroom, Snyder has taught multiple grade levels and courses as both a secondary practitioner and adjunct professor. She also has taught elective courses in creative dramatics, composition, public speaking, and film. She has served as a teacher representative on several committees for the Pennsylvania Department of Education, including those engaged in the revision and development of the Pennsylvania System of School Assessment (PSSA), the Keystone Exams, and the Pennsylvania Common Core. Snyder recently reflected, "I came to teaching, as most teachers do, expecting to touch the hearts and minds of my students. What I never expected was how powerfully they would touch mine." (Rebecca Snyder.)

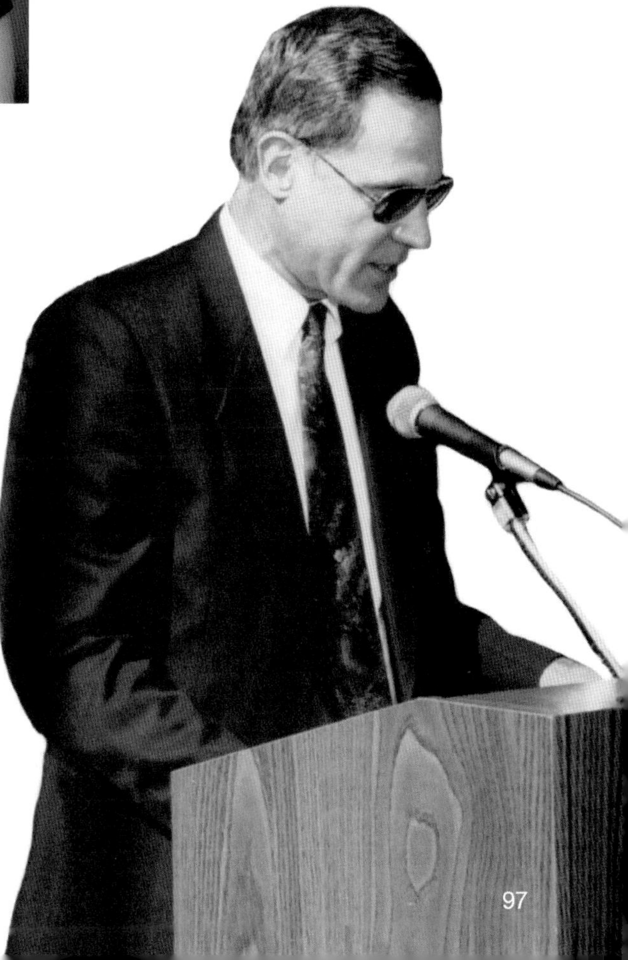

William Stavisky
Dr. William Stavisky, a Shinglehouse, Pennsylvania, native, began his career in education in 1970 as a math and science teacher at the Tunkhannock Area School District near Wilkes-Barre. He advanced through the decades and served a 17-year tenure as superintendent with the Latrobe Area School District. The experience saw him named Pennsylvania Superintendent of the Year by the Pennsylvania Association of School Administrators in 2006. Stavisky said at the time, "Maybe I'm the person who is honored, but this is a team project and it involves administrators, teachers, board members, all of us working as a team, and I want to share the honor." (LAHS.)

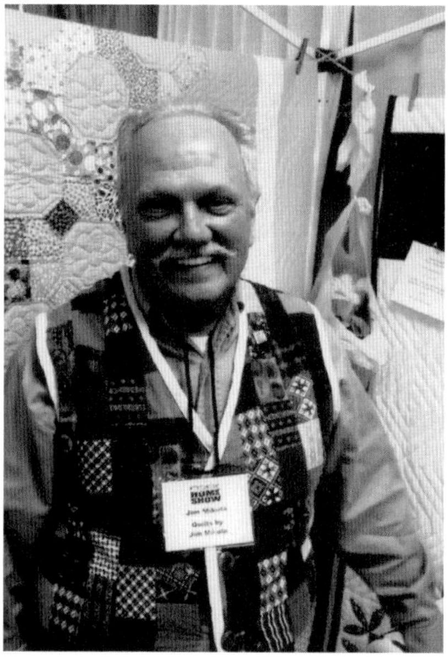

Jim Mikula

Jim Mikula taught English, theater, and film at Latrobe High School from 1968 to 1998 and directed 56 student productions and three faculty shows there. He has been involved in theater for over 50 years, beginning with his high school class play in 1964, and has appeared on stage and as director for many local theaters, including the Valley Players of Ligonier, Apple Hill Playhouse, and the Greensburg Civic Theater, among others. For 40 years, he has hand-quilted, and he was featured in the 2010 book *Men and the Art of Quiltmaking* by Joe Cunningham. Mikula was market manager for the Ligonier Country Market for 11 years and is currently doing the same job for the Latrobe Farmers' Market and the Keystone State Park Farmers' Market. (Jim Mikula.)

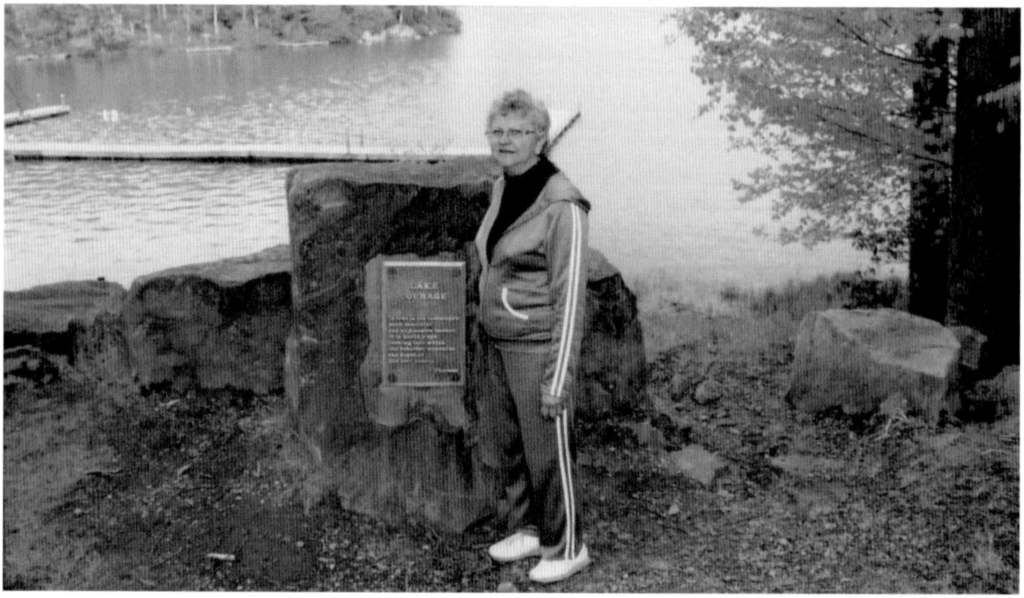

Dawna Bates

Dawna Bates was born in Latrobe in 1948 to Thomas and Velma Richards and graduated from Latrobe High School in 1966. She continued her education at Slippery Rock University, where she earned a bachelor of science in health and physical education. She began her teaching career at Donora High School, but then she returned home to teach physical education for Greater Latrobe, a career that spanned 36 years. She was the first coach of the junior high girls' basketball team and started the district's jump rope demonstration team. She is an instructor trainer of first aid and presently works as a member of the Friends of Flight 93 Memorial, greeting visitors and instructing at a discovery table for children. Bates, pictured at Sixth Grade Camp in 2014, was among the first group of GLSD teachers to attend the annual "outdoor education experience" and was asked to become its director in 2001. (Frank Kegg.)

CHAPTER SEVEN

Military and Hometown Heroes

This chapter honors those from Latrobe who made a difference in the community but didn't ask for anything in return. They are the ordinary individuals who have done extraordinary things. Many served in the armed forces, rallying forth without hesitation to take up arms to defend the nation at home and abroad. Military organizations flourished in the townships surrounding Latrobe from as far back as the American Revolution and before, but it was not until 1861 that the first combat unit, Company C, 11th Pennsylvania Volunteers, was formed within the borough limits. As volunteers, these men served in most of the principal campaigns of the Army of the Potomac during the Civil War, including the bloody battles of Antietam and Gettysburg. They were even present for Lee's surrender at Appomattox. Upon the outbreak of the Spanish-American War, the young men of Latrobe rushed to the colors as their fathers had done before them. Latrobe returned to the regiment's ranks in February 1912. At that time, Thomas B. Anderson was named captain of Company M, 10th Pennsylvania Infantry, and headquarters were established in Mozart Hall. Anderson would go on to serve during the Mexican border dispute in 1916 and become one of Latrobe's most honored World War I heroes when he was killed by machine gun fire on September 5, 1918, while leading a battalion advance near Basileux, France. When the American Legion granted a charter in Latrobe on March 26, 1920, the committee and 15 veterans establish it as the Thomas B. Anderson Post 515. At the time of its induction into federal services in February 1941, Company M was converted from a rifle company to a machine gun company. After training, the regiment was sent to England and then to France during World War II, where it bore itself heroically in the actions in Normandy and the Battle of the Bulge. Since then, men and women of Latrobe have been first in the line of duty when called to serve, some in peacetime and some in war. On the home front, Latrobe businesses and its citizens have always supported the troops by manufacturing machine parts and woolen blankets, collecting money, buying war bonds, welcoming home returning servicemen and women, and honoring those who paid the ultimate sacrifice. Since it is impossible in one chapter to mention by name the many Latrobe-area men and women, living and dead, who served their country in uniform, the few mentioned here will serve to remind readers of the sacrifices of the thousands who have answered the call. When the opportunity arose, Latrobeans have faced challenges and dangers with unmitigated bravery. This chapter highlights hometown heroes who saved lives, created new community organizations, and helped others simply by being good citizens and neighbors. Among them are soldiers, coal miners, a Holocaust survivor, the chief pilot for training at the Tuskegee Institute in Alabama, neighbors, volunteers, and even a meteorologist.

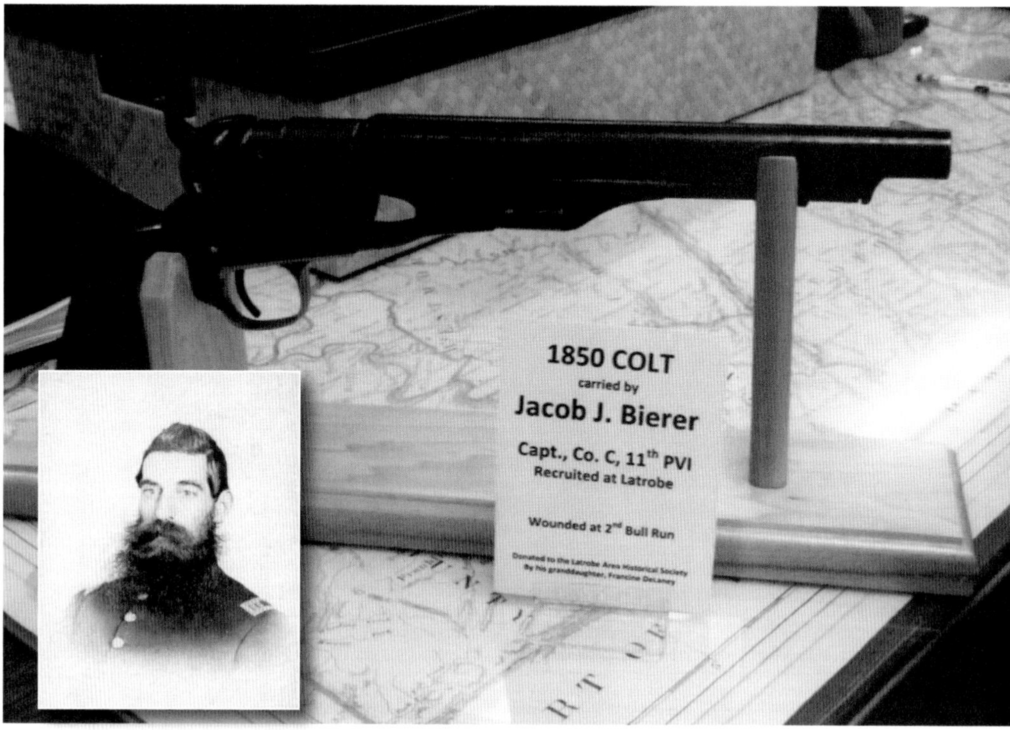

Jacob J. Bierer

Capt. Jacob J. Bierer (inset) was born in Westmoreland County on February 16, 1830, became a carpenter, and later sold real estate and insurance. He was recruited at Latrobe, mustered, and served in the Civil War as a captain of Company C, 11th Regiment, Pennsylvania Volunteers from 1861 to 1864. Pictured is the 1850 Colt he carried. It was donated to the Latrobe Area Historical Society by his granddaughter Francine DeLaney. Bierer and his regiment marched to Gettysburg on July 1, 1863, and were engaged with the enemy there for several days. He was wounded in the Second Battle of Bull Run and discharged. He subsequently served several terms as school director of Latrobe Borough and as chief burgess of Latrobe. (Above, LC; inset, LAHS.)

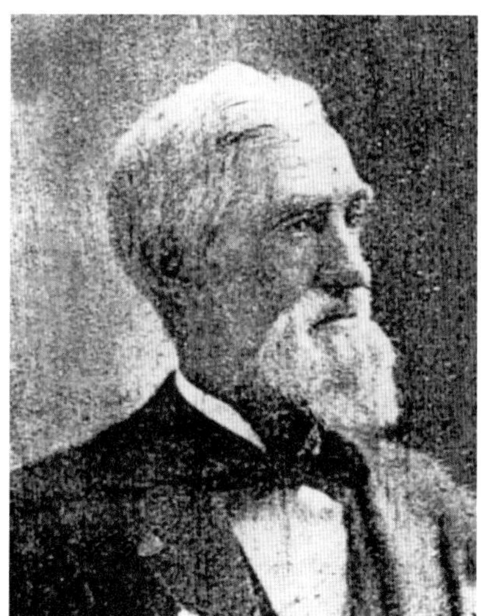

George C. Anderson

Col. George C. Anderson (1836–1919), a Civil War hero, was born in Allegheny County, Pennsylvania, and moved to Latrobe in the summer of 1854. At age 14, he learned the trade of bricklayer and in the spring of 1861 enlisted as a private in Company K, 11th Pennsylvania Volunteers, for three months' service. He then returned home, reenlisted, and became second lieutenant of the 53rd Pennsylvania Veteran Volunteers. The 53rd was assigned to the II Army Corps of the Army of the Potomac. Anderson received wounds in the right side of the head and in the left breast but was able to remain on duty during the entire period of the war. He became a colonel for "bravery and meritorious conduct" and was present at the surrender of General Lee. At the close of his long and faithful service, Anderson operated a lumber mill at Latrobe. (LAHS.)

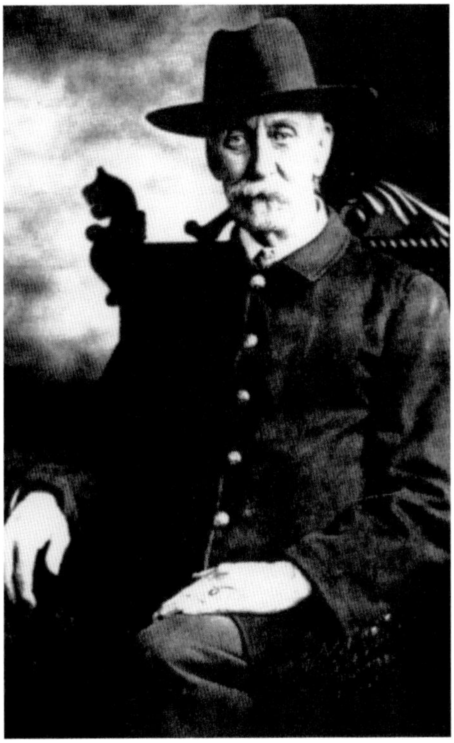

John R. Oursler

John R. Oursler (1838–1914) came to the area with his parents in 1850. His father built an iron foundry, where John worked as a boy. In winter, Oursler attended school in the first schoolhouse built in Latrobe. In 1855, he learned the trade of marble and stone cutting in Greensburg, Pennsylvania, and five years later, John's father started him and his brother Jacob in the marble business in Latrobe under the name of H. Oursler and Sons. They worked together for 40 years, producing stone that was placed all over the country, including seven of the larger monuments on the Gettysburg battlefield. John Oursler was instrumental in local recruitment for the Union army during the Civil War, and in 1861, when President Lincoln issued the first call for volunteers, he was the first man in Westmoreland County to respond. (LAHS.)

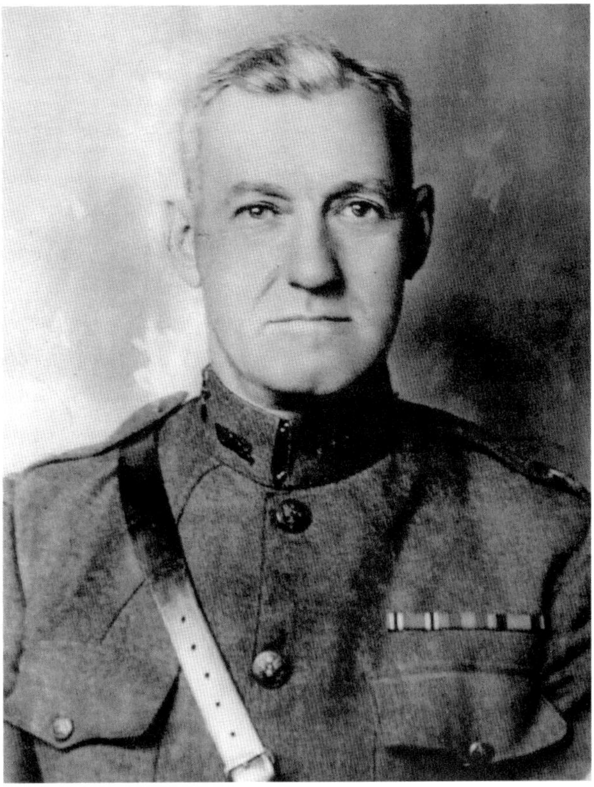

Thomas B. Anderson

Maj. Thomas B. Anderson, US Army, was posthumously awarded the Distinguished Service Cross in 1926 for extraordinary heroism in action while serving near Courmont, France, during World War I. Leading his battalion in an attack on July 30, 1918, Anderson refused to be evacuated when wounded and gassed until the objective had been gained and the position consolidated. His courage was an inspiration to his men. Five weeks later, on September 5, he was killed while leading a patrol across open ground swept by heavy fire against an enemy machine gun nest. Latrobe's American Legion Post 515 is named in his honor. (LAHS.)

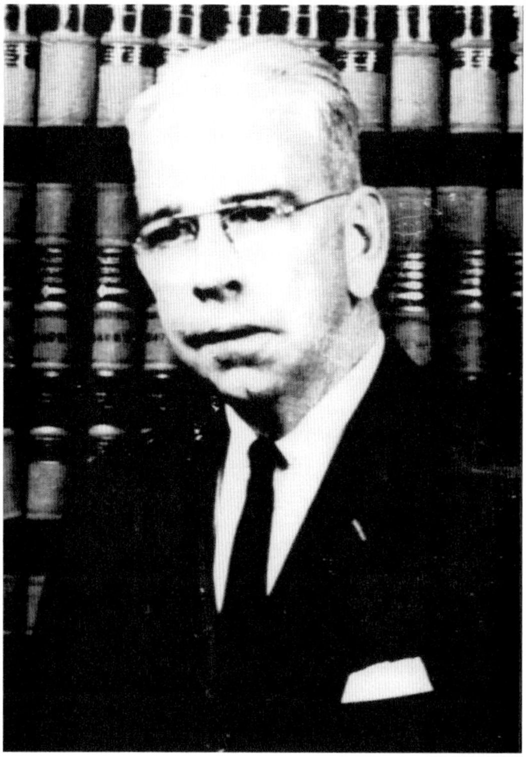

Harold Andrew Stewart

Harold Andrew "Sandy" Stewart (1896–1994) of Latrobe was a 20-year-old student at Bucknell University when he volunteered for the ambulance corps at the start of World War I. He served on the frontlines in France and was just a few miles away when Maj. Thomas B. Anderson was killed. Stewart was awarded the French Croix De Guerre for rescuing a captain and soldiers under direct fire. In later years, he spoke with a gravelly voice, the result of a poison gas attack that burned his throat and lungs. After the war, he earned his law degree from the University of Pittsburgh and set up practice at Latrobe in 1924. He was a leader in many of city's community organizations for many decades and was instrumental in the formation of the Latrobe Municipal Authority, Adam's Memorial Library, Legion Kenner Park, and the Thomas B. Anderson American Legion Post. (LAHS.)

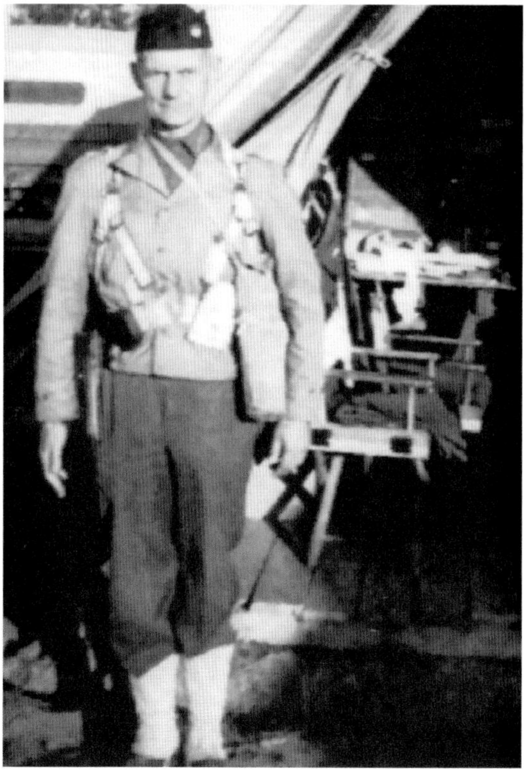

James S. Gallagher

Lt. Col. James S. Gallagher, one of Latrobe's military heroes, stands at attention in October 1941. He was honored as the 20th recipient of the Greater Latrobe Chamber of Commerce Community Service Award for his record on the battlefield and back home in Latrobe. His career began in 1917 when he fought under Maj. Thomas Anderson in France. He was wounded in an air attack and sent home. After World War I, he commanded Company M for 17 years. He returned to active service, serving first in Europe during World War II with the 359th Infantry during the Battle of the Bulge and then later in the Korean War. He was commissioned a brigadier general in 1963. (Steven Patterson.)

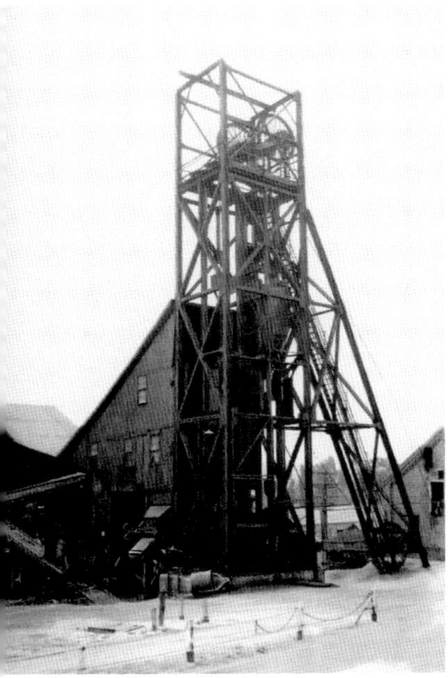

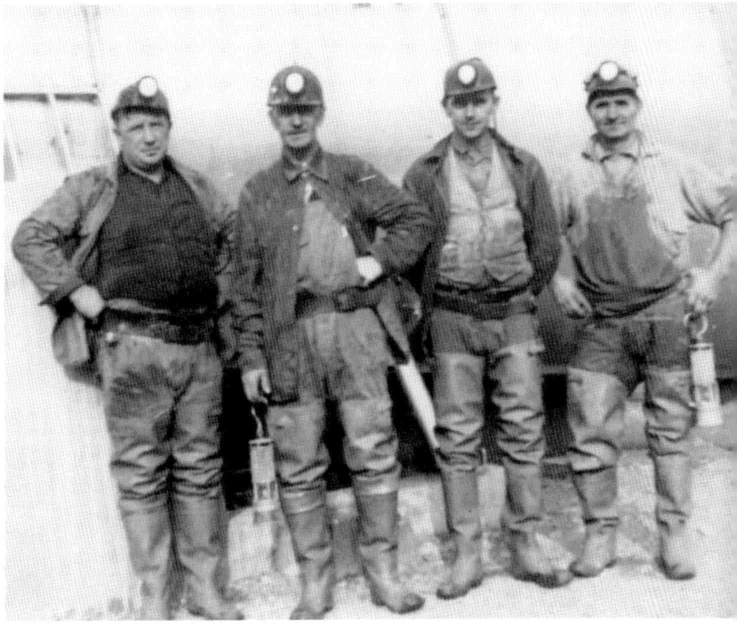

John Lane and Bernard Ransel

John Lane and Bernard "Barney" Ransel were heroes who were simply doing their job to protect others when they gave their lives on May 31, 1937. Lane, 63, a pumper, and Ransel, 50, a machinist, worked for the St. Vincent Mine Shaft. Lane was sent into the mine even though it was a holiday, Decoration Day (now celebrated as Memorial Day), as a pumper was needed in the mine at all times. Ransel was there to escort Robert F. Jones, a fire boss, during his inspection. Ten minutes after Jones left, a wall of water from an underground lake burst through the shaft, trapping and killing the two men remaining and flooding a 25-square-mile area. Only Lane's body was recovered, but not until February 1940, nearly three years after the disaster. His remains were interred in the Dickerson Run Union Cemetery in Fayette County. Pictured at left is the St. Vincent Mine tipple, located on the spur railroad line that fed the main line in Latrobe. Miners of the same era (right), including Stephan Sedlacko (left), pose in front of a 20th-century beehive oven at the Hostetter Mine, also on the spur line. Cleanup efforts from the St. Vincent disaster and other abandoned mine drainage sites continue to this day with the Monastery Run Improvement Project wetlands and sludge basin near the St. Vincent Gristmill. (Left, FF; right, LAHS.)

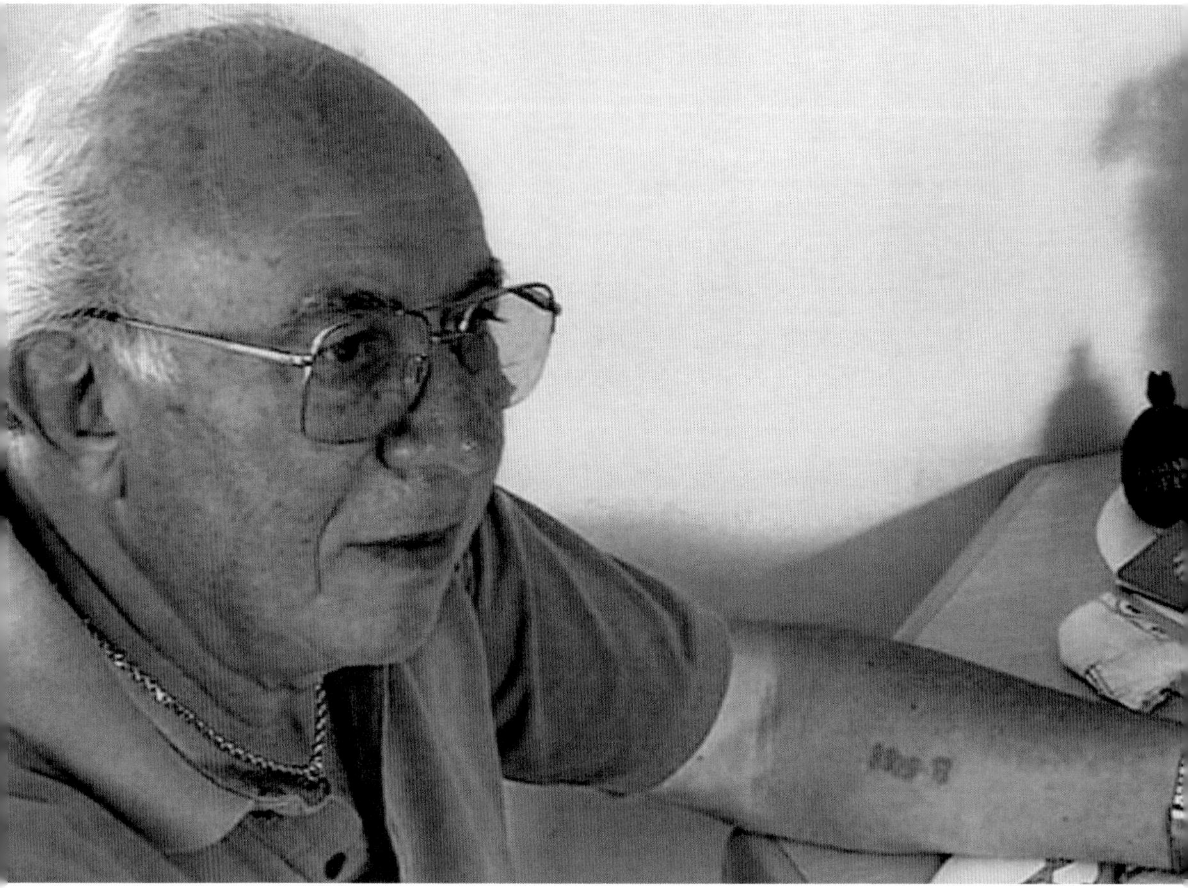

Robert Reibeisen Mendler

Robert Reibeisen "Bob" Mendler (1925–2009), born in Nowy Targ, Poland, was a Holocaust survivor and Latrobe businessman who spent his life educating people about the horrors of the concentration camps. His message was that all prejudice is "ugly and pointless." The only member of his family to survive the Holocaust, he was only 13 when taken to Belzec, the first of 10 concentration camps where he was imprisoned for six years. A survivor of Auschwitz, Mendler often spoke gratefully of the American servicemen who rescued him in 1945. "Thanks to American G.I.s, I'm here today to talk to you," he said to a group of St. Vincent College students in 2007. Despite the horrors he witnessed, his outlook was always positive, and his life was spent in tribute to his mother's last words: "Never forget who you are. Never forget where you come from. Always respect other people." Self-educated, Mendler received an honorary doctor of humane letters degree from St. Vincent College in 2000. In 1996, he was interviewed by Steven Spielberg's Survivors of the Shoah Visual History Foundation. In 1999, he was awarded the New Life Award and the Elie Wiesel Commemorative Medal, presented to survivors for their participation in Holocaust remembrance. In the photograph, Mendler reveals the deep blue tattoo on his left arm that identifies him as Auschwitz prisoner B5188. (Courtesy of Bob Mendler.)

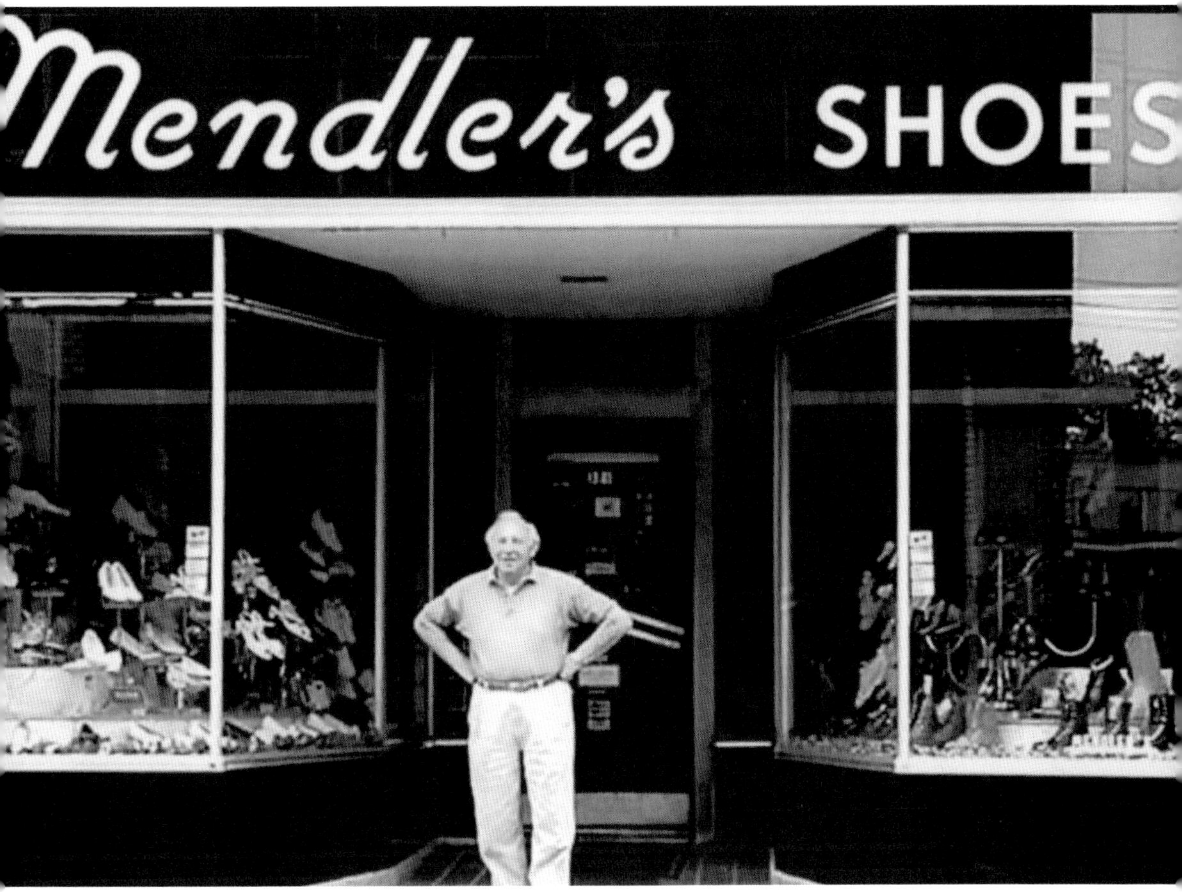

Mendler's Shoes

Bob Mendler came to Latrobe upon discovering the name of an uncle who had escaped the occupation of Poland and was listed in a phone book distributed by the US Army to displaced persons after World War II. He worked at his uncle's shoe store—Mendler's Shoes on Main Street in Latrobe—and later assumed ownership of the business. He sold the business before retiring but fondly remembered that the store was a gathering place for friends and loyal customers. "Our store was an institution. People [often] didn't buy shoes, they came down to say 'hello' and spend some time." (Courtesy of Bob Mendler.)

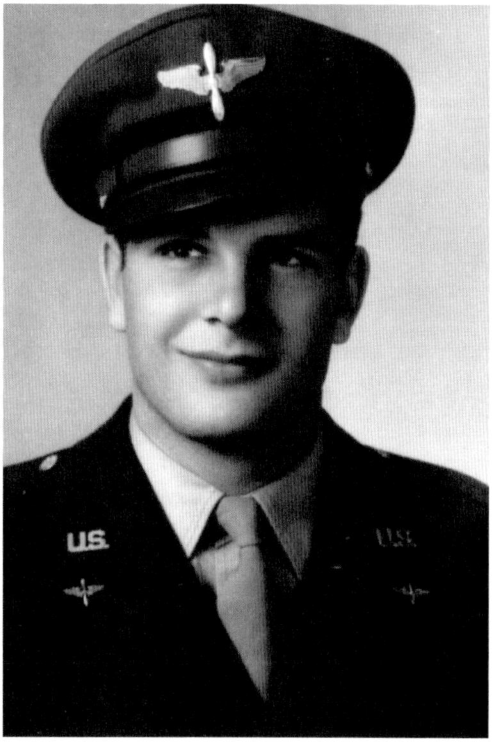

John J. Keltz

John J. "Jack" Keltz (1921–2005) was a World War II veteran, having served in the US Army Air Corps. He flew 15 bombing missions over Southeast Asia as a bombardier and navigator and later wrote about his experience. "I had a job to do and I did my best with the best crew in the USAAC. I circumnavigated the earth and saw a lot of different places that reinforced my belief that the good old USA is the best country to live in." First Lieutenant Keltz returned home and worked as a steelworker for Standard Steel Company in Latrobe. He was vice president of the Latrobe Area Historical Society and a member of the American Legion and Trinity Lutheran Church, volunteering for its Shepherd Shop. (LAHS.)

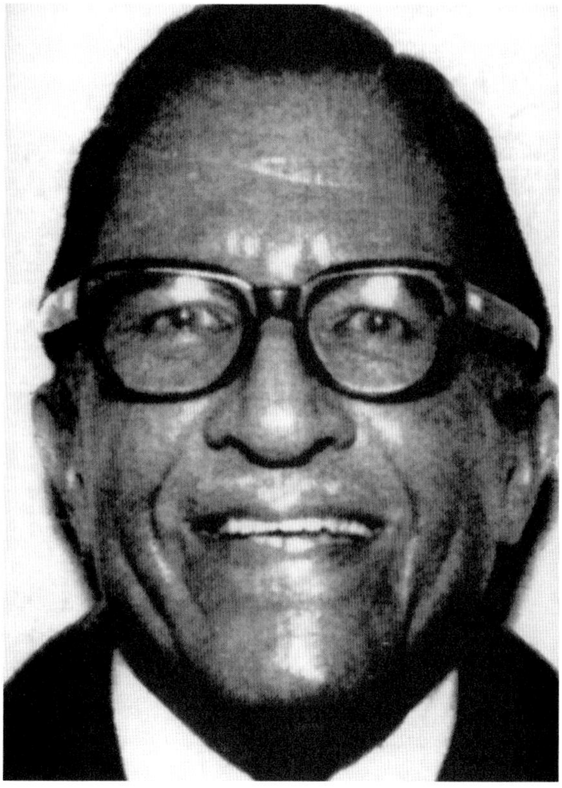

George Allen

George Allen was a drummer with various dance bands in the area, but his dream was to fly. Between gigs, he took flight lessons and made his first solo flight in 1933 at Bettis Field, according to Dr. Richard Wissolik in his book, *A Place in the Sky*. When he got his wings, Allen bought an old Eaglerock OX5 that sat neglected at the Latrobe Airport for $300. He overhauled and repaired it and was soon giving flying lessons. Fred Rogers took lessons from him and said in a PBS interview, "He was so enthusiastic about flying. I know that's why I wanted to learn. The best teacher in the world is somebody who loves what he or she does and just loves it in front of you." Allen was one of the first African American pilots in the Army Air Corps and an instructor to the Tuskegee Airmen during World War II. (Richard Wissolik.)

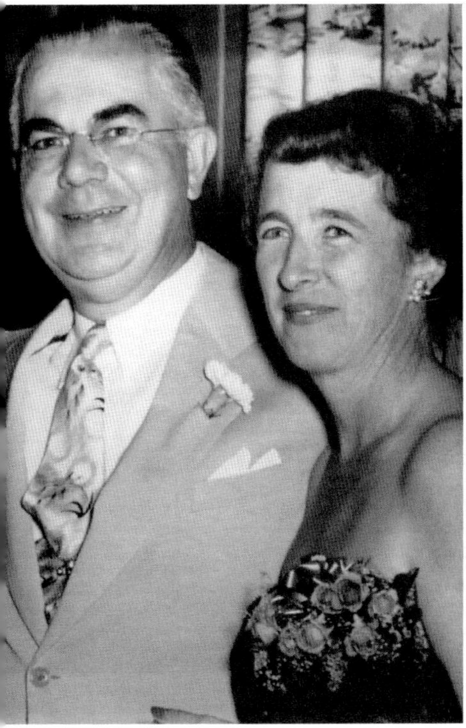

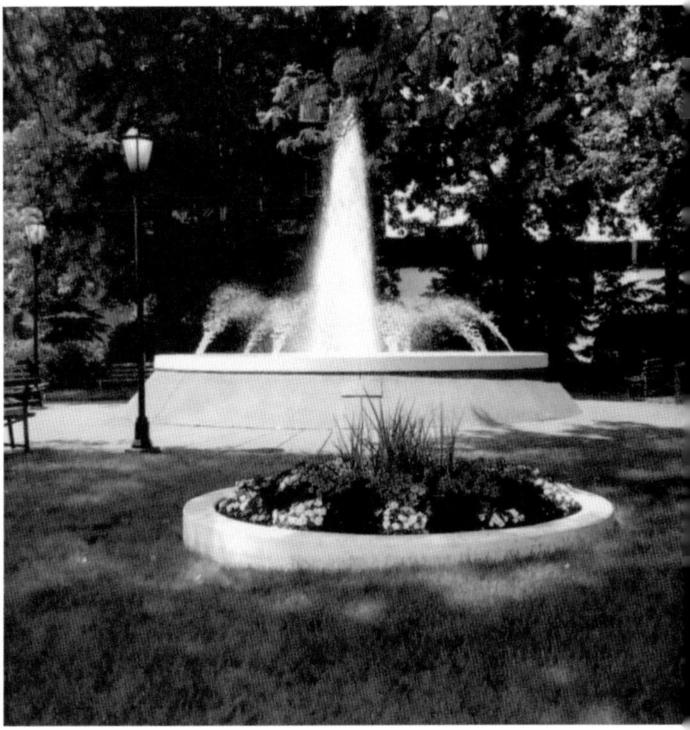

Nancy McFeely Rogers Flagg

Nancy McFeely Rogers Flagg (1903–1981) may be best known for being the mother of children's television pioneer Fred McFeely Rogers, but for many years, she was also one of Latrobe's most prominent citizens and unsung heroes, contributing to many community projects anonymously. Flagg was born in Pittsburgh, the daughter of Fred Brooks McFeely and Nancy Kennedy McFeely. The family moved to Latrobe when she was five. Her humanitarian work began in 1917, when she obtained a driver's license at age 14 and delivered medical supplies to a Latrobe medical center during an influenza epidemic. During World War I, she distributed yarn, knitted for American soldiers, and drove for the local Red Cross. Later, during World War II, she was in charge of surgical dressings for the area. For many years, Flagg was a nurse's aide volunteer in the nursery at Latrobe Area Hospital and, along with her family, donated the meditation chapel there. In addition to knitting for the troops, she also knitted all the sweaters Mr. Rogers wore on his television program. Nancy McFeely Rogers is pictured (left) with her husband, James Hillis Rogers (1900–1970), a very successful Latrobe businessman who prospered as president of McFeely Brick Company. He had a favorite fountain in Clearwater, Florida, where the family wintered, and often wished there was such an attractive water feature back home. After his death, the McFeely-Rogers Foundation, established by Rogers and his family in 1953, honored that wish. Today, the fountain (right) and beautifully landscaped park offer welcome respite to Latrobe residents and visitors alike. In March 2014, it was announced that Fred McFeely Rogers would have a blue and gold historical marker dedicated to him and placed in the park named for his father. (Left, Jonathan Nakles Photography; right, AC.)

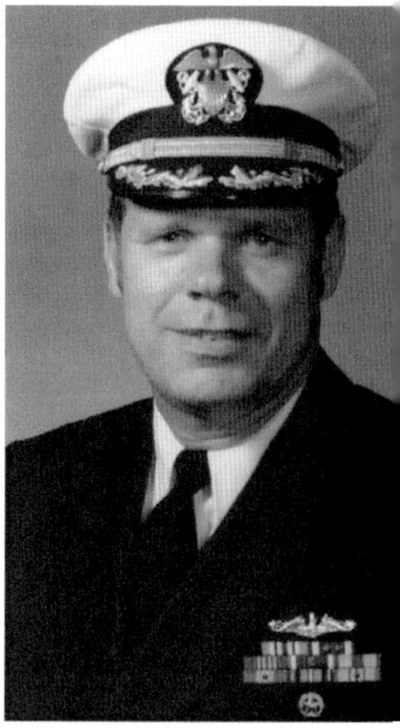

James R. Beatty III

Captain Beatty graduated from Latrobe High School in 1953. He entered the US Naval Academy and was commissioned an ensign in 1957. During his Navy career, which spanned 27 years, he served aboard an aircraft carrier and five submarines, including commanding USS *Trout* (SS 566). Ashore, he attended the US Naval Postgraduate School, earning a master's degree in operations research. His last assignment was as commanding officer at the Fleet Anti Submarine Warfare Training Center. He served during the Cold War, Cuban Missile Crisis, and Vietnam War. His awards include the Legion of Merit, Meritorious Service Medal, Navy Commendation Medal with two gold stars, and Vietnam Service Medal. Following retirement as a captain, in 1984, he was employed as a senior manager for Honeywell and Computer Sciences Corporation. Beatty is married to Carol Beatty (née Parker) of Latrobe. They have one daughter, two sons, and five grandchildren. They currently live in Coronado, California. (Jim Beatty.)

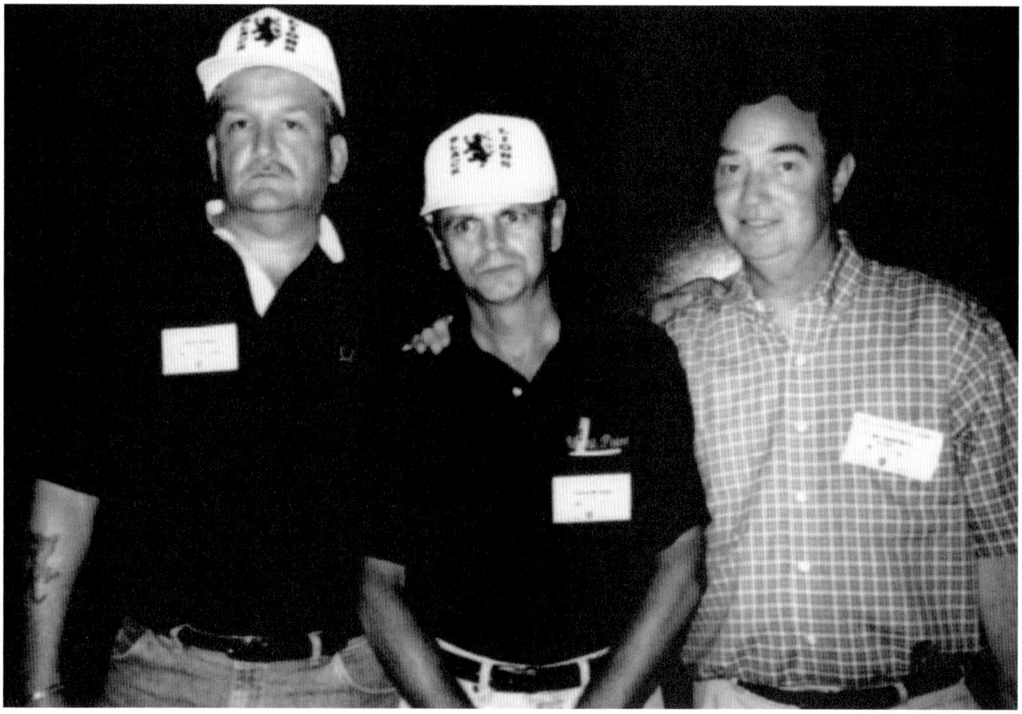

Tom Hinger

Tom Hinger, who grew up in Latrobe, was drafted into the Army for a two-year tour and made a medic. He is a hero of the Vietnam War and is featured in David Maraniss's book *They Marched into Sunlight*, about the ambush of the Black Lion Brigade in 1967. Although wounded himself, Hinger did his job and tended to the other men. He won one of two Purple Hearts that fateful day. Hinger spoke to Mike Porembka's history class at Greater Latrobe High School in 2003. Porembka recalled, "Having Mr. Hinger talk about his experiences made it real for the kids. With a classroom full of 17 and 18 year olds, after listening to Mr. Hinger, they finally understood that kids their age were fighting the War in Vietnam." Pictured in front of the Vietnam Veterans Memorial Wall in Washington, DC, are (from left to right) Steve Goodman, Tom Hinger, and Dave Berry. (Tom Hinger.)

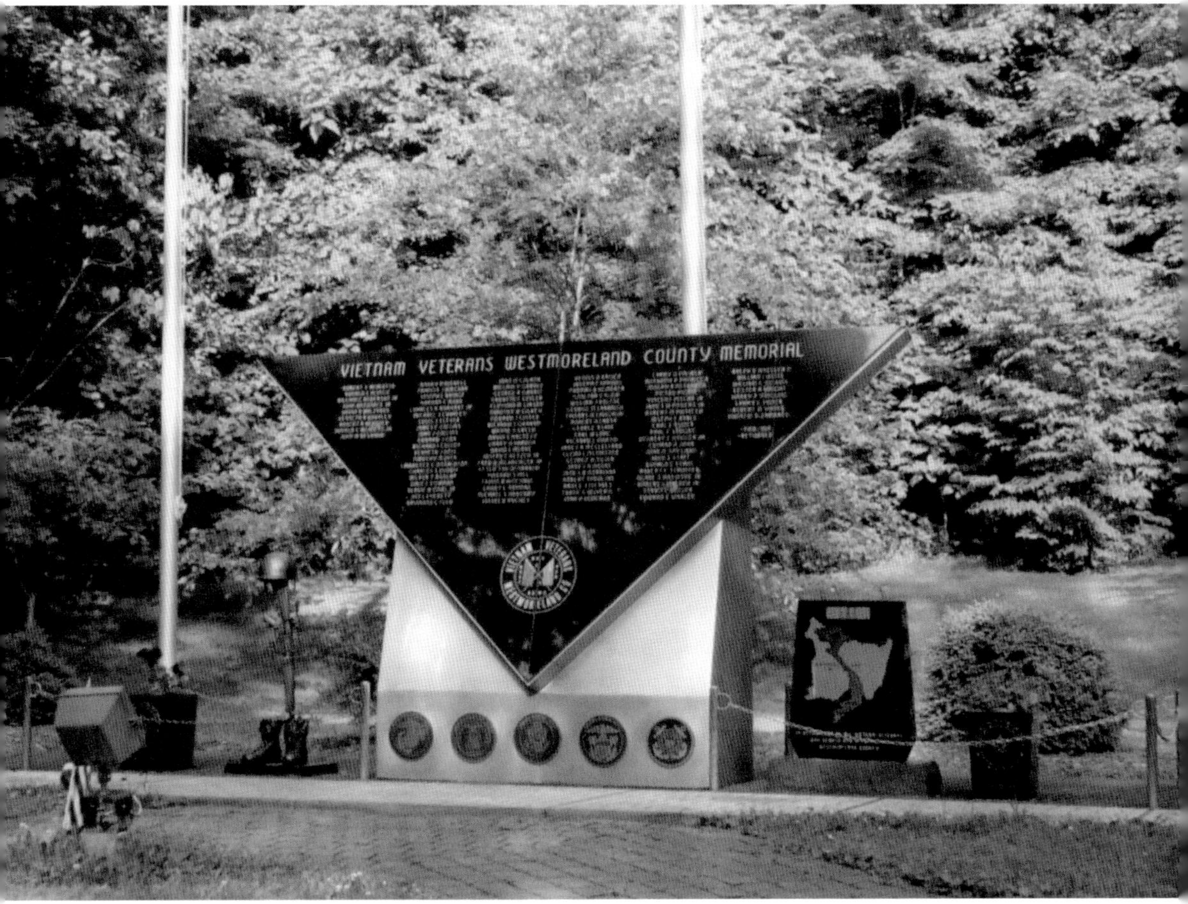

Vietnam Veterans of Westmoreland County Memorial

The Vietnam Veterans of Westmoreland County Memorial at Twin Lakes Park in Greensburg, Pennsylvania, is dedicated to the memory of those from Westmoreland County who gave their lives for their country in Vietnam; it also honors those who served and returned home. The stone came from the same quarry in India as the national memorial in Washington, DC. The names of 97 men who were killed in action or are missing in action are carved in the stone. Latrobe names include Francis Joseph Birchak, Joseph Leonard Bridge, Blaine W. Enos Jr., Jay Leroy Everett, Dennis Dale Kaiser, James Harrison Moore, Robert Michael Priviech, Joseph Edward Roble, and Larry Eugene Yoder. (AC.)

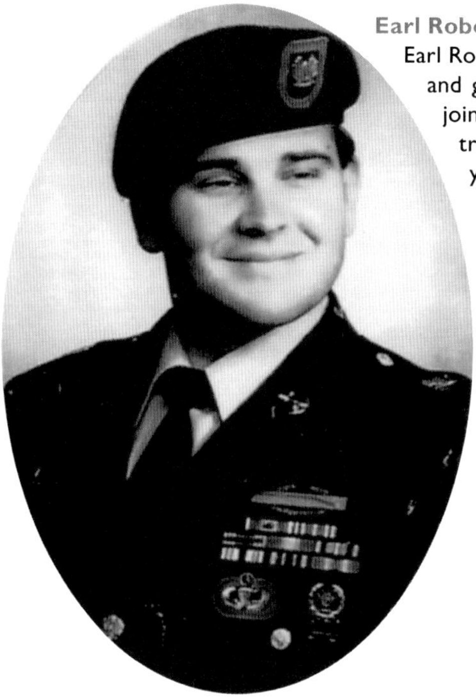

Earl Robert Fillmore Jr.

Earl Robert Fillmore Jr. was born in Latrobe on June 16, 1965, and graduated from Derry Area High School in 1983. He joined the Army at 17, right after high school, getting his training as a medic. When he was 24, he became the youngest soldier ever to be accepted into the Army's elite Delta Force, where he became a counterterrorist. During the Battle of Mogadishu, the fight made famous in the movie *Black Hawk Down*, Fillmore fought through the streets to reach the crash site of a downed helicopter in an attempt to rescue his comrades. He was fatally wounded defending his force and posthumously awarded a Sergeant First Class, US Army, for "conspicuous gallantry and intrepidity in action against hostile enemy forces." (Brenda Fillmore Perry.)

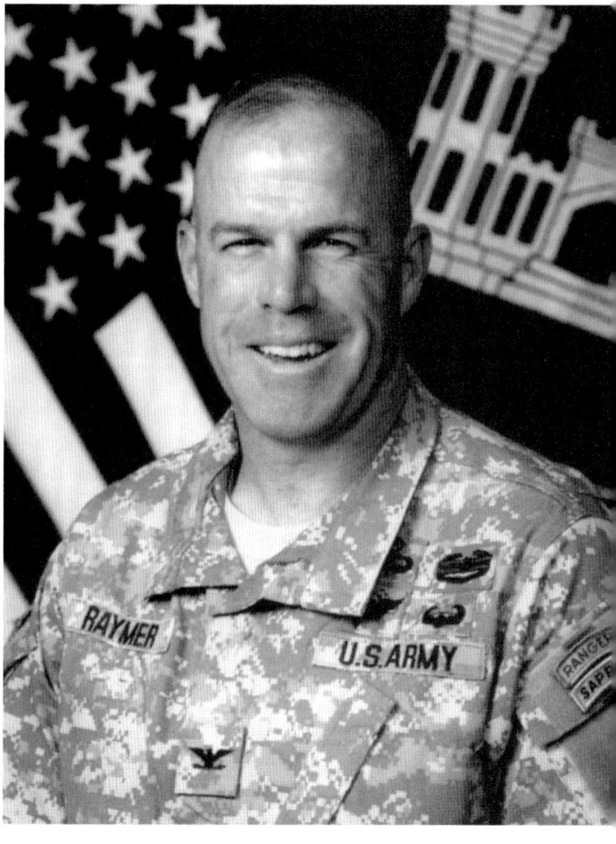

James H. Raymer

Col. James H. Raymer, a native of Latrobe, most recently served in NATO training missions and Combined Security Transition Commands in Afghanistan. Commissioned into the Army from the US Military Academy in 1989, he is currently the 20th Engineer Brigade commander at Fort Bragg, North Carolina. Raymer's awards include the Legion of Merit, Bronze Star, the Meritorious Service Medal, the Joint Service Commendation Medal, and the Army Commendation Medal, among many others. He and his wife, Elizabeth, and their four children reside along the Rio Grande in McAllen, Texas. (James H. Raymer.)

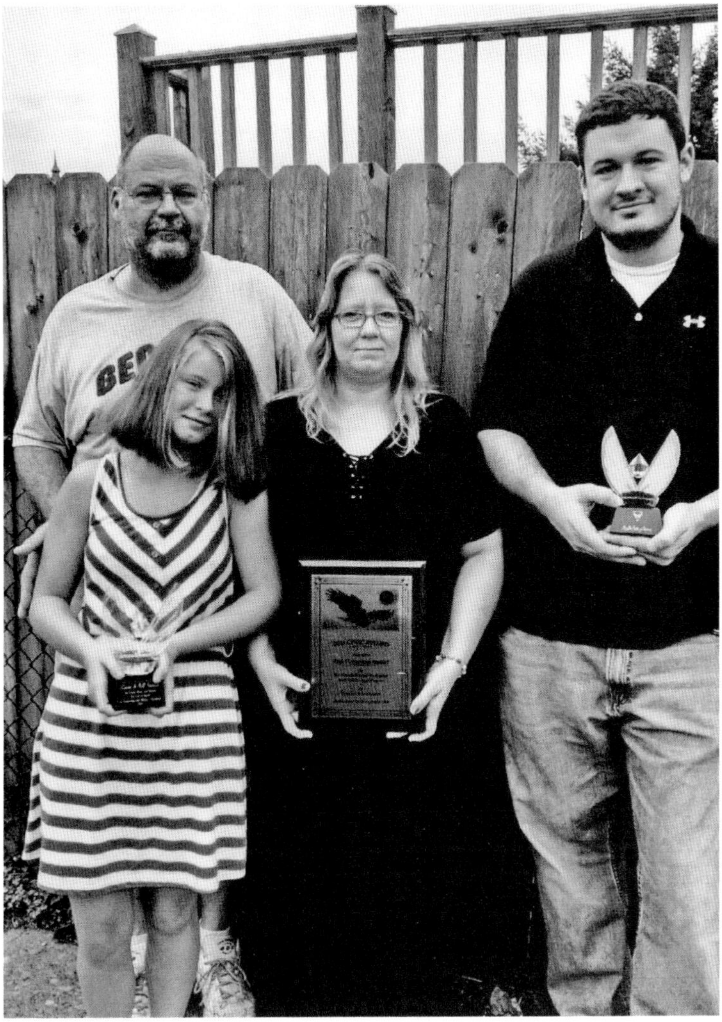

Laura Yuhaniak

Laura Yuhaniak of Latrobe was recognized at the 2011 Patriotic Interfaith Program during the city's annual Fourth of July celebration for her work as local coordinator of Soldiers' Angels, a nonprofit organization based in Pasadena, California, and dedicated to helping military personnel and their families deal with overseas deployment. Speaking at the event, Dorothy Benyacko Carbisiero, leader of the Family Readiness Group of Greensburg, Pennsylvania, eloquently described Yuhaniak's countless selfless actions. "Laura has not only done great things, but she has done them with great love. This angel has truly earned her wings!" Yuhaniak and Soldiers' Angels provided airfare for a mother to cross the country to see her daughter before deployment and have donated thousands of care packages containing a variety of items donated by local groups and individuals. Through the organization's efforts, soldiers have received shop vacuums to keep the desert sand out of their equipment, microwaves for popcorn, freeze pops, fresh bread and meat, clothing, and many of the other items "they yearned for." Of her countless hours spent serving the needs of military members, their families, and the wounded, Yuhaniak recently reflected, "I hope what I do will inspire others to get out there and help their community in whatever way they can, because everyone can do something." Pictured are Yuhaniak (center) and her husband, Bill; son, Jesse; and daughter, Jenny. The family works together to pick up donations, sort and package items, address and affix labels, and ship care packages locally and overseas. (Laura Yuhaniak.)

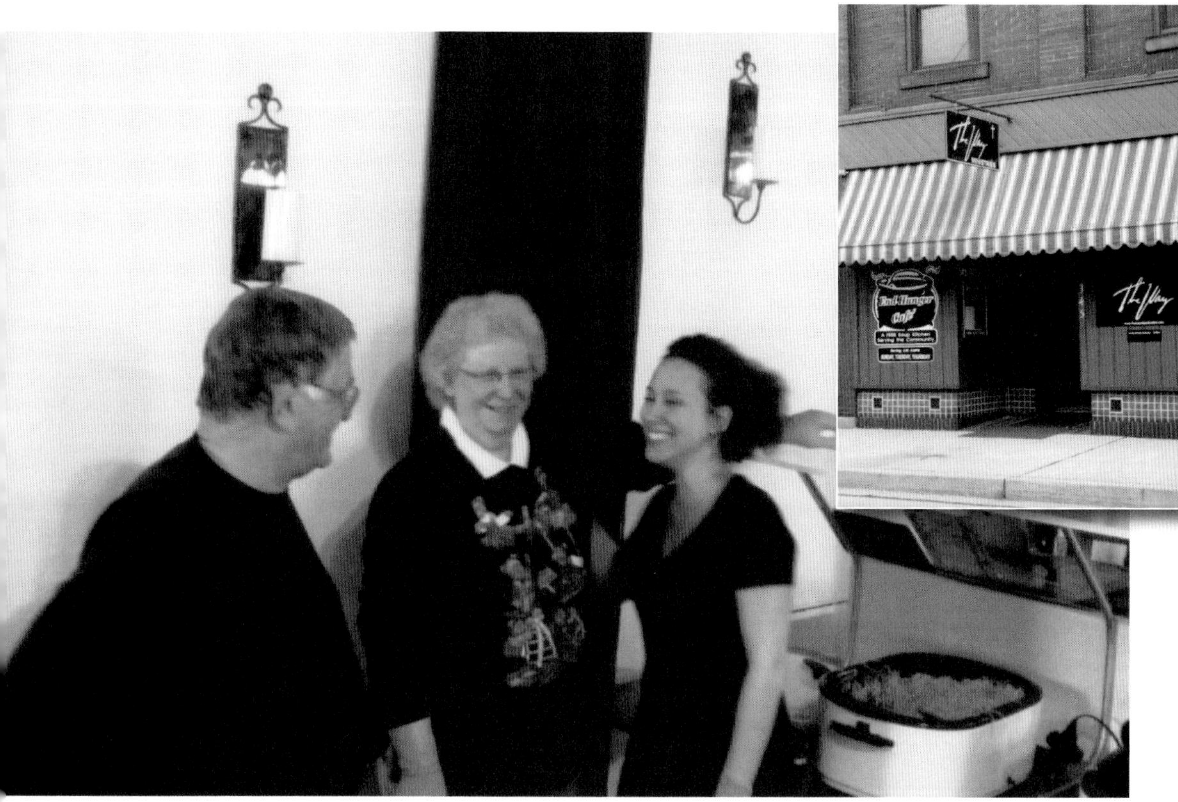

End Hunger Café

The End Hunger Café was the brainchild of Rev. Mark McMahon and Pastor Amy Biddle of The Way, a local nondenominational Christian church. The soup kitchen was launched in the fall of 2010 in rhe Mozart House on Main Street in downtown Latrobe and provides regular food assistance to "send every needy person in the city to bed with a full stomach," according to the current pastor of The Way, Sean Smith. In 2013, the café moved across the street into the facility formerly known as Reeb's Bar and Grill. The kitchen is open year-round, serving fully cooked meals, often with dessert, on Sundays, Tuesdays, and Thursdays from 5:30 to 6:30 p.m. Pastor Smith cites the miracles he has witnessed there. "We feed up to 80 people during the winter months. I don't take a dime from the church. It's all run by volunteers. It is patently impossible for us to keep doing this, but it has been going strong for the two years I've been pastor. Local schools do food drives for us (without being asked), and churches from all over Westmoreland County and private citizens send us money. People come in and say 'I want to buy you an oven' or 'I want to buy you a refrigerator.' A guy drops off hundreds of pounds of beef and pork, and he won't even tell us his name! We didn't ask for it. We just pray." Smith said Latrobe gets much of the credit because most of the support comes from the area. "All we hear is how bad it is. But all I see are caring neighbors." Committed volunteers, from left to right, Walter Maynard, LaVerne Smith, and Tiffany Jackson, believe that together with the people of Latrobe they can end hunger in the city. (Both, Pastor Sean Smith.)

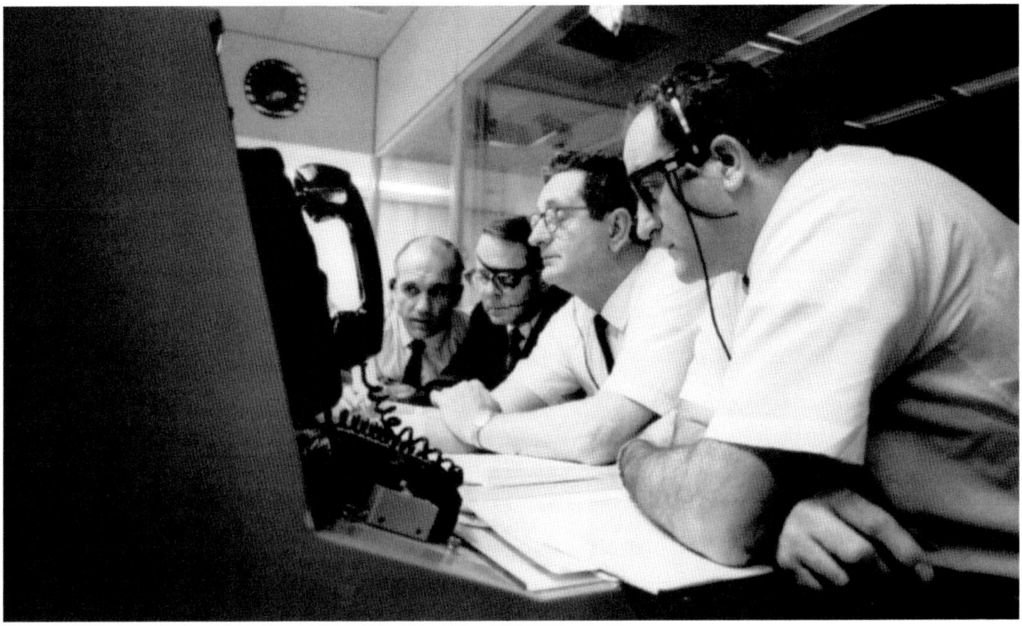

Chester M. Lee

Capt. Chester M. Lee (1919–2000), who survived the kamikaze sinking of a destroyer in World War II and later helped NASA send all manner of spacecraft into the heavens as NASA mission director for Apollo missions, is a Latrobe High School graduate (1936). He spent 23 years at NASA, where he played important roles in the Apollo moon landings, in the first joint space venture between the United States and the Soviet Union, and in the development of the shuttle program. In the photograph from April 16, 1970, Mission Control remains attentive to the crewmen of the problem-plagued Apollo 13 mission. Among those monitoring communications are, from left to right, Thomas H. McMullen, Dale Myers, Chester M. Lee, and Dr. Rocco A. Petrone. (NASA/Apollo Imagery.)

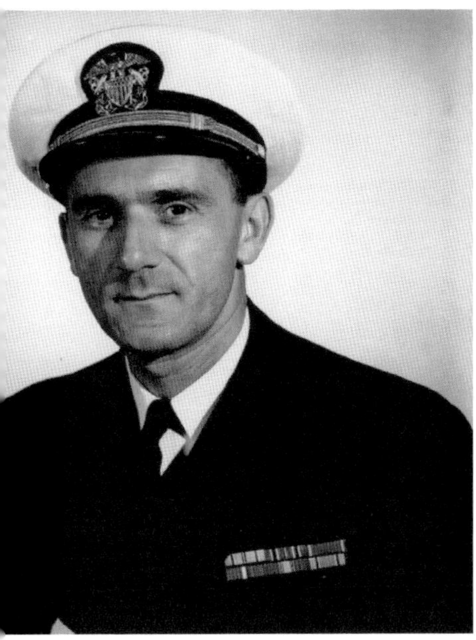

Angelo J. Taiani

Angelo J. Taiani is a native of Latrobe and a graduate of Latrobe High School. He overcame poverty and was the only one of his siblings to attend college. In 1948, he graduated with a bachelor of arts degree in chemistry from St. Vincent College. He served three years in the Navy during World War II and retired as a Navy commander with 41 years of reserve service. During his career at NASA, Taiani worked on numerous projects as a general space engineer, in test support at Cape Canaveral and later the Kennedy Space Center on the Juno project. Later, he worked in support of the Space Shuttle program. He is the namesake of the Angelo J. Taiani Planetarium and Astronaut Exhibit at St. Vincent College. Taiani turned 90 on August 28, 2013, and celebrated his birthday in Cocoa Beach, Florida, with a special family dinner observance. (Angelo J. Taiani.)

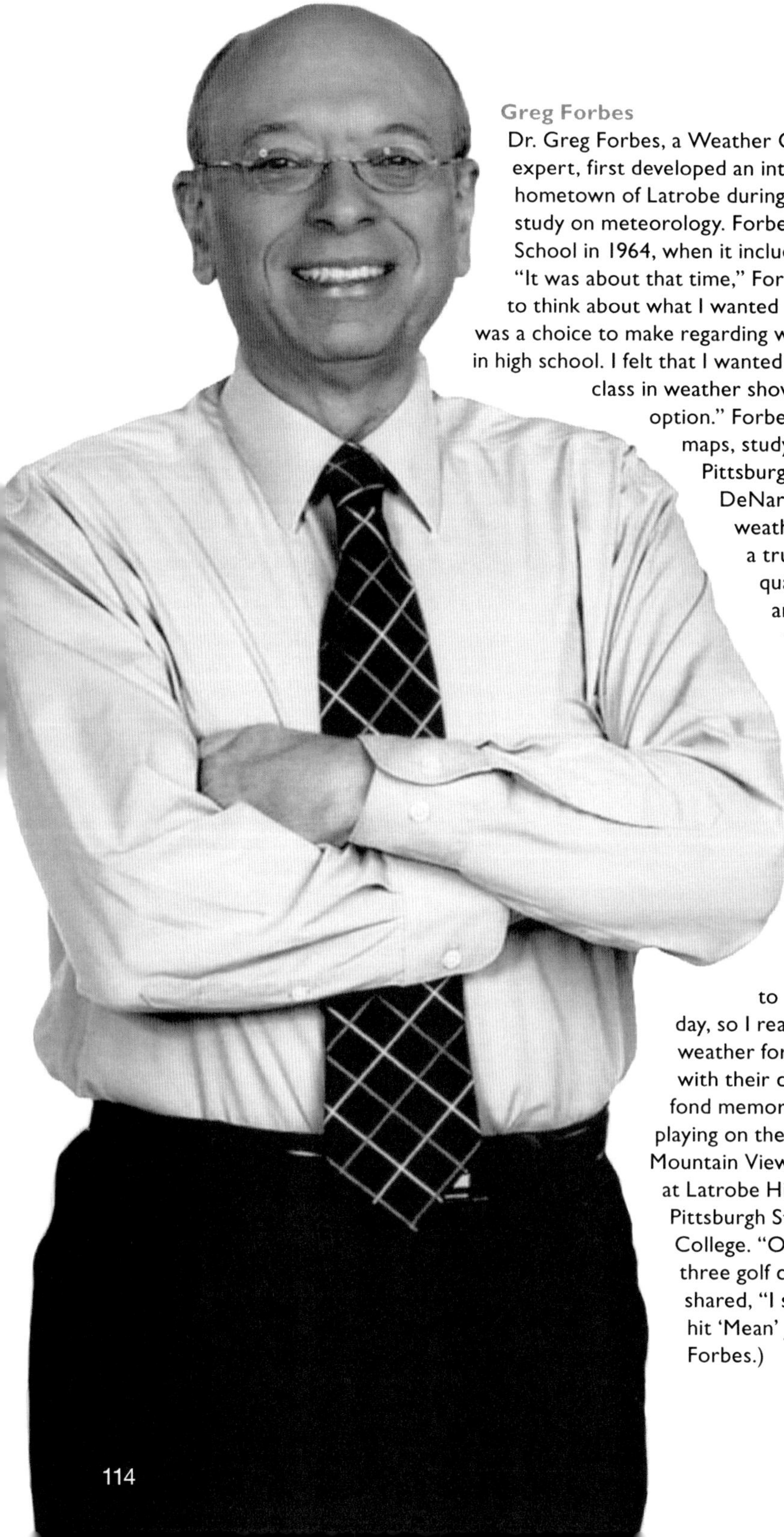

Greg Forbes

Dr. Greg Forbes, a Weather Channel severe weather expert, first developed an interest in weather back in his hometown of Latrobe during a seventh-grade module study on meteorology. Forbes attended Mountain View School in 1964, when it included grades one through eight. "It was about that time," Forbes recalled, "that I started to think about what I wanted to do for a career, and there was a choice to make regarding what curriculum path to take in high school. I felt that I wanted to be a scientist, and the class in weather showed me that this was an option." Forbes enjoyed drawing weather maps, studying clouds, and watching Pittsburgh TV weatherman Joe DeNardo. "Unlike many television weather presenters, DeNardo was a true scientist." Today, Forbes's quality medium-range forecasts and short-term watches and warnings have no doubt saved the lives of hundreds, if not thousands, of people caught in the path of tornadoes, hurricanes, snowstorms, and other weather emergencies, but as a youngster, Forbes simply wanted to help his mother and her neighbors. "I grew up in a rural area and my mother would hang clothes outside to dry on a line if it was a sunny day, so I realized that by becoming a weather forecaster I could help people with their daily lives." Forbes has other fond memories of Latrobe, including playing on the little-league team at Mountain View, being in the marching band at Latrobe High School, and watching the Pittsburgh Steelers practice at St. Vincent College. "One summer at Statler's par-three golf course off Route 30," Forbes shared, "I shanked a shot and nearly hit 'Mean' Joe Greene!" (Dr. Greg Forbes.)

CHAPTER EIGHT

Historians and Preservationists

The local legends in this chapter understand that there is no better way to nurture an interest in history than to start at the smallest level—in your own backyard. Their work includes maintaining records and artifacts, overseeing renovations of historical buildings, and creating or preserving green spaces. They educate the public about its shared history and give area children an appreciation for the works and deeds of those who came before. Most of these individuals and groups are volunteers who receive no financial reimbursement for their efforts. They do it because they have pride in their community and a genuine affection for the people, places, and events of the past. Because of their efforts, current residents are better able to reflect on and appreciate where they are from, and their children and future generations will be provided a wealth of evidence to better understand how they are part of something much larger than themselves.

Winnie Palmer

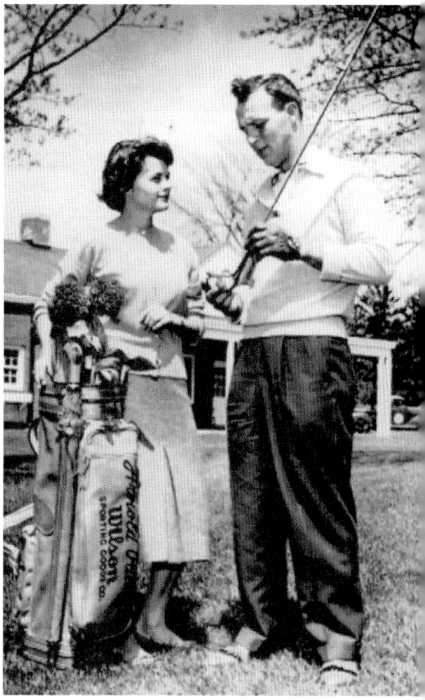

Winifred "Winnie" Palmer (1934–1999), late wife of golf legend Arnold Palmer (right), was born in eastern Pennsylvania but, thanks to her drive and inspiration, will always have real roots in Latrobe. She loved the area and didn't want it to become overcommercialized. She worked hard to save a particular 26-acre tract of land near St. Vincent College from development and hoped to make it an environmental, educational, and recreational area. Shortly after her passing, then Pennsylvania governor Tom Ridge announced that the land would be preserved, thanks to a $500,000 grant from the Pennsylvania Department of Conservation. Today, the Winnie Palmer Nature Reserve Trust's mission is to permanently improve and maintain that property. The reserve provides St. Vincent College students with an outdoor laboratory and a place on campus to relax in a natural setting. (LAHS.)

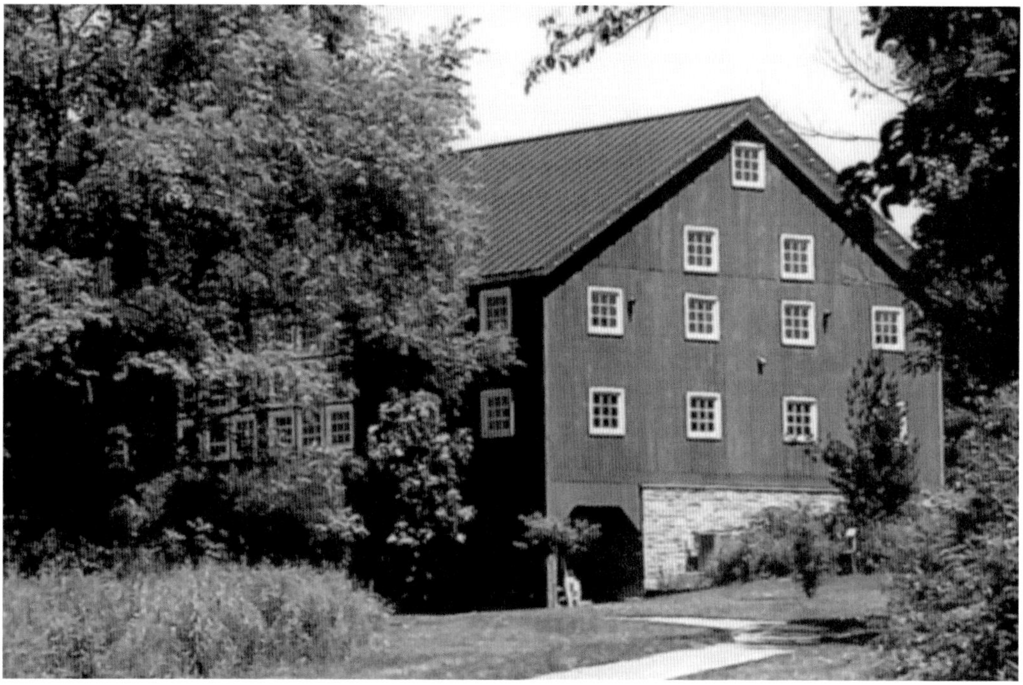

Winnie Palmer Nature Reserve

Nestled between the busy Route 30 corridor and Route 981 is the Winnie Palmer Nature Reserve. This beautiful recreation area includes more than two miles of trails, native plantings, the Historic Lochry Blockhouse, and a 19th-century barn transformed into an environmental education center where students study the environment and conduct field research. (LC.)

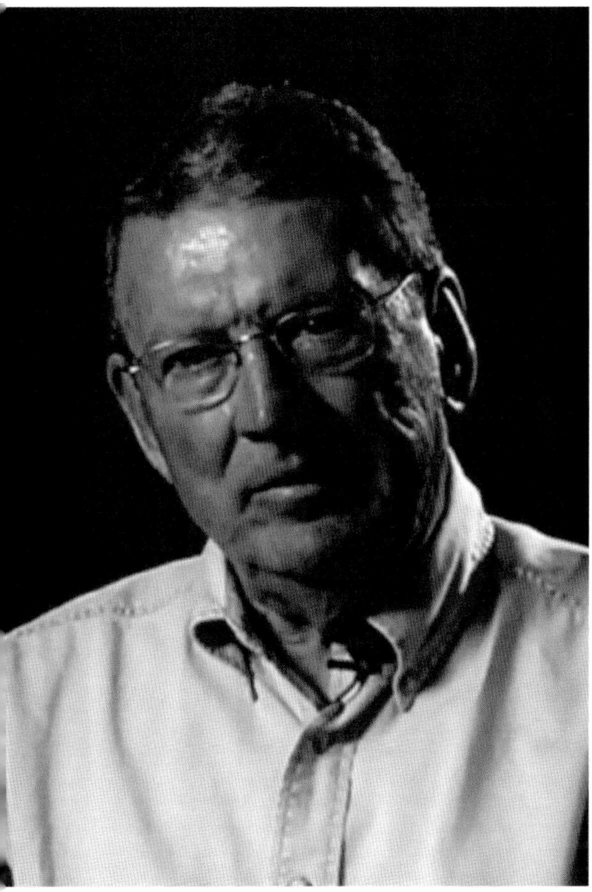

Floyd Eiseman Jr.

Floyd Eiseman Jr., of the Latrobe Area Historical Society, was featured in *Archaeology Magazine* (2002) for discovering the long-lost Lochry Blockhouse under a clump of bushes near St. Vincent College. Eiseman conducted a title search on the property, tracing ownership of the land back to the 18th century and confirming that the blockhouse had been built on land owned by Col. Archibald Lochry. "I knew it had to be there," said Eiseman. "It had been abandoned 30 years ago, and had been vandalized. We had to take it down, fill in the cellar, replace the four logs at the foundation that had rotted out, and then reconstruct the blockhouse to its 1780s appearance." Eiseman is pictured being interviewed about his discovery for *Latrobe: A Video History*, released in 2004 during the city's sesquicentennial celebration. (Steven Patterson.)

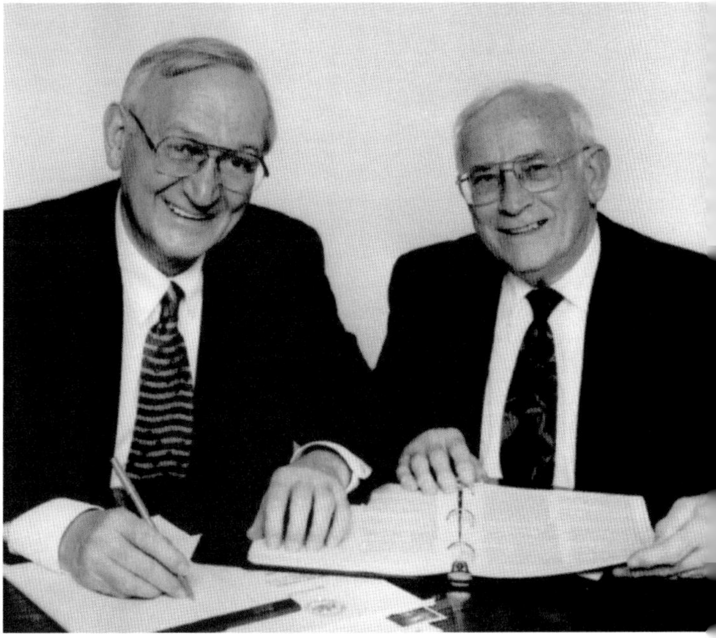

Carl Mattioli

Carl Mattioli (1924–2011), often referred to as "Mr. Latrobe," was the president of the Latrobe Area Historical Society for nearly two decades prior to his passing in 2011. Upon retirement, he intended to pursue recreational activities such as golfing but instead found himself aiding community endeavors. One of the first projects he undertook was to help put together a slide show, "First Ward Memories." He volunteered for the project at the urging of Ned J. Nakles Sr. Once that project was completed, Nakles (left) persuaded Mattioli to become involved with the historical society, and local history became his passion. (LAHS.)

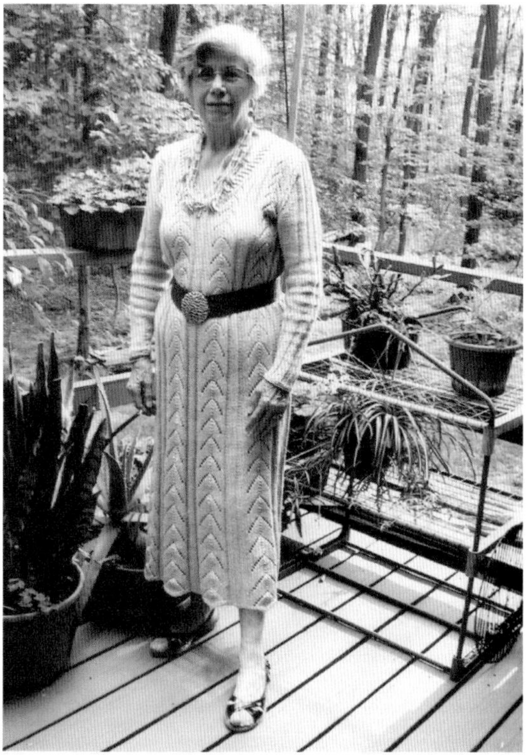

Gertrude S. Myers

Gertrude S. Myers enjoys weaving and photography and is the publisher of *Around Latrobe*, a magazine for the Greater Latrobe area that is published quarterly and was started by her late husband of 62 years, E. Kay Myers. Each issue highlights local news, events, and history, and its "Profiles of the Past" column was first to offer readers insight into local legends and historical figures. Myers is a founding member of the Ligonier Valley Writers Group, a nonprofit organization that encourages interest in the written word and the art and craft of writing. Myers owned and operated Driftwood Yarn Shop in Latrobe in the early 1960s and Ligonier Mountain Outfitters from 1972 to 1988. In addition to *Around Latrobe*, she also published the *Ligonier Free Gazette* and has worked with E. Kay Myers Publishing since 1968. (Gertrude S. Myers.)

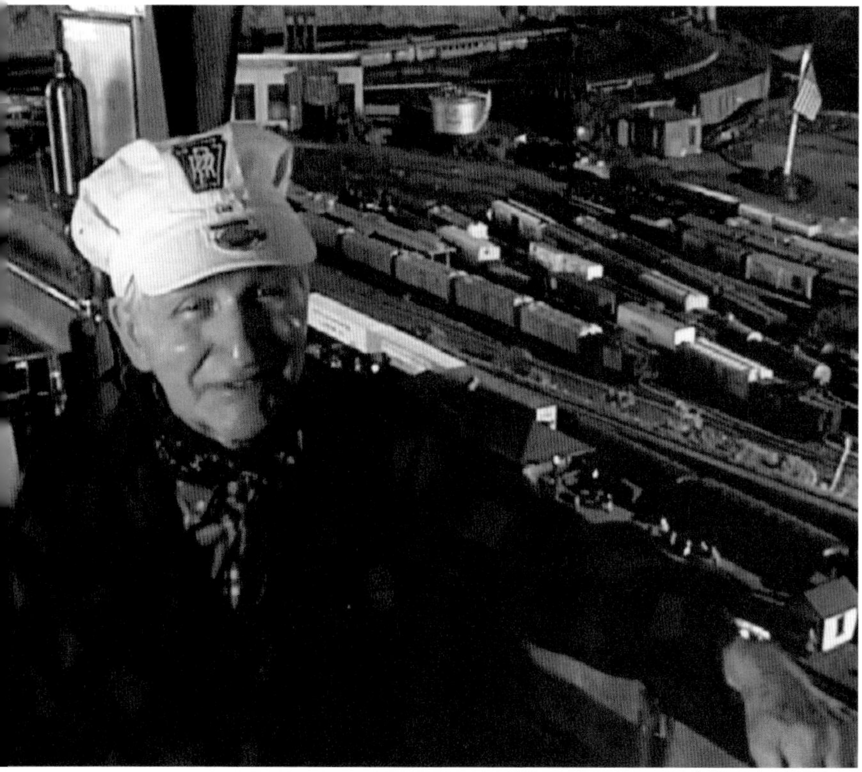

Russel W. Lowden

Russel W. Lowden (1925–2010) was a volunteer with the Latrobe Area Historical Society and its resident expert on the railroad, having worked as a train dispatcher for the Pennsylvania Railroad. He also gave tours of the society's one-room schoolhouse and general store, located in a Latrobe Elementary School classroom. He was a World War II veteran, having served in the Marine Corps. (Steven Patterson.)

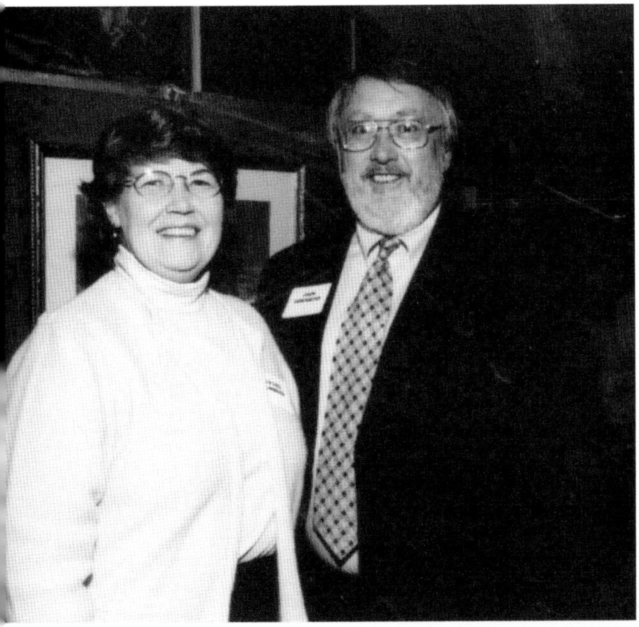

Mary Lou Townsend
Mary Lou Townsend is a retired English teacher, current president of the Latrobe Area Historical Society, and the go-to person if one has any questions about Latrobe-area history. She was featured in *Latrobe: A Video History* (2004) for her expertise on Unity Chapel, and under her leadership, the historical society room, housed in Latrobe Elementary School, has undergone a tremendous transformation, making it much more user-friendly with attractive glass display cases featuring artifacts and documents organized by specific themes. Townsend (left) and her husband, Jack, first developed an interest in local history through studying genealogy. (Mary Lou Townsend.)

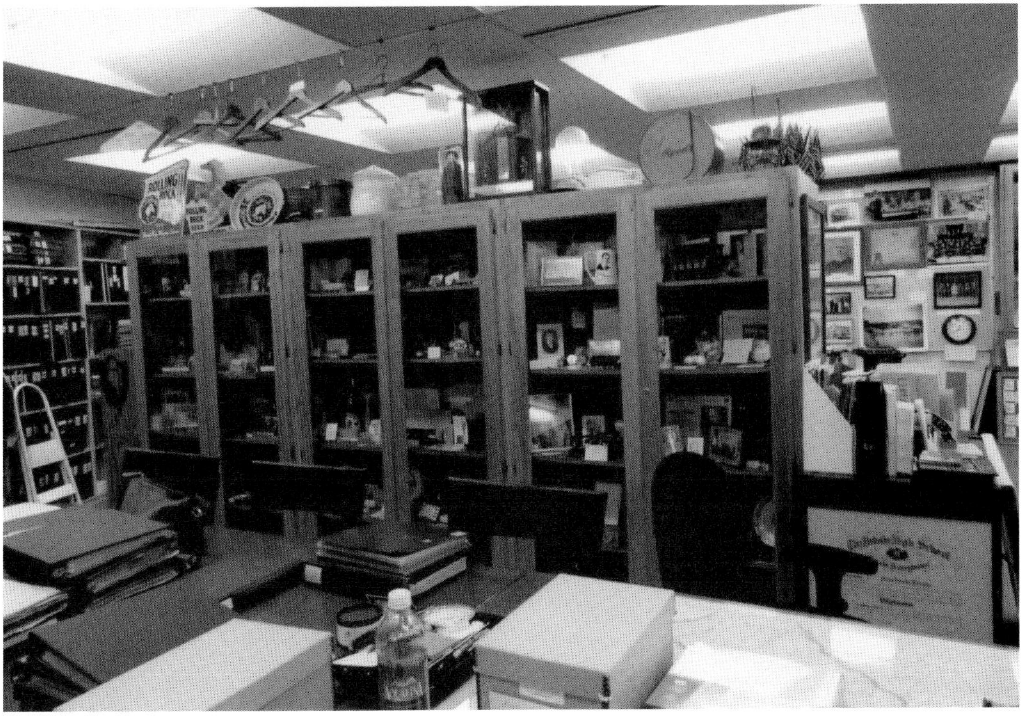

Latrobe Area Historical Society
The Latrobe Area Historical Society is a "hidden treasure," according to Pres. Mary Lou Townsend, for its collection of historical records, documents, photographs, maps, books, and artifacts. Housed in two rooms of Latrobe Elementary School, the treasure trove aids genealogy research, assists local businesses interested in the history of their buildings, and educates school and civic groups on the area's unique history and colorful local legends. (LC.)

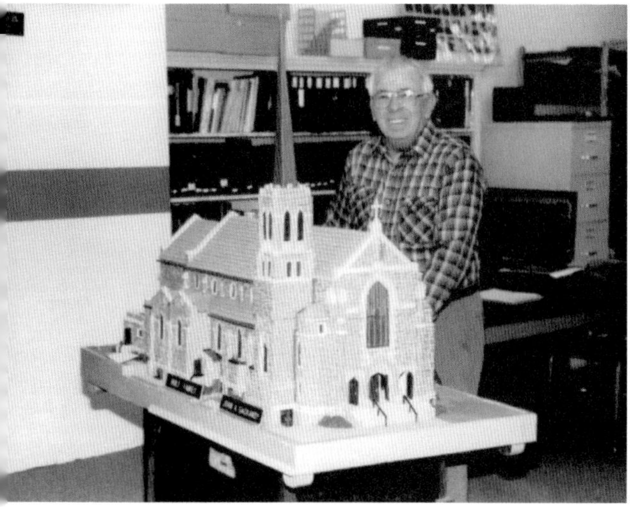

John A. Sackandy

John A. Sackandy (1924–1995) served in the Army during World War II and was a great contributor to the Latrobe Area Historical Society. He was born in Derry, Pennsylvania, and was employed for 41 years at Kennametal. He was the first post historian at the Thomas B. Anderson American Legion Post 515 and one of the original members of the Latrobe Area Historical Society, where he helped build the country store and one-room school as "living museums" for school visits. Sackandy also pasted items and photographs of interest in notebooks and scrapbooks for the historical society and built a beautiful replica of Holy Family Church that is on display there. (LAHS.)

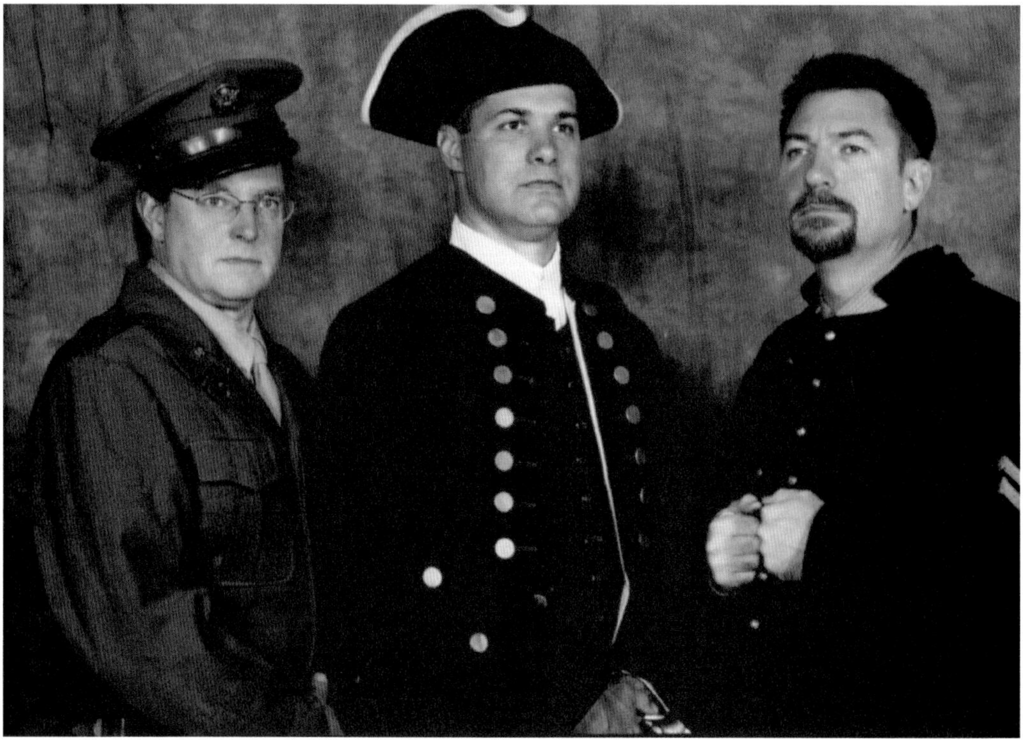

William Snyder II

William Snyder II, a history teacher at Greater Latrobe High School and a Derry Township resident, enjoys bringing history to life for his students. He tells them, "History is not just a record of the past; it's an experience waiting for you!" Many high school students from Derry and Greater Latrobe have assisted Snyder in restoring local historic log buildings, including the barn and blacksmith shop behind the 1817 Fulton House in Derry. He is a lifetime member of the Derry Area Historical Society and has served as a board member and officer there. In 2013, Snyder received the John Pomeroy Award for his contributions to historical preservation and education. Pictured from left to right in period costume are Snyder and his History Department colleagues Brad Wetzel and Jerry Ferraro. (William Snyder II.)

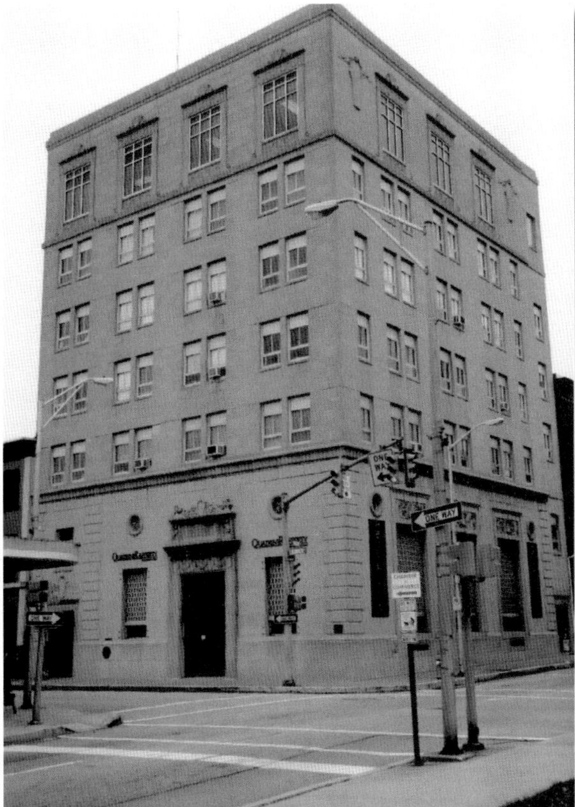

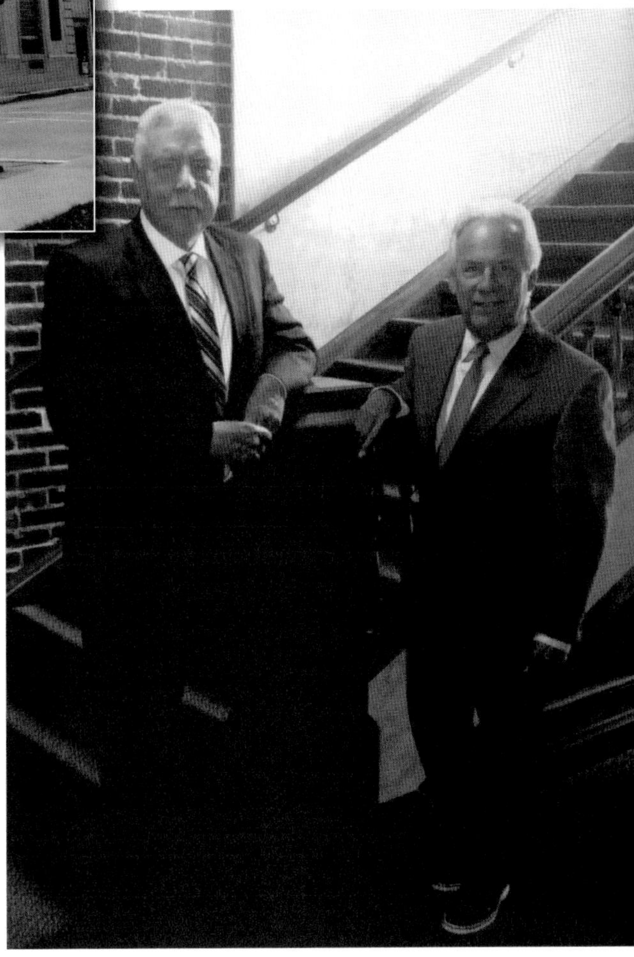

Vincent Quatrini and Dennis Rafferty
Attorney Vincent Quatrini (right) and his law partner, Dennis Rafferty (left), both Latrobe natives, were honored with the 2012 Arthur St. Clair Historic Preservation Award by the Westmoreland County Historical Society for the preservation and reuse by their law practice of the Seventh Ward School in Greensburg and the Citizens National Bank building (above) in downtown Latrobe. Restoration highlights on the first floor of the bank building are the cleaned and preserved original bank vault and the painted and stenciled ceiling. The relationship between Quatrini and Rafferty began when they sat next to one another in first grade at Latrobe's Holy Family grade school. Alphabetical seating order kept them together through eighth grade. They both attended Greater Latrobe High School and St. Vincent College. Quatrini then attended Duquesne University School of Law and Rafferty the University of Pittsburgh School of Law. (Above, AC; right, Quatrini Rafferty Law Firm.)

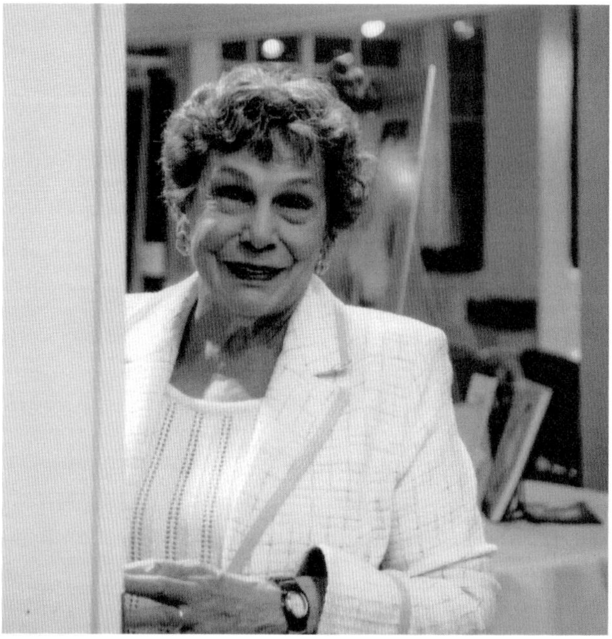

Barbara H. Nakles

Barbara H. Nakles of the GLSD Art Conservation Trust has often said that "art isn't for the elite in Latrobe. It belongs to everybody." This is especially true for the district's art collection. It began more than 75 years ago through the efforts of two visionary educators. The collection lines the corridors of the high school and is accessible to every student every day. Nakles succeeded her late husband, Ned J. Nakles Sr., as chair of the organization and is the author of *A Unique Vision of Art*, first published in 1996. The book includes color reproductions and descriptions for each piece in the collection. (Barbara H. Nakles.)

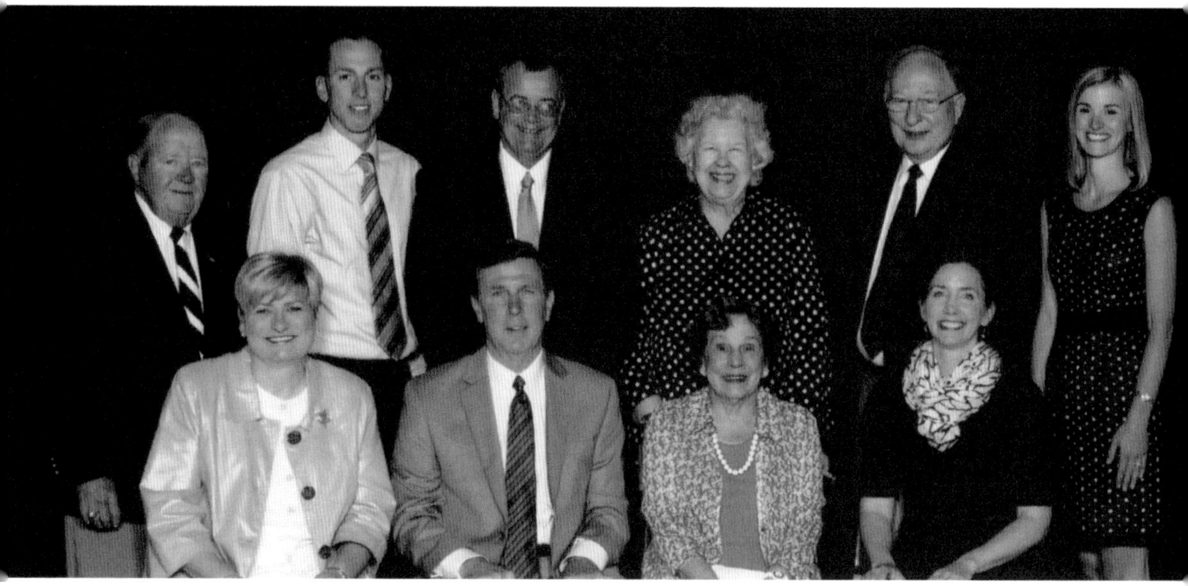

The GLSD Art Conservation Trust

The GLSD Art Conservation Trust was formed to oversee the care and conservation of the Greater Latrobe School District's unique collection of art. The trust is comprised of community members, faculty, school district administrators, and members of the Board of School Directors. From left to right are (first row) Judith A. Swigart, James R. Okonak, chair Barbara H. Nakles, and director of the Center for Student Creativity Jessica O. Golden; (second row) Ronald D. McKenzie, Daniel M. Watson, Steven LoCascio, Kathryn M. Elder, Dr. Gene F. Leonard, and Acacia M. Houck. Not pictured are Carl S. Baumeister, Linda McKenna Boxx, Cynthia S. Busch, George A. Fetkovich, John A. Graziano, William N. Hamilton Jr., Chad M. Krehlik, Susan J. Mains, Norma P. Scherer, Dr. Georgia R. Teppert, Marc L. Tourre, and Keith M. Visconti. (GLSD Art Conservation Trust.)

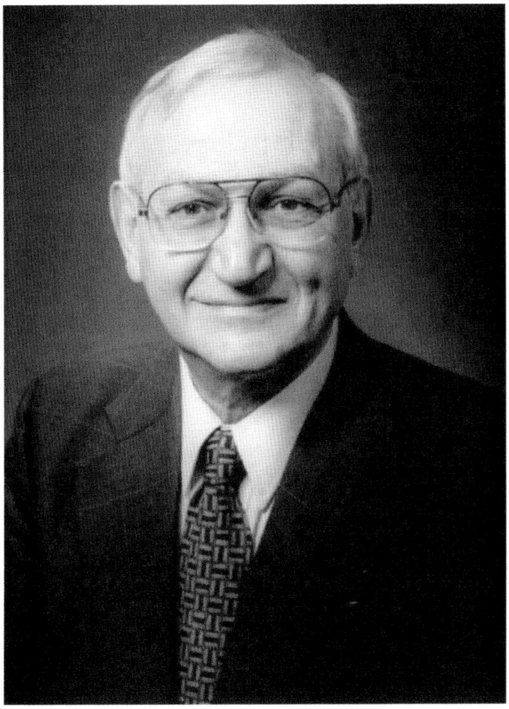

Ned J. Nakles Sr.

Attorney Ned J. Nakles Sr. (1931–1999) was born in Blairsville, Pennsylvania, but spent most of his life in Latrobe. He was the founder of Nakles and Nakles Law Firm in Latrobe and a local advocate of the arts, conservation, and education. He started the GLSD Art Conservation Trust and was its first chairperson. In 1964, Nakles and Greensburg attorney Emmett C. Boyle purchased Laurel Caverns atop Chestnut Ridge, agreeing to do nothing to disturb the 430 acres of the property, even when adding a new visitors' center in 1969. Educational scholarships in Nakles's name have been established and are awarded annually to students of the Latrobe area at Seton Hill University and Thiel College. Following his passing in 1999, the Westmoreland American Inn of Court changed its name to the Ned J. Nakles American Inn of Court, honoring its charter member who was instrumental in promoting legal excellence, professionalism, civility, and ethics. (Barbara H. Nakles.)

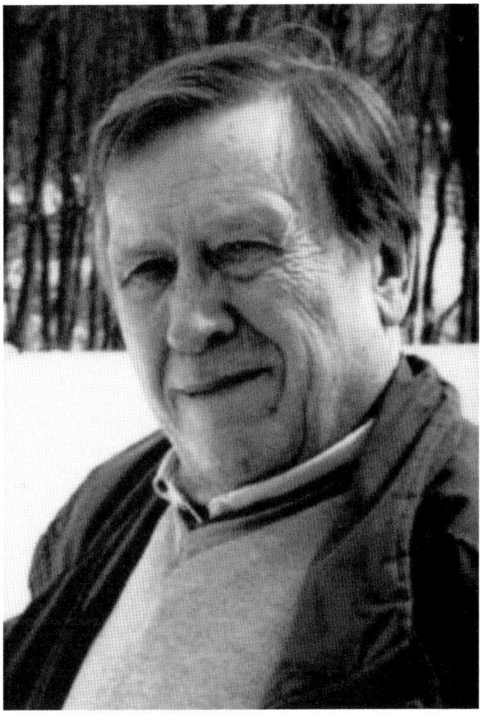

Richard D. Wissolik

Dr. Richard David Wissolik, professor of English and director and founder of St. Vincent College's Center for Northern Appalachian Studies (SVCCNAS), is the author of *Ice Cream Joe: The Valley Dairy Story* and *A Place in the Sky: A History of the Arnold Palmer Regional Airport and Aviation in Southwestern Pennsylvania.* Since 1991, the SVCCNAS has produced more than 20 books on a variety of local historical topics, ranging from *Listen to Our Words*, a collection of oral histories and historical documents of the Jewish community of southwestern Pennsylvania, to the Arnold Palmer Regional Airport. The most popular titles have been *The Long Road, They Say There Was a War, An Honor to Serve*, and *Victorious*, oral histories of local and national veterans of World War II's European theater, as well as *Waiting for Jacob: A Civil War Story* by Edwin P. Hogan. (Dr. Richard D. Wissolik.)

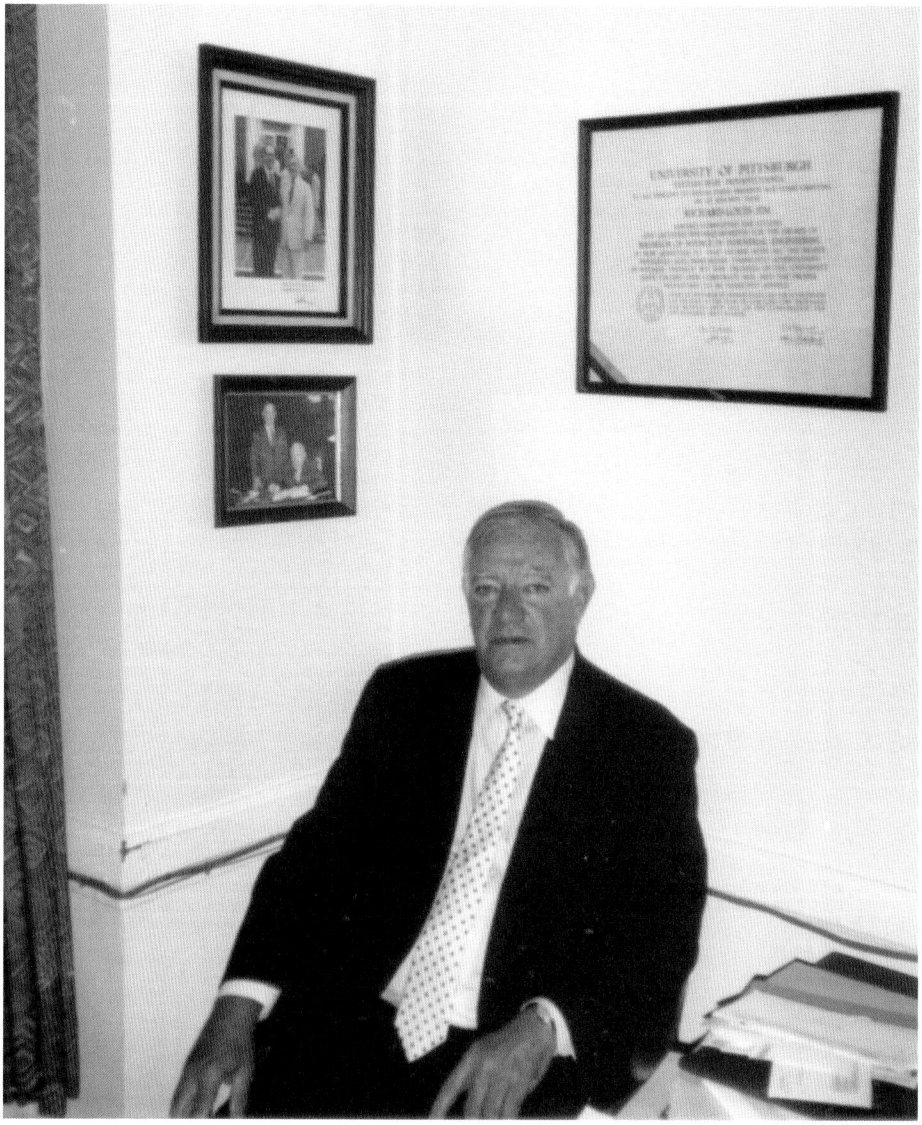

Richard L. Jim

Richard L. Jim is a Latrobe attorney who wrote *The Making of Latrobe* (1986). His book is an overview of the influence of the railroad on the planning of the town of Latrobe and the growth and development of industries in the area. After serving in the Navy, Jim received a bachelor of law degree from the University of Pittsburgh in 1957 and opened his practice in Latrobe. He has served the city as deputy mayor, director of community development, and a city council member. His book was featured in a series of nine installments in the *Latrobe Bulletin*. It provides a lawyer's insight into the town's history, including an examination of early deeds and zoning ordinances, and a modern legal perspective on railroad engineer Oliver W. Barnes's purchase of the Kirk farm: "Oliver W. Barnes today would have been accused of using insider's information with his dealings with Thomas Kirk. He was aware of the potential growth for any municipality that would locate along a right of way of the to-be-constructed Pennsylvania Railroad. Oliver W. Barnes knew his recording of the plan would take place in 1851 and realized the sale of lots, particularly to the Pennsylvania Railroad Company would realize for him sufficient funds to pay for the land he was purchasing." (LAHS.)

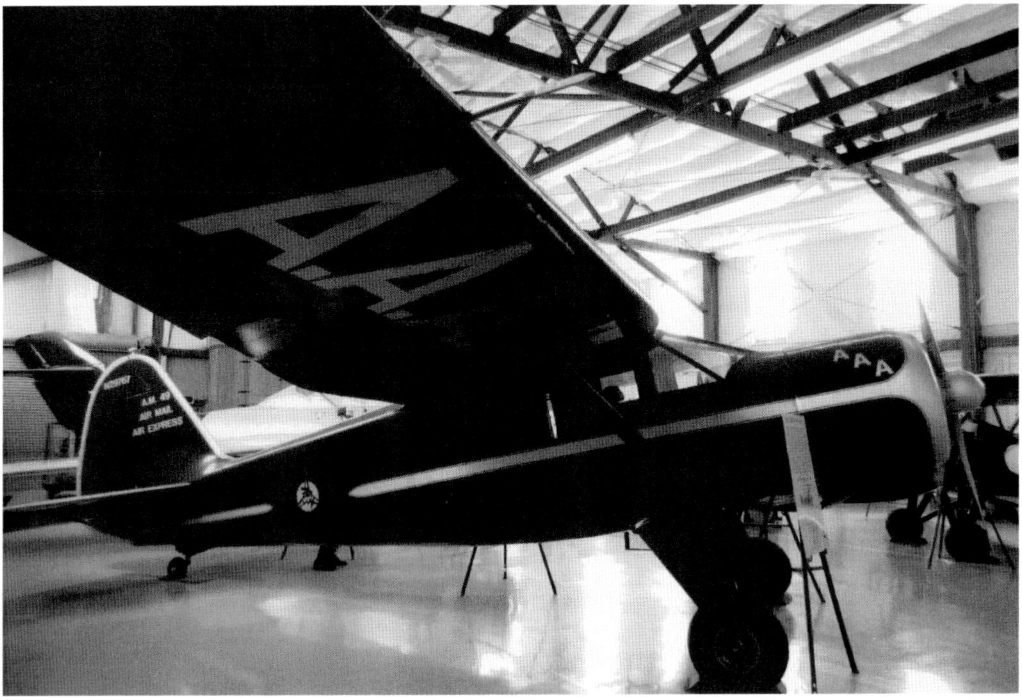

Donald Rossi

Donald "Don" Rossi, of Youngstown, Pennsylvania, is a longtime pilot and board member of the Westmoreland County Airport Authority. He and several other area pilots worked for more than a quarter-century setting up a museum dedicated to aviation history at Arnold Palmer Regional Airport. One of the first acquisitions was a single-engine Stinson Reliant plane (above) similar to the type that was used for the first airmail pickup at the airport beginning in 1939. The initials "A.A.A." on the plane's wing and fuselage stand for All American Aviation, Inc. Since it opened in 2010, the KLBE Aviation Museum has added a 1954 Soviet-made MiG 15-UTI, a 1931 Great Lakes bi-wing aircraft, and a replica of a Curtiss JN-4 "Jenny" biplane. In flight-tracking, "K" signifies US airports and "LBE" is the designator for Latrobe Airport. (AC.)

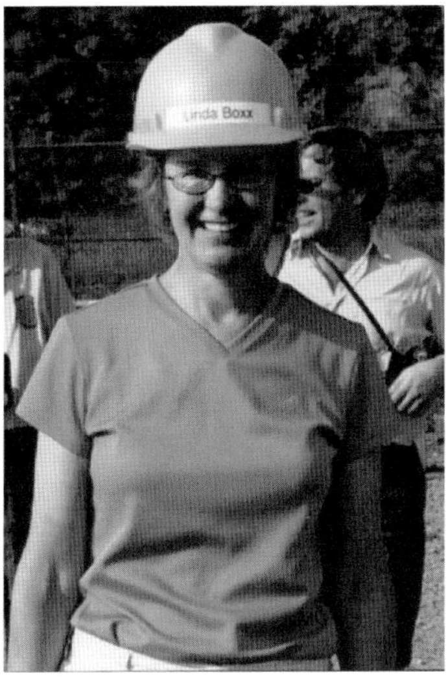

Linda McKenna Boxx

Linda McKenna Boxx is an avid cyclist and was the driving force behind the Allegheny Trail Alliance (ATA) since its inception in 1995. She served as its president and chief executive officer until 2014. Born in Latrobe and a current resident, her ability to inspire and unite the efforts of cities, counties, and volunteer groups, as well as federal, state, and local agencies, is widely credited for the tremendous success of the Great Allegheny Passage (GAP), which, since the time of her involvement, has become one of America's most popular rail-trail destinations. In 2009, McKenna Boxx received a Lifetime Achievement Award for her work on the GAP from the Pennsylvania Environmental Council. (Linda McKenna Boxx.)

INDEX

INDEX

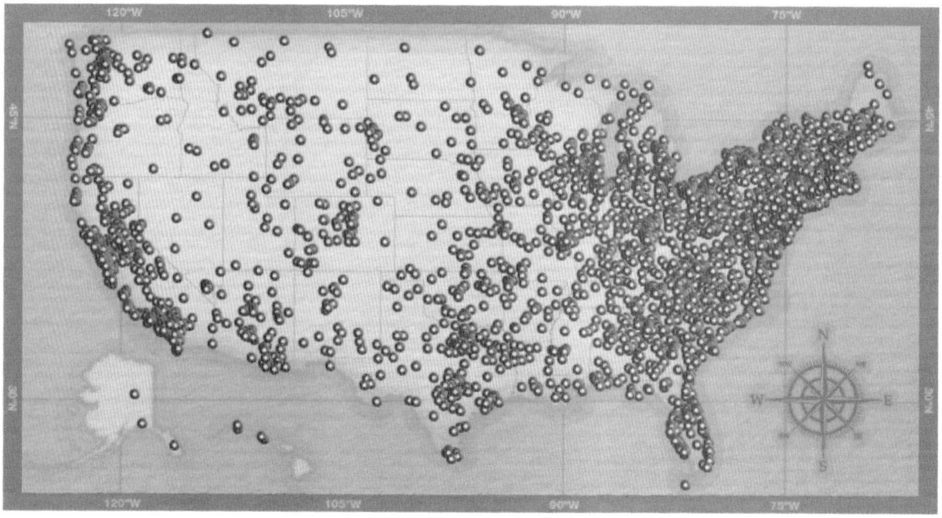
120°W
105°W
90°W
75°W
N
S
E
W